Readings in United States History

Volume II

Seventh Edition

Ron Wright | Larry Watson | Blanche Brick

CENGAGE Learning

Australia • Brazil • Japan • Korea • Mexico • Singapore • Spain • United Kingdom • United States

Readings in United States History: Volume II, Seventh Edition

Senior Manager, Student Engagement:

Linda deStefano

Janey Moeller

Manager, Student Engagement:

Julie Dierig

Marketing Manager:

Rachael Kloos

Manager, Production Editorial:

Kim Fry

Manager, Intellectual Property Project Manager:

Brian Methe

Senior Manager, Production and Manufacturing:

Donna M. Brown

Manager, Production:

Terri Daley

Printed in the United States of America

ACP READ IN US HIST/VOL 2 6ED
Wright

ISBN-13: 978-1-305-00311-8

ISBN-10: 1-305-00311-X

WCN: 01-100-101

Cengage Learning

5191 Natorp Boulevard
Mason, Ohio 45040
USA

Cengage Learning is a leading provider of customized learning solutions with office locations around the globe, including Singapore, the United Kingdom, Australia, Mexico, Brazil, and Japan. Locate your local office at: **international.cengage.com/region.**

Cengage Learning products are represented in Canada by Nelson Education, Ltd.

For your lifelong learning solutions, visit **www.cengage.com/custom.**
Visit our corporate website at **www.cengage.com.**

CREDITS

This page constitutes an extension of the copyright page. We have made every effort to trace the ownership of all copyrighted material and to secure permission from copyright holders. In the event of any question arising as to the use of any material, we will be pleased to make the necessary corrections in future printings. Thanks are due to the following authors, publishers, and agents for permission to use the material indicated.

Dee Brown, "A Trumpet for Heroes," THE YEAR OF THE CENTURY: 1876, Scribner/Simon & Schuster, 1966. Reprinted by permission of Sll/sterling Lord Literistic, INc. Copyright by The Dee Brown Llc.

Andrew Carnegie, "The Gospel of Wealth," 1889.

Booker T. Washington, "The Atlanta Exposition Address," 1895.

W.E.B. DuBois, "The Souls of Black Folk," 1903.

Littlefield, Henry M. "The Wizard of Oz: Parable on Populism," AMERICAN QUARTERLY 16:1 (1964), 47-58. (c) The American Studies Association. Reprinted with permission of The Johns Hopkins University.

John Offner, "Why Did the United States Fight Spain in 1898?" from ORGANIZATION OF AMERICAN HISTORIANS MAGAZINE, Spring, 1998. Used by permission of the Organization of American Historians.

Christopher Lasch, "The Anti-Imperialists, the Philippines, and The Inequality of Man," JOURNAL OF SOUTHERN HISTORY, VOL XXIV, No. 3 (August 1958), pp. 319-331. Copyright 1958 by the Southern Historical Association. Reprinted by permission of the Managing Editor.

Robert M. Crunden, "Progressivism," MINISTERS OF REFORM: THE PROGRESSIVES' ACHIEVEMENT, Perseus Books, 1982. Source: Copyright Clearance Center. Used by permission.

O'Neill, William L. "Divorce in the Progressive Era," AMERICAN QUARTERLY 17:2 (1965), 203-217. (c) The American Studies Association. Reprinted with permission of The Johns Hopkins University Press.

"Theodore Roosevelt, President" by Edmund Morris is reprinted from AMERICAN HERITAGE, Vol. XXXII, 4 (Spring) 1981.

"Woodrow Wilson Wouldn't Yield" by Thomas A. Bailey is reprinted from AMERICAN HERITAGE, Vol. VII-4 (June) 1957.

Herbert Hoover, reprinted from HERBERT HOOVER, AMERICAN INDIVIDUALISM, 1922, Herbert Hoover Foundation, Inc.

William E. Leuchtenburg, "FDR and the Kingfish." Copyright (c) William E. Leuchtenburg. Used by permission of the author.

Robert A. Divine, "The Innocent Bystander," THE RELUCTANT BELLIGERENT, 1965. Source: The McGraw-Hill Companies.

Excerpts from DEATH MARCH, copyright (c) 1981 by Donald Knox, reprinted by permission of Harcourt, Inc.

"The Biggest Decision" by Robert James Maddox is reprinted from AMERICAN HERITAGE May-June 1995.

Donald R. McCoy, "Epilogue," THE PRESIDENCY OF HARRY S. TRUMAN. Copyright (c) 1984 University Press of Kansas. Used by permission of University Press of Kansas.

From Robert D. Marcus, "The Myth of the Placid 1950s," MYTH AMERICA: A HISTORICAL ANTHOLOGY, Vol. II, 1997, pp. 177-184. Copyright (c) 1997 Brandywine Press. Reprinted by permission.

Joann Meyerowitz, "The Myth of the Feminine Mystique," JOURNAL OF AMERICAN HISTORY, March 1993. Used by permission of the Southern Historical Association.

Vaughn D. Bornet, "History Will Judge," THE PRESIDENCY OF LYNDON B. JOHNSON. Copyright (c) 1983 University Press of Kansas. Used by permission of University Press of Kansas.

Arthur M. Schlesinger, Jr., THE DISUNITING OF AMERICA: REFLECTIONS ON A MULTICULTURAL SOCIETY. Source: W.W. Norton & Co., 1998.

Lind, Michael. "Vietnam: A Necessary War" from MAJOR PROBLEMS IN AMERICAN HISTORY, VOLUME II SINCE 1865, pp. 428-36. Houghton Mifflin Company, 2002. Originally published in VIETNAM: A NECESSARY WAR (New York: Free Press, 1999), pp. 1, 4-5, 31-35, 38-41, 52, 54, 60-62, 254, 256-257. Reprinted and edited with permission of The Free Press, a division of Simon & Schuster, Inc. Copyright (c) 1999 by Michael Lind.

Contents

I

The Gilded Age, 1877-1899

I. "A Trumpet Note for Heroes"

Dee Brown

By 1876 the era of the Civil War and Reconstruction was in its final stages, Northern troops were leaving the last southern states and the Republican Party was dead in the South. The conservative elite was once again occupying the state governors' mansions and legislatures, as well as the county courthouses. Blacks had tasted political power for a few years, but were once again relegated to positions of political impotency and economic servitude. More than anything else, Americans wanted to put the war behind them—to forget the pain, end the bitterness, a move on to new things.

Those "new things" were all around them. The Civil War had accelerated the rate of industrialization, bringing millions of Americans into the cities and factories. They left behind their rural past with great misgivings. The frontier and farm had been central elements in American culture, the fountains of self-reliance, individualism, and democracy. City life—with its crowds, pollution, and bureaucracies— seemed to threaten fundamental values. Desperate to preserve wilderness traditions, American culture manufactured heroes in the 1870s, men and women of the West whose exploits were synonymous with ruggedness, courage, and frontier grit. Dee Brown's "...A Trumpet Note for Heroes" describes some of those human symbols.

At high noon of Sunday, June 25, 1876, General George Custer led the 7th U.S. Cavalry Regiment over the last divide between the Rosebud and Little Horn, and there set in motion a series of incidents that before the day's end would create an enduring legend. In the literature of fable, Custer's Last Stand was to hold a fascination for the New World that was as absorbing as the Siege of Troy to the Old World. Its accompanying heroes, gilded by the passing of time, would eventually enter the pantheon of American mythology.

On that summer noonday this future chief of the nation's warrior heroes looked out across the sunbaked loneliness of Montana and studied a line of distant hills which ran in ribbons of green and gray. To the northwest, thin light blue streamers of smoke lifted skyward.

Custer guessed that the smoke cloud was from the cooking fires of Sioux and Cheyenne hostiles, and thereupon made his first reckless decision of the day—to disregard the orders of his superior, General Alfred Terry, to swing south and prevent the Indians' escape but delay an attack until Terry's infantry column could move up for an encirclement.

Having decided to attack with his regiment alone, Custer ordered Captain Frederick Benteen to take one battalion to the left and scout a line of bluffs.

This decision was a violation of a classic principle of war—mass of forces. Two hours later, after marching several miles along Sundance Creek, he sighted dust clouds across the little Horn. His scouts warned him that he was facing superior numbers, but Custer ignored the warning and violated the principle of security by detaching Major Marcus Reno's battalion and sending it galloping across the river while he continued northwestward with the last battalion. During the next two hours he committed his third violation of the principles of war by allowing himself to be outmaneuvered by the warriors of Sitting Bull and Crazy Horse.

When that historic day ended, George Custer and 225 officers and men were dead. Major Reno, trapped in an ambush, had escaped to high ground after suffering heavy casualties. Captain Benteen joined forces with Reno, and the two battalions managed to hold their position until the arrival of Terry and the infantry.

Had Custer survived he probably would have faced a court-martial for disobedience of orders and incompetent leadership, but in the tradition of mythology he died bravely and became a hero. Thus died Hector, chief of the Trojan army, his brother Paris, and Achilles of Agamemnon's army—all courageous, vain, stubborn, foolhardy warriors who squandered their forces and their lives. But in death they joined the gods they had worshipped, and now mortals worshipped them. Few who survived the fall of Troy were heroes; most lived out their lives meanly or in disgrace, shunned by the gods.

Such was the fate of Reno, accused of cowardice, brought before a board of inquiry, hounded until he became a drunkard and had to leave military service. Benteen took his share of the blame, too, and the only reason he and Reno are even remembered is because they were there on the day the gods added a new member to their exclusive circle.

For a decade George Armstrong Custer had been a national celebrity, adored by women, admired by most men, and tolerated by his few enemies. Early in his career he had learned the value of publicity. Before starting on an expedition he usually arranged to have at least one accompanying newspaper correspondent. He was also a writer himself, having published several newspaper and magazine articles and one book.

In December 1875, Custer and his wife Elizabeth were in New York, enjoying the luxuries of civilian life after three years' service in Dakota Territory. They made a brilliant and dashing couple—George with his bright blue eyes and curly yellow hair, Libby with her high spirits and rare beauty. The Redpath lecturing agency offered Custer a contract which would have made him wealthy, but he had to turn it down for lack of time. He knew he would soon be receiving orders to return to Dakota for an Indian campaign. His orders came earlier than expected, but one of his railroad friends supplied a special train so that he and Libby could ride westward in style.

On February 13, they stopped briefly at the Palmer House in Chicago, where the press interviewed them. Custer was quoted *as* saying that he had doffed his

doffed- to remove or take off

military uniform for a sober civilian suit and had begun "to feel as if I were actually settled down to solid comfort, but my dreams were suddenly dissipated by the receipt of telegrams instructing me to get thence forthwith to the West." He heaved a melancholy sigh and added: "It was too bad, wasn't it?"

[illegible]ed him to estimate the size of the hostile Indian forces, [illegible]re probably between eight and ten thousand warriors [illegible] know, there are two Sitting Bulls," he explained. "This [illegible] agency and *is* a dangerous character." Asked if she felt any apprehension about the coming campaign, Mrs. Custer replied cheerfully: [illegible]

[illegible]ers reached Fort Abraham Lincoln, he received a sum[illegible]o appear before the House Committee on Expenditures in the War Department, ostensibly to discuss construction of new forts on the Yellowstone River. This was not the real reason, however. Chairman of that committee was Heister Clymer, the Democrat, who had recently exposed the Republican Administration's Secretary of War, William Belknap, for accepting graft in connection with the Fort Sill post-tradership. Clymer was eager to broaden the charges before beginning impeachment proceedings against Belknap, and he believed that Custer could supply valuable evidence. In his recent book, *My Life on the Plains,* Custer had been extremely critical of Grant's Indian policies.

On March 16, Custer wrote Clymer from Dakota, explaining that he was preparing for an expedition and requesting permission to submit his views to the committee by mail. Clymer, however, wanted Custer in person; he too knew the value of publicity and was certain the newspapers would report every move and statement of the celebrated cavalry leader.

Custer arrived in Washington late in March. An old friend, General Rufus Ingalls, now on the President's staff, invited him to share his lodgings. Custer also made a courtesy call at the White House, but Grant was suffering from a cold that day and was seeing no visitors. Heister Clymer arranged for him to be given the privileges of the House floor, and important Democrats began wooing him with receptions and informal parties.

On March 29, Clymer put Custer on the witness stand, and immediately got him to talking about a "ring" of post-traders. Most of Custer's evidence was hearsay, and after discussing fraudulent practices he had learned about at second or third hand, Custer said flatly that he had always regarded Secretary Belknap as "a silent partner in the transactions." Under Clymer's adroit questioning, he then related an incident which implicated the President's brother, Orville Grant, in the sale of corn stolen from the Indian Bureau. Custer went on to criticize Grant's order extending the Great Sioux Reservation, intimating that it only gave the post-traders more opportunity for illegal profits.

During the next few days, Republican ranks closed against Custer. Telegrams flew back and forth between Washington and Custer's departmental commander, General Alfred Terry in St. Paul. Terry's records discredited much of Custer's testimony against Orville Grant, and Belknap's attorneys immediately announced that they were collecting additional evidence that would bring Custer to trial by court-martial for swearing falsely before the Clymer committee.

Custer remained unruffled, and late in April when Clymer released him as a witness, he decided to return to Fort Abraham Lincoln by way of New York. He stopped over in Philadelphia for a look at the completed buildings on the Centennial Exhibition grounds. In New York he conferred with editors who had been showering him with offers for articles about his experiences, and then made arrangements for correspondents from the *Herald* and *Tribune* to accompany his expedition against Sitting Bull. On the 25th his busy schedule was interrupted by a telegram from Clymer summoning him back to Washington.

The Belknap impeachment proceedings were now under way, and when Custer appeared in the hearing room on April 28 he was the center of attention, dressed in a fashionable black coat, white vest and light trousers. He was not called to testify, however, and the next day when he received an urgent telegram from General Terry requesting him to report immediately to Fort Abraham Lincoln, Chairman Clymer released him again. Influential newspapers were beginning to criticize Custer's previous testimony as showing no proof of fraudulent activities but only stating opinions, and Clymer probably felt that the usefulness of his stellar performer had come to an end.

Custer went immediately to General Sherman's office to report his departure from Washington, but Sherman was out of town. He left a written message, and hurried on to the White House. He was unable to obtain an interview with Grant, and as the day was Saturday, he had to delay his departure until Monday. At ten o'clock Monday morning, when the President's anteroom was opened, Custer entered with several other callers and awaited his turn.

By one o'clock all except Custer had been admitted, transacted their business and departed, leaving him sitting alone. About two o'clock General Ingalls, coming in, was surprised to see Custer still there, surrounded by a new group of callers. "How long have you been waiting?" Ingalls asked him. "Since ten o'clock," Custer replied.

Ingalls promised to intercede with Grant, and if we may believe his own report of his conversation with the President, he spoke rather candidly. "It is not fair to Custer to serve him in this way," Ingalls said to Grant. "If you do not want to see him you should have sent him word this morning, and not kept him out there among the crowd waiting the entire day."

Ingalls' words had no effect, however. At three o'clock, the hour the anteroom closed, Grant sent Custer's card back to him with a message declining to see him.

Grant had been giving Custer the treatment that many an army officer often gives a bumptious lieutenant. Undoubtedly the President was exceedingly angry with this lieutenant-colonel who bore the temporary rank of general. He believed that Custer had gone out of his way to slur his Administration by giving testimony made up of assertions and opinions. "I did not mean to allow Custer to smirch the administration," Grant afterwards explained to a friend. It should be remembered that in April the President was not yet fully recovered from the ailment diagnosed by his physicians as "neuralgia of the brain," and was inclined neither to forgive nor forget any criticism of his Administration.

But George Custer was also a proud and impatient man. Believing that he had done his duty by waiting on the President for three days, he boarded a train and started for Fort Abraham Lincoln. When he arrived in Chicago, May 4, the long arm of Grant had reached out ahead of him, and a staff officer was waiting to escort him to General Sheridan's Chicago headquarters. There, Custer learned that the War Department had ordered Sheridan to intercept and detain him. Later in the day Custer received a telegram from the War Department demanding an explanation as to why he had left Washington without permission.

After an exchange of lengthy telegrams, Custer received authorization to proceed to Fort Abraham Lincoln, but he was also informed that he would not be permitted to join the expedition.

By this time, journalists had learned about the Grant-Custer quarrel and were spreading it across the pages of the press. Even the pro-Administration newspapers chided the President for his actions, accusing him of using his power to the detriment of the Army.

For the first time Custer seemed to realize that he was embroiled in the dangerous game of politics. He was dismayed over the prospect that his long-desired promotion to permanent rank of colonel would be delayed again; his very career was jeopardized. He swallowed his pride and wrote a letter to the President: "I appeal to you as a soldier to spare me the humiliation of seeing my regiment march to meet the enemy and I not share its dangers." Terry, Sheridan and Sherman all interceded for him, and at the last moment Grant yielded. Custer would lead the 7th Regiment, with Terry in command of the whole expedition.

Perhaps Grant himself was a victim of the Custer legend, and believed with other Americans that the yellow-haired cavalryman possessed magic powers against warrior Indians. Or perhaps he merely felt that Custer had learned his lesson and would not meddle in politics again. Whatever the reason, Grant relented, and in relenting sent Custer to his mortal doom.

The impact of the Last Stand upon all Americans was extraordinary. For two or three days, newspapers published special editions, adding more and more details until by July 8 most of the story was as complete as it would ever be. "A sight fit to appall the stoutest heart ... All along the slopes and ridges and in the ravines, lying as they had fought, line behind line, showing where defensive positions had been successfully taken up and held till none were left to fight, lay the bodies of the fallen soldiers; then huddled in a narrow compass horses and men were piles promiscuously.

"At the highest point of the ridge lay Gen. Custer, surrounded by a chosen band. Here were his two brothers and his nephew, Mr. Reed, Col. Yates and Col.

Cooke, and Capt. Smith, all lying in a circle of a few yards, their horses beside them. Here, behind Col. Yates' company, *the last stand* had been made, and here, one after another, these last survivors of Gen. Custer's five companies had met their death. The companies had successively thrown themselves across the path of the advancing enemy and had been annihilated. Not a man has escaped to tell the tale, but the story was inscribed on the surface of the barren hills in a language more eloquent than words."

Walt Whitman, singer of America, composed the first literary tribute to the fallen hero. Within twenty-four hours after the news reached him in Camden, New Jersey, Whitman mailed "A Death Song for Custer" to Whitelaw Reid for the New York *Tribune*, putting a price tag of ten dollars on the manuscript... It was published July 10.

From far Dakota's canons
Land of the wild ravine, the dusky Sioux, the lonesome stretch, the silence,
Haply today a mournful wait haply a trumpet note for heroes.
Thou of the tawny flowing hair in battle,
I erewhile saw, with erect head, pressing ever in front, bearing a bright sword in thy hand,
Now ending well in death the splendid fever of thy deeds.

Significantly in the 26 lines of verse were at least two errors of fact-the "flowing hair" and the "bright sword." Custer's hair was cut short for the battle, and all sabers had been left at the base camp. Another poem published in the New York *Herald* by an anonymous author implied that Custer had been reckless in his attack on the Indians because he was angry with politicians in Washington, and had revenged himself by rushing headlong into an ambush. In years to come, these errors and many more would multiply in hundreds of books and articles, in dozen of paintings, plays, pageants, Wild West shows, motion pictures, and television dramas. In 1939 a comprehensive bibliography of Custerana contained 641 items, a number which has probably doubled since that date. Much of this mass of chronicle, which has made Custer more widely known than any other American military hero, is misted with fantasy, giving it a dreamlike quality that is suited to legendry and the perpetuation of heroes.

In the immediate aftermath of the tragedy, the nation turned to the survivors, grieving with the widow who like Aphrodite wept, for her lost Adonis. The press chronicled in detail the sad journey of Elizabeth Custer from Dakota to Michigan. In Chicago she stopped at the Palmer House, as she and George had always done when passing through the city, and announced that she wished to give her husband's numerous staghounds and foxhounds to anyone who would pay express charges and provide good homes for them. She kept up a brave front until she reached Monroe, Michigan, where her first sight of the Custers' hometown brought back such a rush of poignant memories that she fainted. Libby Custer, however, did not remain for long an inactive mourner of a dead hero. For the remaining fifty-seven years of her life she would devote her pen and her energies to the preservation of his legend.

Meanwhile in many cities public prayers were held for Custer and his comrades; throughout the summer in military posts and at fashionable summer resorts funds were raised for Custer monuments. Congress passed a bill to provide pensions for Custer's father and mother. Every scrap of news from the West made headlines: the supposed recovery of Custer's rifle from a warrior killed in the Black Hills; the surrender of nineteen of Sitting Bull's warriors; the tall tales of Curley the Crow scout who was allegedly the only surviving witness; false reports of the deaths of Crazy Horse and Sitting Bull.

No man becomes completely a hero in death unless it can be shown that his adversary also was touched by the magic power of the gods. Sitting Bull was the monstrous villain, hated but respected. Many fanciful accounts of his life appeared in print; *Harpers' Weekly* published Sitting Bull's autobiography in a special supplement, illustrating it with the Sioux medicine man's own remarkable drawings. No one seemed to remember Custer's remark that there were two Sitting Bulls, one friendly, the other hostile. What was known about both of them was combined and woven into one character, which made the mythical Sitting Bull a complex Indian hero indeed—for a hero he became with the passing of time. He has fared far better in our mythology than Crazy Horse, who fought bravery and with real generalship. Bull did not fight at all that day. As though prescient of his destiny, he sat on a hill making medicine and communing with the gods.

Before the end of the centennial summer, both Buffalo Bill and Wild Bill Hickok also entered American mythology. Like Custer, Wild Bill Hickok died violently, but Buffalo Bill was one of those unusual mortals who is permitted by the gods to live out his legend. William E Cody did not have to die to become a myth; he only had to kill an Indian, a Cheyenne named Yellow Hand.

Both Cody and Hickok were linked with Custer, having served as scouts for him through several campaigns. In fable, heroes usually seek the company of heroes, so it was fitting that the paths of Wild Bill and Buffalo Bill crossed frequently during the turbulent postwar decade on the Western frontier.

Cody was not merely a flamboyant showman. He was a genuine plainsman—daring, resourceful, tough as rawhide. As a teenage boy he rode for the Pony Express. He soldiered in the ranks during the Civil War; he hunted buffalo to supply meat for workmen building the Union Pacific Railroad; he scouted for the Army.

But there were hundreds of young Americans roaming the West who were just as leathery as he—bullwhackers, teamsters, stagecoach drivers, miners, buffalo hunters, soldiers, cowboys, gamblers, peace officers. Dozens of them bore the nickname "Buffalo Bill." By chance, Buffalo Bill Cody met a writer. Edward

Z. C. Judson, who signed his dime novels as "Ned Buntline." Buntline borrowed Cody's nickname for a story, *Buffalo Bill, the King of the Border Men,* which began running serially in the *New York Weekly* in December 1869.

Buntline's novel had nothing to do with Cody's real life adventures; it would have been a better story if it had, but it did mark the beginning of the Buffalo Bill legend. What was more important, Cody's relationship with Buntline opened the way to a stage career for the young plainsman. Buntline also wrote plays of a sort, and in 1872 he persuaded Cody to appear in a preposterous drama entitled *Scouts of the Prairie; or, Red Deviltry As it Is.* Dialogue and action could not have been cruder; the reviewers condemned it, but because of the novelty of the cast, audiences packed the Chicago theater where the play opened. In Eastern cities, *Scouts of the Prairie* was an even greater financial success.

During the following three years Cody toured theaters in the winter months, returning to the frontier each summer to guide hunting parties or scout for the Army. One year he invited Wild Bill Hickok to make a stage tour, but Wild Bill was too reckless with his shooting irons, inflicting powder burns on several of the minor actors, and Cody had to let him go before the season ended.

As late as the spring of 1876, Buffalo Bill was still a third-rate actor traveling about the country performing in third-rate melodramas set in the Wild West. To achieve immortality he must perform a heroic deed that would give him special distinction, an exploit worthy of a god. His opportunity came in July of that year, occurring only a few days after the nationwide shock of the last Stand, on the same lonely sagebrush plains, and luckily in view of appreciative newspaper correspondents.

On June 10, 1876, Cody joined General Wesley Merritt's 5th Cavalry Regiment at Fort Laramie as scout, and set out on his strawberry roan to capture "all the Sitting Bulls and Crazy Horses in the Sioux tribe." Less than a month afterward, July 7, while the 5th Regiment was camped on Sage Creek in eastern Wyoming, he heard the awesome news that Sitting Bull and Crazy Horse had wiped out Custer's battalion.

A few days later, General Merritt received orders to move rapidly eastward to intercept a thousand Cheyenne warriors who had suddenly departed their Nebraska reservation to join the victorious Indians in the north.

After a forced march of eighty miles, the cavalrymen unsaddled under a screen of bluffs along Hat Creek (sometimes called War Bonnet Creek). Horses and men were exhausted, and as soon as the animals were picketed, everyone except the guards rolled up in blankets for a sound sleep.

Before dawn of July 17, Cody was saddling his horse, ready to start scouting for the expected Cheyennes. He must have had a vision that this would be a day of great importance (gods possess the power of divination). Instead of donning his buckskins he chose to wear a stage costume which he had packed in his saddlebags—a Mexican vaquero outfit of black and scarlet, trimmed with silver buttons and lace.

As though following a prepared script, Cody rode out, located the Cheyennes, and returned to camp in time to alert the cavalry. At one of the outposts, he joined a small group which included Lieutenant Charles King, who would writing variations of the ensuing incident in dozens of novels about the Indian-fighting cavalry.

Shortly after sunrise the first Cheyenne horsemen appeared on a ridge two miles to the east, and at about the same time the regiment's supply train from Fort Laramie came into view from the southwest. Screened by bluffs along Hat Creek, the cavalrymen remained invisible to the Cheyennes; the Indians in turn could not be seen by the soldiers with the wagon train.

Suddenly a war party of thirty or forty Cheyennes came dashing down a ravine below Lieutenant King's outpost. At first King and Cody were puzzled as to the warriors' intentions, but when they glanced toward the supply train they saw two soldiers galloping far out in front of the lead wagon. The two horsemen were couriers who had sighted signs of the cavalry camp, and, not expecting to find enemies in the area, were hastening forward to deliver their messages to General Merritt. In another minute or so they would run headlong into the concealed war party.

Cody leaped into his saddle immediately and started to the rescue, Lieutenant King ordering eight men from the outpost to follow him in support. As soon as Cody and his party were down the slope and into the trail, they sought what cover they could find and waited for the approaching Cheyennes.

The action which followed was witnessed and recorded by a correspondent for the New York *Herald:* "Down they came nearer and nearer, the sun flashing from their brilliantly painted bodies and their polished ornaments... The Indians... turned savagely on Buffalo Bill and the little party at the outpost. The latter sprang from their horses and met the daring charge with a volley. Yellow Hand, a young Cheyenne brave, came foremost, singling Bill as a foeman worthy of his steel. Cody coolly knelt, and taking deliberate aim sent his bullet through the chief's leg and into his horse's head. Down went the two, and, before his friends could reach him, a second shot laid the redskin low. On came the others, bent on annihilating the little band that opposed them, when to their amazement, a long blue line popped up in their very front, and K Company, with Colonel Mason at its head, dashed at them..."

That was all there was to it. The Cheyennes scattered, most of them returning to their reservation, and the 5th Regiment and Buffalo Bill were back in Fort Laramie four days later.

Within such incidents is the genesis of legends. Before the end of summer the encounter between Cody and Yellow Hand had become folklore, a classical confrontation of two mythical beings—a Hector opposing an Ajax, David against Goliath, Sir Gawain and the Green Knight.

Because the nation's attention was fixed upon the Indian War, the story was told and retold, new versions embellished and amplified. It came a personal vendetta between two longstanding enemies, a duel which lasted for several minutes while the other Indians and the cavalrymen stood by as admiring noninterfering spectators. On September 25, the *New York Weekly* began publication of *The Crimson Trail; or, On Custer's Last Warpath.* In this story, as Buffalo Bill lifts Yellow Hand's topknot he shouts, "The first scalp for Custer!" Thus was forged a link with the heroic cavalry leader.

Cody's four years on the stage had taught him the value of publicity, and he contributed to the legend by sending trophies of his feat to Rochester, New York, his temporary family home. There Yellow Hand's scalp, war bonnet, and shield were placed on exhibition. Photographs of this gory display soon appeared for sale around the country; newspapers and magazines reproduced them in drawings.

That winter Buffalo Bill turned the Indian War into drama on the stage, and after he organized his Wild West show which traveled the world for a third of a century, his duel with Yellow Hand was submerged into a mythical near rescue of Custer at the Last Stand. Simultaneously his legend thrived in more than 500 Buffalo Bill dime novels, most of them from the fertile imagination of Prentiss Ingraham.

When the old showman died in Denver, Colorado, in 1917, four states contended for burial rights. Almost five months passed before Colorado settled the matter by enclosing his body in a steel vault and sinking it into solid granite lined with cement, a crypt from which even a god would have difficulty in escaping.

In the clanship of the gods, it was inevitable that James Butler Hickok, good friend of William F. Cody and George Armstrong Custer, should fill out the triumvirate. The forces which made this possible were set in motion in June 1876 when Hickok arrived in Cheyenne, Wyoming, en route to the Black Hills.

Wild Bill's career in many ways paralleled that of Buffalo Bill. They drove wagon trains and stagecoaches; they both fought in the Union Army; they served as scouts against hostile Indians. Wild Bill became a celebrity two years before Cody when *Harpers' New Monthly Magazine* of February 1867 introduced him to the nation in an illustrated article glorifying his frontier exploits.

During the brawling era of cattle drives from Texas, he was marshal at Hays and Abilene, establishing his reputation as a gunfighter by killing several "bad men." He entered the acting profession with Buffalo Bill's show, but was no success. He turned to gambling, wandering about the West, occasionally becoming involved in gunplay in which he was always successful. But he grew increasingly wary as his eyesight began to fail, and after a long and interrupted courtship of Agnes Lake, widow of a showman, he married her in March 1876, resolving to settle down *as* soon as he could recoup his fading fortune. Apparently Hickok hoped to accomplish this by staking a gold claim in the Black Hills. He left his wife in Cincinnati and joined a small group of old friends in Cheyenne. In late June, just about the time Custer was marching into Sitting Bull's stronghold, Hickok and his friends started north for the Black Hills.

On June 30, John Hunton who owned a ranch between Cheyenne and Fort Laramie noted in his diary that a "large party of Black Hillers passed with Wild Bill." Next day the party was at Fort Laramie where they were delayed two or three days for assembly of a wagon train large enough to offer protection against Indian attacks. With this wagon train were several prostitutes who had been practicing their trade near the fort, and were transferring to booming Deadwood in hopes of larger profits. One of them was Martha Jane Cannary, better known as Calamity Jane. She and Wild Bill may have met before, but neither had any special attraction for the other.

By remarkable coincidence, at a 5th Cavalry camp on Sage Creek, Wild Bill and Buffalo Bill met for the last time July 7, and on that same day learned of Custer's death. Four days later, Hickok arrived in Deadwood, renewed acquaintanceship with friends, and staked out a gold claim.

His reputation as a gunfighter was known everywhere now, and he was quite aware that he had enemies as well as friends—outlaws he had humiliated in the old trail towns of Kansas, lesser gunmen resentful of his prowess. In Deadwood when he was asked to demonstrate his fast draw and marksmanship, he used shiny tin cans as targets, and no one suspected that his eyesight was dimming. But he knew it, and probably brooded on his weakness, telling friends that he had a presentiment he would be killed in Deadwood, writing his wife on August 1 that if he should never see her again he would breathe her name while firing his last shot.

Wild Bill never had an opportunity to fire that last shot. On the afternoon of August 2, while he was playing poker in a saloon, a twenty-five-year-old malcontent named Jack McCall shot him in the back, killing him instantly.

The death of Wild Bill was reported in most Eastern newspapers, although the coverage by no means compared with the extensive treatment given Custer or Buffalo Bill. "Everybody in the country has heard of Wild Bill," a delayed dispatch from Denver began, "noted scout, buffalo hunter and plainsman, and who on account of his reckless bravery was made marshal at different times of several frontier towns when it was necessary because of the lawlessness that prevailed in their early settlement to have peace officers who could kill in order to uphold their authority."

The story went on to explain that Hickok had killed a man named Sutherland in Kansas, and that "Sutherland's avenger kept the trail like a sleuth-hound. Wild Bill..." was a tall handsome fellow about forty years of age, as straight as an Indian, and like most of his class, wore his hair, which was as black as a crow, falling over his shoulders... By some means Bill drifted into the Black Hills, and on the 2nd day of the month he was shot in the back of the head and killed at Deadwood City by a man named Sutherland, a brother of the man of that name whom Wild Bill killed in a Kansas trail town... Wild Bill's friends say Sutherland will never live to get out of the country"

It was true that McCall used the alias Sutherland in Deadwood (although most of the gamblers knew his real name). But the story that Hickok had killed his brother was pure fantasy invented by McCall. Leander P. Richardson, a writer for *Scribner's Magazine,* who was in Deadwood reported that McCall was "hired to do his work by gamblers who feared the time when better citizens should appoint Bill the champion of law and order." McCall's real motive, however, was that of a nobody who wanted to become the greatest gunfighter of the west.

The prediction that the killer would "never live to get out of the country" proved false. A hastily convened and illegal jury found McCall not guilty, and the judge freed him, ordering him to leave town.

Hickok's friends were irate, some threatening a lynching, but a few were wise enough to know that the law could still punish the killer. Not long afterward a United States marshal tracked McCall down in Wyoming and arrested him when he was overheard boasting that he had killed Wild Bill. Like all Western villains he met his just deserts, death by hanging on March 1, 1877.

The legend of Wild Bill matured slowly, much of it by oral transmission in the tradition of purest folklore. Calamity Jane's name appeared in none of the contemporary accounts of his death or the two trials of Jack McCall, and during the 1880s when the first dime novels about Calamity and Wild Bill began to appear, the authors gave no special romantic treatment to their relationship. In *Calamity Jane, the Heroine of Whoop-Up,* 1885, her true love was Deadwood Dick.

But with the passing of time, Wild Bill and Calamity Jane were linked as irrevocably as Pyramus and Thisbe, Tristram and Isolde, or Paris and Helen of Troy. One of the later romancers brought Calamity into the saloon where Bill lay dying; as she knelt by his side she heard his last whisper: "My heart was yours, from the first."

Barroom anecdotes and campfire tales about their undying love spread across the West so that fact and fancy became inextricably mingled. When John Hunton, the Wyoming rancher who knew both of them, decided to record the "facts" about the famous pair, he fell victim to one of these myths and said that a mob led by a furiously grieving Calamity had lynched Jack McCall. Another myth that would not die was their supposed marriage which produced a child. As late as 1896, however, Calamity herself was making no claim on Wild Bill as a former lover. Her ghostwritten autobiography published that year mentions him only twice, the incident of the wagon train journey from Fort Laramie, and a lurid account of how she attempted to avenge his death by pursuing Jack McCall with a meat cleaver.

During the next seven years, *as* Calamity sank lower in the social scale and became a besotted, maundering wanderer of the Black Hills, selling her pamphlet autobiography and photographs to tourists, she discovered that everyone wanted to hear about her life with Wild Bill. By this time she may have come to believe some of the myths herself. Anyway she soon found that a good tale about her love for Bill was an excellent opening for a handout or a free beer.

When she visited Deadwood in July 1903, she arranged to have her photograph made at Wild Bill's grave, posing her ruined face so that it simulated anguish for a long-dead lover. Calamity did not profit very much from this photograph. A few weeks later she was dead. Whether it is true that she expressed a final wish to be buried beside Wild Bill is doubtful, but to the citizens of Deadwood it was the fitting thing to do.

Today Calamity Jane and Wild Bill lie together, sealed forever in the myth of the harlot with a heart of gold, the gunfighter with the fastest draw in the West, a profane Artemis in men's buckskins, an Orion astride the sky with a pair of six-shooters glittering like stars.

To round out this gallery of rogues, the American people needed a legendary hero who robbed the rich to help the poor, a native American Robin Hood. The likeliest candidates were four Missouri cousins, a pair of brothers—Bob and Cole Younger, Frank and Jesse James. Their specialties were stagecoach, train, and bank robberies. During 1876 this quartet, with their merry band of robbers, reached the zenith of their careers.

For various reasons the Robin Hood mantle was to fall upon the shoulders of Jesse James. His name was alliterative, suited to dime novel titles, easy to remember. He was the planner of most of the robberies; he was the most elusive; he had a prankish sense of humor. Like Robin Hood who sent impudent messages to the Sheriff of Nottingham, Jesse wrote insulting letters to Pinkerton detectives and to newspapers, either denying the exploits he was accused of or daring his pursuers to capture and convict him. Jesse also looked the part. In one of his early photographs he wore an antique powder horn and a hat with the brim upturned so that it resembled the jaunty bonnet of a denizen of Sherwood Forest.

[illegible] 1875, the James boys successfully robbed at least eleven [illegible] and three stagecoaches. How many more they robbed [illegible] usually had alibis to prove they were somewhere else, [illegible] away from the scenes of their crimes.

In 1876 as if purposely setting a pattern for posterity to remember them by, the James-Younger combination planned and executed three robberies, each one a different demonstration of their professional skills—a stagecoach holdup in Texas, a train robbery in Missouri, and the disastrous robbery of the Northfield, Minnesota, bank.

The Austin-San Antonio stagecoach holdup on May 12 was a model of perfection. Two months later they were back in their home state of Missouri, and being in need of cash, decided to rob a train. Assembling half a dozen or more of their trusted yeomen, they selected Rocky Cut east of Otterville on the Missouri Pacific Railroad as a suitable site.

About ten o'clock on the night of July 7, the engineer of an eastbound train saw a red signal lantern flashing ahead in the railroad cut. Believing it to be a warning from a trackwalker, he reached for the air brake. A few moments later his locomotive crashed into a pile of ties and lumber. As the train came to a rocking stop, masked men swarmed alongside, yelling and firing off pistols. Two jumped aboard the locomotive, covering the engineer and fireman with huge revolvers and threatening to kill them if they offered resistance. At the same time three other robbers climbed into the side door of the express car, demanding the keys to the safe. The baggageman told them be had no keys, that the express messenger carried them, but had disappeared immediately after the train's sudden halt.

Two of the robbers then marched the baggageman through the train, ordering him to point out the express messenger when they came to him. In this way they passed through every car in the train, terrorizing the passengers, many of whom crouched down under seats. Not until they reached the rear sleeper did they find the expressman. He had given his keys to the brakeman to hide in his shoes, but he had already discovered that escape from the train was impossible because of the robbers outside who were galloping up and down, yelling like devils and firing off their weapons. The two masked men took the keys, returned to the express car, opened both safes, and crammed $16,000 into a large wheat sack. A few minutes later the gang raced away on their horses.

By morning, central Missouri was in turmoil with several posses in hot pursuit of the robbers. But as usual Jesse James and his merry men scattered to prearranged hideouts, vanishing into the Ozark hills. A few weeks later, after newspapers reported that the robbery was the work of the James-Younger boys, Jesse in his usual fashion wrote a letter to the Kansas City *Times* claiming he could prove his presence in another part of Missouri at the time of the robbery. He then concluded by accusing one of the posse leaders of committing the train robbery.

About the time his letter was published, Jesse and seven of his chief yeomen were on a train bound for Minnesota. One of the seven was Bill Chadwell, who had spent considerable time in Minnesota. He had convinced Jesse that not only were the banks in Minnesota filled with money, but that robbery should be easy because the crime was so seldom practiced there.

After a leisurely inspection of several Minnesota towns, they selected Northfield. It was a county seat, the First National was the only bank in the prosperous area, and the quiet dusty village looked vulnerable. A bank robbery should be mere child's play.

Early on the afternoon of September 7, three of the gang rode casually into town, hitched their horses to a rail, and waited for the first act of the drama. It came suddenly—three riders galloping in from one direction, two from another, all five yelling and shooting. This was a signal for the three dismounted outlaws to enter the bank, draw their revolvers, and order the three bank employees to hand over all the money in the safe.

The cashier, unaware that he was facing three of the most competent bank robbers in the Republic, not only refused to comply but made an attempt to slam the safe door shut. A pistol butt crashed into his head, knocking him to the floor. While this was happening one of the tellers leaped toward the rear door of the bank. A bullet tore into his shoulder, but he escaped.

The recklessly brave cashier meanwhile had arisen and was reaching for a drawer, trying to get his hands on a pistol. A screaming bullet caught him in the head, killing him instantly.

Outside the bank, aroused citizens of North-field had brought rifles and shotguns into play against the five outlaws in the street, wounding Bill Chadwell and Cole Younger, killing Clell Miller.

Warned by the gunfire outside, the three men inside the bank abandoned their plans to rob the safe, grabbed what money was in sight, and fled into the battleground of the street. What happened next was described by so many contradictory eyewitnesses that the version of a contemporary dime novel author is probably as accurate as any:

> *Jesse mounted his horse with the reins in his teeth and a revolver in each hand, old guerrilla fashion, charged again and again up the street, clearing it each time. But the houses were being filled with armed men and a continuous rain of bullets rattled around him.*
>
> *The sharp cracking had increased to a steady roar, and they knew it was only a question of time when they should all be shot down.*
>
> *"Mount quick!" cried Jesse. "We must leave this accursed town or we shall all be killed."*

Before they escaped that "accursed town," two of the original eight outlaws were dead in the street, and every one of the surviving six was wounded.

By nightfall posses were swarming throughout southeastern Minnesota, but the James-Younger boys had been in tight places before. Instead of running, they holed up for four days within sixteen miles of Northfield, nursing their wounds and waiting for the pursuers to relax their vigilance. The Minnesotans, however, remained alert, and when the outlaws came out of cover the chase was resumed.

On September 21, two weeks after the robbery, a posse surrounded them in a thick patch of woods. In the furious battle which followed, one robber was killed, three captured. Two escaped.

Although it was a disaster for the outlaws, the Northfield bank robbery was so faultless in its plot line that dime novel writers were left with nothing to invent. *The James Boys in Minnesota* ended the story this way:

> *Frank and Jesse James were the only outlaws of the eight who had gone on the disastrous expedition to Northfield, Minnesota, who escaped. They were pursued vigilantly to the very border lines, and far*

beyond, but no man can yet boast that he has ever captured one of the wonderful James boys.

They were already heroes, Frank and Jesse. The three who were captured were Bob, Cole, and Jim Younger; their long prison sentences kept them among the mortals.

There would be three more train robberies, a stage holdup, and a bank robbery, but the James boys were running out of yeomen. Time ran out for Jesse on April 3, 1882, when Robert Ford shot him in the back in hopes of receiving a $10,000 reward from the state of Missouri. Frank later gave himself up, was tried and acquitted. He lived out the rest of his long life too uneventfully to remain a hero.

So It was Jesse who became the American Robin Hood, Jesse James, the leader of a robber gang which took almost half a million dollars from the rich. The poor who received it were themselves, their relatives, and their women, as wide a distribution of stolen property perhaps as was made by the original bandit of Sherwood Forest.

A sadistic murderer of at least a dozen men was a legend before he was out of his teens. In 1876 at the age of seventeen, William H. Bonney was roaming the southwestern ranges, robbing, killing, making love to fair Mexican maidens who would soon play guitars and sing about Billy their boy-bandit king.

Billy the Kid, born on New York City's Bowery, grew up in the West during [illegible] n he was only twelve years old, he killed his first man with [illegible] hting remark about his mother. Not long after that he was [illegible] on as a gunman, quick-tempered young savage, hostile to authority, as dangerous as a rattlesnake when crossed. In his photographs Billy's face appears adenoidal, almost moronic, resembling that of a predatory rodent.

But when a mortal wins the sympathy of the gods, great transformations are possible. In American mythology Billy is a Hermes (who on the day of his birth rustled fifty heifers from the divine herd of Apollo) with a face fine and fair, who started out in life with a chance to be square, but was led astray by the dark forces of destiny.

Billy spent most of the centennial year rustling cattle, an activity which brought him into the Lincoln County War of 1877-78. He was arrested for killing a sheriff, then escaped by killing two guards, and the law had to hunt him down like the dangerous wild animal he was. Six months after his death in 1881, *The True Life of Billy the Kid* was being sold on the streets of the city where he was born. The legend was on its way.

Myra Belle Shirley who became Belle Starr was no more admirable a character than Billy the Kid. Like Billy, Belle was a teen-age rebel. She was a sexually promiscuous wood nymph, leaving home at the age of eighteen after being seduced by Cole Younger, and before the end of her career had in turn seduced far more men than Billy the Kid slew with his six-gun.

In 1876 Belle had not yet achieved national fame, but she had begun her life of crime, during which she exchanged one male partner for another through a long line of husbands and paramours that included Sam Starr. It was while she was married to Sam that she secured most of her publicity as Belle Star. A six-month sentence was the sole conviction any court was able to return against her, although she was involved in enough violent robberies to fill a large catalog. Only a bullet could stop Belle Starr's blazing career, and that was how she [illegible] ne day in 1889.

[illegible] on, Belle has never quite reached the upper ranks of [illegible] remains a wood nymph, cavorting with centaurs and [illegible]

The affinity of the gods for bad men and loose women is beyond the control of mortals. Mortals also usually fail when they attempt to fill out obvious lacunae in their mythology. A case in point is the cowboy, America's most romantic figure. No cowboy was ever chosen to join the gods.

To fill the need for a cowboy hero, some well-meaning mortal created a synthetic being called Pecos Bill. No amount of literary endeavor has succeeded in breathing life into Pecos Bill. He is but a pale imitation of such real trail drivers as Shanghai Pierce, Charles Goodnight, and Richard King, all active rawhiders in the 1870's. Or Tom Candy Ponting who drove the first Longhorns from Texas to New York City. Or Nelson Story who trailed a herd from Texas to Montana through an Indian war and blizzard. Perhaps the real cowboys worked too hard on roundups, endured too much on the range, were too honest, and displayed too little wickedness in the sinful trail towns to win the notice of the gods.

First choice for a hero of American stagecoach drivers would be Hank Monk who boasted that he always "got through on time." The Gold Hill (Nevada) *News* saluted him on his fiftieth birthday in 1876: "Of all the drivers who have drawn strings over kyuse and mustang horses that no one but a western man would think of harnessing, Hank Monk is probably the best man." Hank celebrated the nation's centennial by setting a new record on the stagecoach run between Virginia City and Carson City—one hour and eight minutes. But not even Mark Twain, who extolled him in *Roughing It,* could make an enduring hero of Hank Monk.

[illegible] er's Last Stand, Captain William J. Fetterman and [illegible] ramatic massacre at Fort Phil Kearny, and Colonel [illegible] aved the fort from disaster. Both remain in the shadows of history, almost forgotten.

In December 1876, Frank Eclestadt, civilian dispatch rider for the Army, performed a remarkable feat. While carrying messages on horseback from Hat Creek to Red Cloud Agency he was surrounded by twelve circling Cheyennes.

Eclestadt fought them off, killed two, then made a mad dash through their line only to have his mount shot from under him. He got to his feet with two revolvers at ready, dived into a cottonwood thicket, kept the Cheyennes at bay until dark, and then made his way on foot to the agency to deliver his dispatches. Along with thousands of others like him, Eclestadt has almost vanished from the memory of man.

There is no accounting for the caprices of mythmakers. Gods and heroes are made by poets and balladers, folktellers in rhyme or prose. No matter what heroic deeds mortals may perform, without minstrels to sing of them or scribblers to set them down, they fade into the vast limbo of unrecorded legend. And if the gods are not listening, all the Homers and sweet-voiced minstrels combined can never sing a mortal to the heights of Olympus.

caprice- a sudden, unpredictable change

2. The Gospel of Wealth

Andrew Carnegie

Andrew Carnegie (1835-1919), a Scottish immigrant who made a reality of the "rags to riches" myth, was one of the most successful and richest businessmen of the "Gilded Age." He reflected upon his great wealth and in 1889 wrote a tract, "The Gospel Wealth," in which he justified laissez-faire capitalism and the accumulation of huge fortunes. In the following excerpt Carnegie considers the options a rich person faces in disposing of great wealth.

The Problem of the Administration of Wealth

The problem of our age is the proper administration of wealth, so that the ties of brotherhood may still bind together the rich and poor in harmonious relationship. The conditions of human life have not only been changed, but revolutionized, within the past few hundred years. In former days there was little difference between the dwelling, dress, food, and environment of the chief and those of his retainers. The Indians are today where civilized man then was. When visiting the Sioux, I was led to the wigwam of the chief. It was like the others in external appearance, and even within the difference was trifling between it and those of the poorest of his braves. The contrast between the palace of the millionaire and the cottage of the laborer with us today measures the change which has come with civilization. This change, however, is not to be deplored, but welcomed as highly beneficial. It is well, nay, essential, for the progress of the race that the houses of some should be homes for all that is highest and best in literature and the arts, and for all the refinements of civilization, rather than that none should be so. Much better this great irregularity than universal squalor. Without wealth there can be no Maecenas. The "good old times" were not good old times. Neither master nor servant was as well situated then as to-day. A relapse to old conditions would be disastrous to both—not the least so to him who serves—and would sweep away civilization with it. But whether the change be for good or ill, it is upon us, beyond our power to alter, and therefore to be accepted and made the best of. It is a waste of time to criticize the inevitable.

It is easy to see how the change has come. One illustration will serve for almost every phase of the cause. In the manufacture of products we have the whole story. It applies to all combinations of human industry, as stimulated and enlarged by the inventions of this scientific age. Formerly, articles were manufactured at the domestic hearth, or in small shops which formed part of the household. The master and his apprentices worked side by side, the latter living with the master, and therefore subject to the same conditions. When these apprentices rose to be masters, there was little or no change in their mode of life, and they, in turn, educated succeeding apprentices in the same routine. There was, substantially, social equality, and even political equality, for those engaged in industrial pursuits had then little or no voice in the State.

The inevitable result of such a mode of manufacture was crude articles at high prices. To-day the world obtains commodities of excellent quality at prices which even the preceding generation would have deemed incredible. In the commercial world similar causes have produced similar results, and the race is benefited thereby. The poor enjoy what the rich could not before afford. What were the luxuries have become the necessaries of life. The laborer has now more comforts than the farmer had a few generations ago. The farmer has more luxuries than the landlord had, and is more richly clad and better housed. The landlord has books and pictures rarer and appointments more artistic than the king could then obtain.

The price we pay for this salutary change, is, no doubt, great. We assemble thousands of operatives in the factory, in the mine, and in the counting-house, of whom the employer can know little or nothing, and to whom the employer is little better than a myth. All intercourse between them is at an end. Rigid castes are formed, and, as usual, mutual ignorance breeds mutual distrust. Each caste is without sympathy for the other, and ready to credit anything disparaging in regard to it. Under the law of competition, the employer of thousands is forced into the strictest economies, among which the rates paid to labor figure prominently, and often there is friction between the employer and the employed, between capital and labor, between rich and poor. Human society loses homogeneity.

The price which society pays for the law of competition, like the price it pays for cheap comforts and luxuries, is also great; but the advantages of this law are also greater still, for it is to this law that we owe our wonderful material development, which brings improved conditions in its train. But, whether the law be benign or not, we must say of it, as we say of the change in the conditions of men to which we have referred: It is here; we cannot evade it; no substitutes for it have been found; and while the law may be sometimes hard for the individual, it is best for the race, because it insures the survival of the fittest in every department. We accept and welcome, therefore, as conditions to which we must accommodate ourselves, great inequality of environment, the concentration of business, industrial and commercial, in the hands of a few, and the law of competition between these, as being not only beneficial, but essential for the future progress of the race. Having accepted these, it follows that there must be great scope for the exercise of special ability in the merchant and in the manufacturer who has to conduct affairs upon a great scale. That this talent for organization and management is rare among men is proved by the fact that it invariably secures enormous rewards for it possessor, no matter where or under what laws or conditions. The experienced in affairs always rate the MAN whose services can be obtained as a partner as not only the first consideration, but such as render the question of his capital scarcely worth considering: for able men soon create capital; in the hands of those without the special talent required, capital soon takes wings. Such men become interested in firms or corporations using millions; and, estimating only simple interest to be made upon the capital invested, it is inevitable that their income must exceed their expenditure and that they must, therefore, accumulate wealth. Nor is there any middle ground which such men can occupy, because the great manufacturing or commercial concern which does not earn at least interest upon its capital soon becomes bankrupt. It must either go forward or fall behind; to stand still is impossible. It is a condition essential to its successful operation that it should be thus far profitable, and even that, in addition to interest on capital, it should make profit. It is a law, as certain as any of the others named, that men possessed of this peculiar talent for affairs, under the free play of economic forces must, of necessity, soon be in receipt of more revenue than can be judiciously expended upon themselves; and this law is as beneficial for the race as the others.

Objections to the foundations upon which society is based are not in order, because the condition of the race is better with these than it has been with any other which have been tried. Of the effect of any new substitutes proposed we cannot be sure. The Socialist or Anarchist who seeks to overturn present conditions is to be regarded as attacking the foundation upon which civilization itself rests, for civilization took its start from the day that the capable, industrious workman said to his incompetent and lazy fellow, "If thou dolt not sow, thou shalt not reap," and thus ended primitive Communism by separating the drones from the bees. One who studies this subject will soon be brought face to face with the conclusion that upon the sacredness of property civilization itself depends—the right of the laborer to his hundred dollars in the savings bank, and equally the legal right of the millionaire to his millions. Every man must be allowed "to sit under his own vine and fig-tree, with none to make afraid," if human society is to advance, or even to remain so far advanced as it is. To those who propose to substitute Communism for this intense Individualism the answer therefore is: The race has tried that. All progress from that barbarous day to the present time has resulted from its displacement. Not evil, but good, has come to the race from the accumulation of wealth by those who have had the ability and energy that produce it. But even if we admit for a moment that it might be better for the race to discard its present foundation, Individualism—that is a nobler ideal that man should labor, not for himself alone, but in for a brotherhood of his fellows, and share with them all in common, realizing Swedenborg's idea of heaven, where is, as he says, the angels derive their happiness, not from laboring for self, but for each other—even admit all this, and a sufficient answer is, This is not evolution, but revolution. It necessitates the changing of human nature itself—a work of eons, even if it were good to change it, which we cannot know.

It is not practicable in our day or in our age. Even if desirable theoretically, it belongs to another and long-succeeding sociological stratum. Our duty is with what is practicable now—with the next step possible in our day and generation. It is criminal to waste our energies in endeavoring to uproot, when all we can profitably accomplish is to bend the universal tree of humanity a little in the direction most favorable to the production of good fruit under existing circumstances. We might as well urge the destruction of the highest existing type of man because he failed to reach our ideal as to favor the destruction of Individualism, Private Property, the Law of Accumulation of Wealth, and the Law of Competition; for these are the highest result of human experience, the soil in which society, so far, has produced the best fruit. Unequally or unjustly, perhaps, as these laws sometimes operate, and imperfect as they appear to the Idealist, they are, nevertheless, like the highest type of man, the best and most valuable of all that humanity has yet accomplished.

We start, then, with a condition of affairs under which the best interests of the race are promoted, but which inevitably gives wealth to the few. Thus far, accepting conditions as they exist, the situation can be surveyed and pronounced good. The question then arises—and if the foregoing be correct, it is the only question with which we have to deal,—What is the proper mode of administering wealth after the laws upon which civilization is founded have thrown it into the hands of the few? And it is of this great question that I believe I offer the true solution. It will be understood that fortunes are here spoken of, not moderate sums saved by many years of effort, the returns from which are required for the comfortable maintenance and education of families. This is not wealth, but only competence, which it should be the aim of all to acquire, and which it is for the best interests of society should be acquired.

There are but three modes in which surplus wealth can be disposed of. It can be left to the families of the decedents; or it can be bequeathed for public purposes; or, finally, it can be administered during their lives by its possessors. Under the first and second modes most of the wealth of the world that has reached the few has hitherto been applied. Let us in turn consider each of these modes. The first is the most injudicious. In monarchical countries, the estates and the greatest portion of the wealth are left to the first son, that the vanity of the parent may be gratified by the thought that his name and title are to descend to succeeding generations unimpaired. The condition of this class in Europe today teaches the failure of such hopes or ambitions. The successors have become impoverished through their follies, or from the fall in the value of land. Even in Great Britain the strict law of entail has been found inadequate to maintain an hereditary class. Its soil is rapidly passing into the hands of the stranger. Under republican institutions the division of property among the children is much fairer; but the question which forces itself upon thoughtful men in all lands is, Why should men leave great fortunes to their children? If this is done from affection, is it not misguided affection? Observation teaches that, generally speaking, it is not well for the children that they should be so burdened. Neither is it well for the State. Beyond providing for the wife and daughters moderate sources of income, and very moderate allowances indeed, if any, for the sons, men may well hesitate; for it is no longer questionable that great sums bequeathed often work more for injury than for the good of the recipients. Wise men will soon conclude that, for the best interests of the members of their families, and of the State, such bequests are an improper use of their means.

It is not suggested that men who have failed to educate their sons to earn a livelihood shall cast them adrift in poverty. If any man has seen fit to rear his sons with a view to their living idle lives, or, what is highly commendable, has instilled in them the sentiment that they are in a position to labor for public ends without reference to pecuniary considerations, then, of course, the duty of the parent is to see that such are provided for in moderation. There are instances of millionaires' sons unspoiled by wealth, who, being rich, still perform great services to the community. Such are the very salt of the earth, as valuable as, unfortunately, they are rare. It is not the exception, however, but the rule that men must regard; and, looking at the usual result of enormous sums conferred upon legatees, the thoughtful man must shortly say, "I would as soon leave to my son a curse as the almighty dollar," and admit to himself that it is not the welfare of the children, but family pride, which inspires these legacies.

As to the second mode, that of leaving wealth at death for public uses, it may be said that this is only a means for the disposal of wealth, provided a man is content to wait until he is dead before he becomes of much good in the world. Knowledge of the results of legacies bequeathed is not calculated to inspire the brightest hopes of much posthumous good being accomplished by them. The cases are not few in which the real object sought by the testator is not attained, nor are they few in which the real object sought by the testator is not attained, nor are they few in which his real wishes are thwarted. In many cases the bequests are so used as to become only monuments of his folly. It is well to remember that it requires the exercise of not less ability than that which acquires it, to use wealth so as to be really beneficial to the community. Besides this, it may fairly be said that no man is to be extolled for doing what he cannot help doing, nor is he to be thanked by the community to which he only leaves wealth at death. Men who leave vast sums in this way may fairly be thought men who would not have left it at all had they been able to take it with them. The memories of such cannot be held in grateful remembrance, for there is no grace in their gifts. It is not to be wondered at that such bequests seem so generally to lack the blessing.

The growing disposition to tax more and more heavily large estates left at death is a cheering indication of the growth of a salutary change in public opinion. The State of Pennsylvania now takes—subject to some exceptions—one tenth of the property left by its citizens. The budget presented in the British Parliament the other day proposes to increase the death-duties; and, most significant of all, the new tax is to be a graduated one. Of all forms of taxation, this seems the wisest. Men who continue hoarding great sums all their lives, the proper use of which for public ends would work good to the community from which it chiefly came, should be made to feel that the community, in the form of the State, cannot thus be deprived of its proper share. By taxing estates heavily at death the State marks its condemnation of the selfish millionaire's unworthy life.

It is desirable that nations should go much further in this direction. Indeed, it is difficult to set bounds to the share of a rich man's estate which should go at his death to the public through the agency of the State, and by all means such taxes should be graduated, beginning at nothing upon moderate sums to dependents, and increasing rapidly as the amounts swell, until of the millionaire's hoard, as of Shylock's, at least

The other half
Comes to the privy coffer of the State.

This policy would work powerfully to induce the rich man to attend to the administration of wealth during his life, which is the end that society should always have in view, as being by far the most fruitful for the people. Nor need it be feared that this policy would sap the root of enterprise and render men less anxious to accumulate, for, to the class whose ambition it is to leave great fortunes and be talked about after their death, it will attract even more attention, and, indeed, be a somewhat nobler ambition, to have enormous sums paid over to the State from their fortunes.

There remains, then, only one mode of using great fortunes; but in this we have the true antidote for the temporary unequal distribution of wealth, the reconciliation of the rich and the poor—a reign of harmony, another ideal, differing, indeed, from that of the Communist in requiring only the further evolution of existing conditions, not the total overthrow of our civilization. It is founded upon the present most intense Individualism, and the race is prepared to put it in practice by degrees whenever it pleases. Under its sway we shall have an ideal State, in which the surplus wealth of the few will become, in the best sense, the property of the many, because it is administered for the common good; and this wealth, passing through the hands of the few, can be made a much more potent force for the elevation of our race than if it had been distributed in small sums to the people themselves. Even the poorest can be made to see this, and to agree that great sums gathered by some of their fellow-citizens and spent for public purposes, from which the masses reap the principal benefit, are more valuable to them than if scattered among themselves through the course of many years in trifling amounts.

If we consider the results which flow from the Cooper Institute, for instance, to the best portion of the race in New York not possessed of means, and compare these with those which would have ensued for the good of the masses from an equal sum distributed by Mr. Cooper in his lifetime in the form of wages, which is the highest form of distribution, being for work done and not for charity, we can form some estimate of the possibilities for the improvement of the race which lie embedded in the present law of the accumulation of wealth. Much of this sum, if distributed in small quantities among the people, would have been wasted in the indulgence of appetite, some of it in excess, and it may be doubted whether even the part put to the best use, that of adding to the comforts of the home, would have yielded results for the race, as a race, at all comparable to those which are flowing and are to flow from the Cooper Institute from generation to generation. Let the advocate of violent or radical change ponder well this thought.

We might even go so far as to take another instance—that of Mr. Tilden's bequest of five millions of dollars for a free library in the city of New York; but in referring to this one cannot help saying involuntarily: How much better if Mr. Tilden had devoted the last years of his own life to the proper administration of this immense sum; in which case neither legal contest nor any other cause of delay could have interfered with his aims. But let us assume that Mr. Tilden's millions finally become the means of giving to this city a noble public library, where the treasures of the world contained in books will be open to all forever, without money and without price. Considering the good of that part of the race which congregates in and around Manhattan Island, would its permanent benefit have been better promoted had these millions been allowed to circulate in small sums through the hands of the masses? Even the most strenuous advocate of Communism must entertain a doubt upon this subject. Most of those who think will probably entertain no doubt whatever.

Poor and restricted are our opportunities in this life, narrow our horizon, our best work most imperfect; but rich men should be thankful for one inestimable boon. They have it in their power during their lives to busy themselves in organizing benefactions from which the masses of their fellows will derive lasting advantage, and thus dignify their own lives. The highest life is probably to be reached, not by such imitation of the life of Christ as Count Tolstoi gives us, but, while animated by Christ's spirit, by recognizing the changed conditions of this age, and adopting modes of expressing this spirit suitable to the changed conditions under which we live, still laboring for the good of our fellows, which was the essence of his life and teaching, but laboring in a different manner.

This, then, is held to be the duty of the man of wealth: To set an example of modest, unostentatious living, shunning display or extravagance; to provide moderately for the legitimate wants of those dependent upon him; and after doing so, to consider all surplus revenues which come to him simply as trust funds, which he is called upon to administer, and strictly bound as a matter of duty to administer in the manner which, in his judgment, is best calculated to produce the most beneficial results for the community—the man of wealth thus becoming the mere agent and trustee for his poorer brethren, bringing to their service his superior wisdom, experience, and ability to administer, doing for them better than they would or could do for themselves.

We are met here with the difficulty of determining what are moderate sums to leave to members of the family; what is modest, unostentatious living; what is the test of extravagance. There must be different standards for different conditions. The answer is that it is as impossible to name exact amounts or actions as it is to define good manners, good taste, or the rule of propriety; but, nevertheless, these are verities, well known, although indefinable. Public sentiment is quick to know and to feel what offends these. So in the case of wealth. The rule in regard to good taste in the dress of men or women applies here. Whatever makes one conspicuous offends the canon. If any family be chiefly known for display, for extravagance in home, table, or equipage, for enormous sums ostentatiously spent in any form upon itself—if these be its chief distinctions, we have no difficulty in estimating its nature or culture. So likewise in regard to the use or abuse of its surplus wealth, or to generous, free-handed cooperation in good public uses, or to unabated efforts to accumulate and hoard to the last, or whether they administer or bequeath. The verdict rests with the best and most enlightened public sentiment. The community will surely judge, and its judgments will not often be wrong.

The best uses to which surplus wealth can be put have already been indicated. Those who would administer wisely must, indeed, be wise; for one of the serious obstacles to the improvement of our race is indiscriminate charity. It were better for mankind that the millions of the rich were thrown into the sea than so spent as to encourage the slothful, the drunken, the unworthy. Of every thousand dollars spent in so-called charity to-day, it is probable that nine hundred and fifty dollars is unwisely spent—so spent, indeed, as to produce the very evils which it hopes to mitigate or cure. A well-known writer of philosophic books admitted the other day that he had given a quarter of a dollar to a man who approached him as he was coming to visit the house of his friend. He knew nothing of the habits of this beggar, knew not the use that would be made of this money, although he had every reason to suspect that it would be spent improperly. This man professed to be a disciple of Herbert Spencer; yet the quarter-dollar given that night will probably work more injury than all the money will do good which its thoughtless donor will ever be able to give in true charity. He only gratified his own feelings, save himself from annoyance—and this was probably one of the most selfish and very worst actions of his life, for in all respects he is most worthy.

In bestowing charity, the main consideration should be to help those who will help themselves; to provide part of the means by which those who desire to improve may do so; to give those who desire to rise the aids by which they may rise; to assist, but rarely or never to do all. Neither the individual nor the race is improved by alms-giving. Those worthy of assistance, except in rare cases, seldom require assistance. The really valuable men of the race never do, except in case of accident or sudden change. Every one has, of course, cases of individuals brought to his own knowledge where temporary assistance can do genuine good, and these he will not overlook. But the amount which can be wisely given by the individual for individuals is necessarily limited by his lack of knowledge of the circumstances connected with each. He is the only true reformer who is as careful and as anxious not to aid the unworthy as he is to aid the worthy, and, perhaps, even more so, for in alms-giving more injury is probably done by rewarding vice than by relieving virtue.

The rich man is thus almost restricted to following the examples of Peter Cooper, Enoch Pratt of Baltimore, Mr. Pratt of Brooklyn, Senator Stanford, and others, who know that the best means of benefiting the community is to place within its reach the ladders upon which the aspiring can rise—free libraries, parks, and means of recreation, by which men are helped in body and mind; works of art, certain to give pleasure and improve the public taste; and public institutions of various kinds, which will improve the general condition of the people; in this manner returning their surplus wealth to the mass of their fellows in the forms best calculated to do them lasting good.

Thus is the problem of rich and poor to be solved. The laws of accumulation will be left free; the laws of distribution free. Individualism will continue, but the millionaire will be but a trustee for the poor, intrusted for a season with a great part of the increased wealth of the community, but administering it for the community far better than it could or would have done for itself. The best minds will thus have reached a stage in the development of the race in which it is clearly seen that there is no mode of disposing of surplus wealth creditable to thoughtful and earnest men into whose hands it flows, save by using it year by year for the general good. The day already dawns. Men die without incurring the pity of their fellows, still sharers in great business enterprises from which their capital cannot be or has not been withdrawn, and which is left chiefly at death for public uses; yet the day is not far distant when the man who dies leaving behind him millions of available wealth, which was free for him to administer during life, will pass away "unwept, unhonored, and unsung," no matter to what uses he leaves the dross which he cannot take with him. Of such as these the public verdict will then be: "The man who dies thus rich dies disgraced."

Such, in my opinion, is the true gospel concerning wealth, obedience to which is destined some day to solve the problem of the rich and the poor, and to bring "Peace on earth, among men good will."

3. The Atlanta Exposition Address

Booker T. Washington

Booker T. Washington (1856-1915), born of a slave mother and a white father in pre-Civil War Virginia, overcame great adversity to become an esteemed educator. He helped found the Tuskegee Institute in Alabama, a leading college for African Americans. In considering the future of black people at a time of great prejudice and segregation, Washington argued that African Americans should first forge a strong economic base before they could expect full civil and political rights. In 1895, he argued his case in a famous speech he gave at the Atlanta Cotton States and International Exposition.

The Atlanta Exposition, at which I had been asked to make an address as a representative of the Negro race, . . . opened with a short address from Governor Bullock. After other interesting exercises, including an invocation from Bishop Nelson, of Georgia, a dedicatory ode by Albert Howell, Jr., and addresses by the President of the Exposition and Mrs. Joseph Thompson, the President of the Woman's Board, Governor Bullock introduced me with the words, "We have with us to-day a representative of Negro enterprise and Negro civilization."

When I arose to speak, there was considerable cheering, especially from the coloured people. As I remember it now, the thing that was uppermost in my mind was the desire to say something that would cement the friendship of the races and bring about hearty cooperation between them. So far as my outward surroundings were concerned, the only thing that I recall distinctly now is that when I got up, I saw thousands of eyes looking intently into my face. The following is the address which I delivered:—

Mr. President and Gentlemen of the Board of Directors and Citizens:

One third of the population of the South is of the Negro race. No enterprise seeking the material, civil, or moral welfare of this section can disregard this element of our population and reach the highest success. I but convey to you, Mr. President and Directors, the sentiment of the masses of my race when I say that in no way have the value and manhood of the American Negro been more fittingly and generously recognized than by the managers of this magnificent Exposition at every stage of its progress. It is a recognition that will do more to cement the friendship of the two races than any occurrence since the dawn of our freedom.

Not only this, but the opportunity here afforded will awaken among us a new era of industrial progress. Ignorant and inexperienced, it is not strange that in the first years of our new life we began at the top instead of at the bottom; that a seat in Congress or the state legislature was more sought than real estate or industrial skill; that the political convention or stump speaking had more attractions than starting a dairy farm or truck garden.

A ship lost at sea for many days suddenly sighted a friendly vessel. From the mast of the unfortunate vessel was seen a signal, "Water, water; we die of thirst!" The answer from the friendly vessel at once came back, "Cast down your bucket where you are." A second time the signal, "Water, water; send us water!" ran up from the distressed vessel, and was answered, "Cast down your bucket where you are." And a third and fourth signal for water was answered, "Cast down your bucket where you are." The captain of the distressed vessel, at last heeding the injunction, cast down his bucket, and it came up full of fresh, sparkling water from the mouth of the Amazon River. To those of my race who depend upon bettering their condition in a foreign land or who underestimate the importance of cultivating friendly relations with the Southern white man, who is their next-door neighbor, I would say: "Cast down your bucket where you are"—cast it down in making friends, in every manly way, of the people of all races by whom we are surrounded.

Cast it down in agriculture, mechanics, in commerce, in domestic service, and in the professions. And in this connection it is well to bear in mind that whatever other sins the South may be called to bear, when it comes to business, pure and simple, it is in the South that the Negro is given a man's chance in the commercial world, and in nothing is this Exposition more eloquent than in emphasizing this chance. Our greatest danger is that in the great leap from slavery to freedom we may overlook the fact that the masses of us are to live by the productions of our hands, and fail to keep in mind that we shall prosper in proportion as we learn to dignify and glorify common labor and put brains and skill into the common occupations of life; shall prosper in proportion as we learn to draw the line between the superficial and the substantial, the ornamental gewgaws of life and the useful. No race can prosper till it learns that there is as much dignity in tilling a field as in writing a poem. It is at the bottom of life we must begin, and not at the top. Nor should we permit our grievances to overshadow our opportunities.

To those of the white race who look to the incoming of those of foreign birth and strange tongue and habits for the prosperity of the South, were I permitted, I would repeat what I say to my own race, "Cast down your bucket where you are." Cast it down among the eight million Negroes whose habits you know, whose fidelity and love you have tested in days when to have proved treacherous meant the ruin of your firesides. Cast down your bucket among these people who have, without strikes and labor wars, tilled your fields, cleared your forests, builded your railroads and cities, brought forth treasures from the bowels of the earth, and helped make possible this magnificent representation of the progress of the South. Casting down your bucket among my people, helping and encouraging them as you are doing on these grounds, and to education of head, hand, and heart, you will find that they will buy your surplus land, make blossom the waste places in your fields, and run your factories. While doing this, you can be sure in the future, as in the past, that you and your families will be surrounded by the most patient, faithful, law-abiding, and unresentful people that the world has seen. As we have proved our loyalty to you in the past, in nursing your children, watching by the sick bed of your mothers and fathers, and often following them with tear-dimmed eyes to their graves, so in the future, in our humble way, we shall stand by you with a devotion that no foreigner can approach, ready to lay down our lives, if need be, in defense of yours, interlacing our industrial, commercial, civil, and religious life with yours in a way that shall make the interests of both races one. In all things that are purely social we can be *as* separate as the fingers, yet one as the hand in all things essential to mutual progress.

There is no defense or security for any of us except in the highest intelligence and development of all. If anywhere there are efforts tending to curtail the fullest growth of the Negro, let these efforts be turned into stimulating, encouraging, and making him the most useful and intelligent citizen. Effort or means so invested will pay a thousand per cent interest. These efforts will be twice blessed—"blessing him that gives and him that takes."

There is no escape through law of man or God from the inevitable:

The laws of changeless justice bind
Oppressor with oppressed
And close as sin and suffering joined
We march to fate abreast.

Nearly sixteen millions of hands will aid you in pulling the load upward, or they will pull against you the load downward. We shall constitute one third and more of the ignorance and crime of the South, or one third its intelligence and progress; we shall contribute one third to the business and industrial prosperity of the South, or we shall prove a veritable body of death, stagnating, depressing, retarding every effort to advance the body politic.

Gentlemen of the Exposition, as we present to you our humble effort at an exhibition of our progress, you must not expect overmuch. Starting thirty years ago with ownership here and there in a few quilts and pumpkins and chickens (gathered from miscellaneous sources), remember the path that has led from these to the inventions and production of agricultural implements, buggies, steam engines, newspapers, books, statuary, carving, paintings, the management of drug-stores and banks, has not been trodden without contact with thorns and thistles. While we take pride in what we exhibit as a result of our independent efforts, we do not for a moment forget that our part in this exhibition would fall far short of your expectations but for the constant help that has come to our educational life, not only from the Southern states, but especially from Northern philanthropists, who have made their gifts a constant stream of blessing and encouragement.

The wisest among my race understand that the agitation of questions of social equality is the extremest folly, and that progress in the enjoyment of all the privileges that will come to us must be the result of severe and constant struggle rather than of artificial forcing. No race that has anything to contribute to the markets of the world is long, in any degree, ostracized. It is important and right that all privileges of the law be ours, but it is vastly more important that we be prepared for the exercises of these privileges. The opportunity to earn a dollar in a factory just now is worth infinitely more than the opportunity to spend a dollar in an opera house.

In conclusion, may I repeat that nothing in thirty years has given us more hope and encouragement, and drawn us so near to you of the white race, as this opportunity offered by the Exposition; and here bending, as it were, over the altar that represents the results of the struggles of your race and mine, both starting practically empty-handed three decades ago, I pledge that in your effort to work out the great and intricate problem which God has laid at the doors of the South, you shall have at all times the patient, sympathetic help of my race; only let this be constantly in mind, that, while from representations in these buildings of the product of field, of forest, of mine, of factory, letters, and art, much good will come, yet far above and beyond material benefits will be that higher good, that, let us pray God, will come, in a blotting out of sectional differences and racial animosities and suspicions, in a determination to administer absolute justice, in a willing obedience among all classes to the mandates of law. This, coupled with our material prosperity, will bring into our beloved South a new heaven and a new earth.

Some days after its delivery I sent a copy of my address to the President of the United States, the Hon. Grover Cleveland. I received from him the following autograph reply:

GRAY GABLES, BUZZARD'S BAY,
MASS.,

October 6, 1895

BOOKER T. WASHINGTON, ESQ:

MY DEAR SIR: I thank you for sending me a copy of your address delivered at the Atlanta Exposition.

I thank you with much enthusiasm for making the address. I have read it with intense interest, and I think the Exposition would be fully justified if it did not do more than furnish the opportunity for its delivery. Your words cannot fail to delight and encourage all who wish well for your race; and if our coloured fellow-citizens do not from your utterances gather new hope and form new determinations to gain every valuable advantage offered them by their citizenship, it will be strange indeed.

Yours very truly,
GROVER CLEVELAND

Mr. Cleveland has not only shown his friendship for me in many personal ways, but has always consented to do anything I have asked of him for our school. This he has done, whether it was to make a personal donation or to use his influence in securing the donations of others. Judging from my personal acquaintance with Mr. Cleveland, I do not believe that he is conscious of possessing any colour prejudice. He is too great for that. In my contact with people I find that, as a rule, it is only the little, narrow people who live for themselves, who never read good books, who do not travel, who never open up their souls in a way to permit them to come into contact with other souls—with the great outside world. No man whose vision is bounded by colour can come into contact with what is highest and best in the world. In meeting men, in many places, I have found that the happiest people are those who do the most for others; the most miserable are those who do the least. I have also found that few things, if any, are capable of making one so blind and narrow as race prejudice. I often say to our students, in the course of my talks to them on Sunday evenings in the chapel, that the longer I live and the more experience I have of the world, the more I am convinced that, after all, the one thing that is most worth living for—and dying for, if need be—is the opportunity of making some one else more happy and more useful.

The coloured people and the coloured newspapers at first seemed to be greatly pleased with the character of my Atlanta address, as well as with its reception. But after the first burst of enthusiasm began to die away, and the coloured people began reading the speech in cold type, some of them seemed to feel that they had been hypnotized. They seemed to feel that I had been too liberal in my remarks toward the Southern whites, and that I had not spoken out strongly enough for what they termed the "rights" of the race. For a while there was a reaction, so far as a certain element of my own race was concerned, but later these reactionary ones seemed to have been won over to my way of believing and acting. . . .

I am often asked to express myself more freely than I do upon the political condition and the political future of my race. These recollections of my experience in Atlanta give me the opportunity to do so briefly. My own belief is, although I have never before said so in so many words, that the time will come when the Negro in the South will be accorded all the political rights which his ability, character, and material possessions entitle him to. I think, though, that the opportunity to freely exercise such political rights will not come in any large degree through outside or artificial forcing, but will be accorded to the Negro by the Southern white people themselves, and that they will protect him in the exercise

of those rights. Just *as* soon as the South gets over the old feeling that it is being forced by "foreigners," or "aliens," to do something which it does not want to do, I believe that the change in the direction that I have indicated is going to begin. In fact, there are indications that it is already beginning in a slight degree.

I believe it is the duty of the Negro—as the greater part of the race is already doing—to deport himself modestly in regard to political claims, depending upon the slow but sure influences that proceed from the possession of property, intelligence, and high character for the full recognition of his political rights. I think that the according of the full exercise of political rights is going to be a matter of natural, slow growth, not an over-night, gourd-vine affair. I do not believe that the Negro should cease voting, for a man cannot learn the exercise of self-government by ceasing to vote, any more than a boy can learn to swim by keeping out of the water, but I do believe that in his voting he should more and more be influenced by those of intelligence and character who are his next-door neighbours.

I know coloured men who, through the encouragement, help, and advice of Southern white people, have accumulated thousands of dollars' worth of property, but who, at the same time, would never think of going to those same persons for advice concerning the casting of their ballots. This, it seems to me, is unwise and unreasonable, and should cease. In saying this I do not mean that the Negro should buckle, or not vote from principle, for the instant he ceases to vote from principle he loses the confidence and respect of the Southern white man even.

I do not believe that any state should make a law that permits an ignorant and poverty-stricken white man to vote, and prevents a black man in the same condition from voting. Such a law is not only unjust, but it will react, as all unjust laws do, in time; for the effect of such a law is to encourage the Negro to secure education and property, and at the same time it encourages the white man to remain in ignorance and poverty. I believe that in time, through the operation of intelligence and friendly race relations, all cheating at the ballot-box in the South will cease. It will become apparent that the white man who begins by cheating a Negro out of his ballot soon learns to cheat a white man out of his, and that the man who does this ends his career of dishonesty by the theft of property or by some equally serious crime. In my opinion, the time will come when the South will encourage all of its citizens to vote. It will see that it pays better, from every standpoint, to have healthy, vigorous life than to have that political stagnation which always results when one-half of the population has no share and no interest in the Government.

As a rule, I believe in universal, free suffrage, but I believe that in the South we are confronted with peculiar conditions that justify the protection of the ballot in many of the states, for a while at least, either by an educational test, a property test, or by both combined; but whatever tests are required, they should be made to apply with equal and exact justice to both races.

4. The Souls of Black Folk, 1903

W.E.B. DuBois

W.E.B. DuBois (1868-1963) was born in Massachusetts and became a renowned African American educator, author and political activist. He was one of the severest critics of Booker T Washington's accommodation strategy, referring to Washington's approach as the "gospel of Work and Money" DuBois called for "ceaseless agitation" for civil rights for black Americans and emphasized the importance of education and political action in achieving that goal Soon after Washington's Atlanta Exposition Address, which DuBois ridiculed as the Atlanta Compromise," DuBois spoke out against Washington's ideas in an essay published in his book "The Souls of Black Folk."

Of Mr. Booker T. Washington and Others

Easily the most striking thing in the history of the American Negro since 1876 is the ascendancy of Mr. Booker T. Washington. It began at the time when war memories and ideals were rapidly passing; a day of astonishing commercial development was dawning; a sense of doubt and hesitation overtook the freedmen's sons,—then it was that his leading began. Mr. Washington came, with a simple definite programme, at the psychological moment when the nation was a little ashamed of having bestowed so much sentiment on Negroes, and was concentrating its energies on Dollars. His programme of industrial education, conciliation of the South, and submission and silence as to civil and political rights, was not wholly original; the Free Negroes from 1830 up to war-time had striven to build industrial schools, and the American Missionary Association had from the first taught various trades; and Price and others had sought a way of honorable alliance with the best of the Southerners. But Mr. Washington first indissolubly linked these things; he put enthusiasm, unlimited energy, and perfect faith into this programme, and changed it from a by-path into a veritable Way of Life. And the tale of the methods by which he did this is a fascinating study of human life.

It startled the nation to hear a Negro advocating such a programme after many decades of bitter complaint; it startled and won the applause of the South, it interested and won the admiration of the North; and after a confused murmur of protest, it silenced if it did not convert the Negroes themselves.

To gain the sympathy and cooperation of the various elements comprising the white South was Mr. Washington's first task; and this, at the time Tuskegee was founded, seemed, for a black man, well-nigh impossible. And yet ten years later it was done in the word spoken at Atlanta: "In all things purely social we can be as separate as the five fingers, and yet one as the hand in all things essential to mutual progress." This "Atlanta Compromise" is by all odds the most notable thing in Mr. Washington's career. The South interpreted it in different ways: the radicals received it as a complete surrender of the demand for civil and political equality; the conservatives, as a generously conceived working basis for mutual understanding. So both approved it, and to-day its author is certainly the most distinguished Southerner since Jefferson Davis, and the one with the largest personal following.

Next to this achievement comes Mr. Washington's work in gaining place and consideration in the North. Others less shrewd and tactful had formerly essayed to sit on these two stools and had fallen between them; but as Mr. Washington knew the heart of the South from birth and training, so by singular insight he intuitively grasped the spirit of the age which was dominating the North. And so thoroughly did he learn the speech and thought of triumphant commercialism, and the ideals of material prosperity, that the picture of a lone black boy poring over a French grammar amid the weeds and dirt of a neglected home soon seemed to him the acme of absurdities. One wonders what Socrates and St. Francis of Assisi would say to this.

And yet this very singleness of vision and thorough oneness with his age is a mark of the successful man. It is as though Nature must needs make men narrow in order to give them force. So Mr. Washington's cult has gained unquestioning followers, his work has wonderfully prospered, his friends are legion, and his enemies are confounded. To-day he stands as the one recognized spokesman of his ten million fellows, and one of the most notable figures in a nation of seventy millions. One hesitates, therefore, to criticise a life which, beginning with so little, has done so much. And yet the time is come when one may speak in all sincerity and utter courtesy of the mistakes and shortcomings of Mr. Washington's career, as well as of his triumphs, without being thought captious or envious, and without forgetting that it is easier to do ill than well in the world.

Mr. Washington represents in Negro thought the old attitude of adjustment and submission; but adjustment at such a peculiar time as to make his programme unique. This is an age of unusual economic development, and Mr. Washington's programme naturally takes an economic cast, becoming a gospel of Work and Money to such an extent as apparently almost completely to overshadow the higher aims of life. Moreover, this is an age when the more advanced races are coming in closer contact with the less developed races, and the race-feeling is therefore intensified; and Mr. Washington's programme practically accepts the alleged inferiority of the Negro races. Again, in our own land, the reaction from the sentiment of war time has given impetus to race-prejudice against Negroes, and Mr. Washington withdraws many of the high demands of Negroes as men and American citizens. In other periods of intensified prejudice all the Negro's tendency to self-assertion has been called forth; at this period a policy of submission is advocated. In the history of nearly all other races and peoples the doctrine preached at such crises has been that manly self-respect is worth more than lands and houses, and that a people who voluntarily surrender such respect, or cease striving for it, are not worth civilizing.

In answer to this, it has been claimed that the Negro can survive only through submission. Mr. Washington distinctly asks that black people give up, at least for the present, three things,

First, political power,

Second, insistence on civil rights,

Third, higher education of Negro youth—and concentrate all their energies on industrial education, the accumulation of wealth, and the conciliation of the South. This policy has been courageously and insistently advocated for over fifteen years, and has been triumphant for perhaps ten years. As a result of this tender of the palm-branch, what has been the return? In these years there have occurred:

1. The disfranchisement of the Negro.
2. The legal creation of a distinct status of civil inferiority for the Negro.
3. The steady withdrawal of aid from institutions for the higher training of the Negro.

These movements are not, to be sure, direct results of Mr. Washington's teachings; but his propaganda has, without a shadow of doubt, helped their speedier accomplishment. The question then comes: Is it possible, and probable, that nine millions of men can make effective progress in economic lines if they are deprived of political rights, made a servile caste, and allowed only the most meagre chance for developing their exceptional men? If history and reason give any distinct answer to these questions, it is an emphatic *No.* And Mr. Washington thus faces the triple paradox of his career:

1. He is striving nobly to make Negro artisans business men and property-owners; but it is utterly impossible, under modern competitive methods, for workingmen and property-owners to defend their rights and exist without the right of suffrage.
2. He insists on thrift and self-respect, but at the same time counsels a silent submission to civic inferiority such as is bound to sap the manhood of any race in the long run.
3. He advocates common-school and industrial training, and depreciates institutions of higher learning; but neither the Negro common-schools, nor Tuskegee itself, could remain open a day were it not for teachers trained in Negro colleges, or trained by their graduates.

This triple paradox in Mr. Washington's position is the object of criticism by two classes of colored Americans. One class is spiritually descended from Toussaint the Savior, through Gabriel, Vesey, and Turner, and they represent the attitude of revolt and revenge; they hate the white South blindly and distrust the white race generally, and so far as they agree on definite action, think that the Negro's only hope lies in emigration beyond the borders of the United States. And yet, by the irony of fate, nothing has more effectually made this programme seem hopeless than the recent course of the United States toward weaker and darker peoples in the West Indies, Hawaii, and the Philippines—for where in the world may we go and be safe from lying and brute force?

The other class of Negroes who cannot agree with Mr. Washington has hitherto said little aloud. They deprecate the sight of scattered counsels, of internal disagreement; and especially they dislike making their just criticism of a useful and earnest man an excuse for a general discharge of venom from small-minded opponents. Nevertheless, the questions involved are so fundamental and serious that it is difficult to see how men like the Grimkes, Kelly Miller, J. W. E. Bowen, and other representatives of this group, can much longer be silent. Such men feel in conscience bound to ask of this nation three things:

1. The right to vote.
2. Civic equality.
3. The education of youth according to ability.

They acknowledge Mr. Washington's invaluable service in counselling patience and courtesy in such demands; they do not ask that ignorant black men vote when ignorant whites are debarred, or that any reasonable restrictions in the suffrage should not be applied; they know that the low social level of the mass of the race is responsible for much discrimination against it, but they also know, and the nation knows, that relentless color-prejudice is more often a cause than a result of the Negro's degradation; they seek the abatement of this relic of barbarism, and not its systematic encouragement and pampering by all agencies of social power from the Associated Press to the Church of Christ. They advocate, with Mr. Washington, a broad system of Negro common schools supplemented by thorough industrial training; but they are surprised that a man of Mr. Washington's insight cannot see that no such educational system ever has rested or can rest on any other basis than that of the well-equipped college and university, and they insist that there is a demand for a few such institutions throughout the South to train the best of the Negro youth as teachers, professional men, and leaders.

First, it is the duty of black men to judge the South discriminatingly. The present generation of Southerners are not responsible for the past, and they should not be blindly hated or blamed for it. Furthermore, to no class is the indiscriminate endorsement of the recent course of the South toward Negroes more nauseating than to the best thought of the South. The South is not "solid"; it is a land in the ferment of social change, wherein forces of all kinds are fighting for supremacy; and to praise the ill the South is to-day perpetrating is just as wrong as to condemn the good. Discriminating and broad-minded criticism is what the South needs,—needs it for the sake of her own white sons and daughters, and for the insurance of robust, healthy mental and moral development.

To-day even the attitude of the Southern whites toward the blacks is not, as so many assume, in all cases the same; the ignorant Southerner hates the Negro, the workingmen fear his competition, the money-makers wish to use him as a laborer, some of the educated see a menace in his upward development, while others—usually the- sons of the masters—wish to help him to rise. National opinion has enabled this last class to maintain the Negro common schools, and to protect the Negro partially in property, life, and limb. Through the pressure of the money-makers, the Negro is in danger of being reduced to semi-slavery, especially in the country districts; the workingmen, and those of the educated who fear the Negro, have united to disfranchise him, and some have urged his deportation; while the passions of the ignorant are easily aroused to lynch and abuse any black man. To praise this intricate whirl of thought and prejudice is nonsense; to inveigh indiscriminately against "the South" is unjust; but to use the same breath in praising Governor Aycock, exposing Senator Morgan, arguing with Mr. Thomas Nelson Page, and denouncing Senator Ben Tillman, is not only sane, but the imperative duty of thinking black men.

It would be unjust to Mr. Washington not to acknowledge that in several instances he has opposed movements in the South which were unjust to the Negro; he sent memorials to the Louisiana and Alabama constitutional conventions, he has spoken against lynching, and in other ways has openly or silently set his influence against sinister schemes and unfortunate happenings. Notwithstanding this, it is equally true to assert that on the whole the distinct impression left by Mr. Washington's propaganda is, first, that the South is justified in its present attitude toward the Negro because of the Negro's degradation; secondly, that the prime cause of the Negro's failure to rise more quickly is his wrong education in the past; and, thirdly, that his future rise depends primarily on his own efforts. Each of these propositions is a dangerous half-truth. The supplementary truths must never be lost sight of: first, slavery and race-prejudice are potent if not sufficient causes of the Negro's position; second, industrial and common-school training were necessarily slow in planting because they had to await the black teachers trained by higher institutions,—it being extremely doubtful if any essentially different development was possible, and certainly a Tuskegee was unthinkable before 1880; and, third, while it is a great truth to say that the Negro must strive and strive mightily to help himself, it is equally true that unless his striving be not simply seconded, but rather aroused and encouraged, by the initiative of the richer and wiser environing group, he cannot hope for great success.

In his failure to realize and impress this last point, Mr. Washington is especially to be criticised. His doctrine has tended to make the whites, North and South, shift the burden of the Negro problem to the Negro's shoulders and stand aside as critical and rather pessimistic spectators; when in fact the burden belongs to the nation, and the hands of none of us are clean if we bend not our energies to righting these great wrongs.

The South ought to be led, by candid and honest criticism, to assert her better self and do her full duty to the race she has cruelly wronged and is still wronging. The North—her co-partner in guilt—cannot salve her conscience by plastering it with gold. We cannot settle this problem by diplomacy and suaveness, by "policy" alone. If worse come to worst, can the moral fibre of this country survive the slow throttling and murder of nine millions of men?

The black men of America have a duty to perform, a duty stern and delicate,—a forward movement to oppose a part of the work of their greatest leader. So far as Mr. Washington preaches Thrift, Patience, and Industrial Training for the masses, we must hold up his hands and strive with him, rejoicing in his honors and glorying in the strength of this Joshua called of God and of man to lead the headless host. But so far as Mr. Washington apologizes for injustice, North or South, does not rightly value the privilege and duty of voting, belittles the emasculating effects of caste distinctions, and opposes the higher training and ambition of our brighter minds,—so far as he, the South, or the North, does this,—we must unceasingly and firmly oppose them. By every civilized and peaceful method we must strive for the rights which the world accords to men, clinging unwaveringly to those great words which the sons of the Fathers would fain forget: "We hold these truths to be self-evident: That all men are created equal; that they are endowed by their Creator with certain unalienable rights; that among these are life, liberty, and the pursuit of happiness."

Of the Training of Black Men

So here we stand among thoughts of human unity, even through conquest and slavery; the inferiority of black men, even if forced by fraud; a shriek in the night for the freedom of men who themselves are not yet sure of their right to demand it. This is the tangle of thought and afterthought wherein we are called to solve the problem of training men for life.

But when we have vaguely said that Education will set this tangle straight, what have we uttered but a truism? Training for life teaches living; but what training for the profitable living together of black men and white? . . . No secure civilization can be built in the South with the Negro as an ignorant, turbulent proletariat. Suppose we seek to remedy this by making them laborers and nothing more: they are not fools, they have tasted of the Tree of Life, and they will not cease to think, will not cease attempting to read the riddle of the world. By taking away their best equipped teachers and leaders, by slamming the door of opportunity in the faces of their bolder and brighter minds, will you make them satisfied with their lot? or will you not rather transfer their leading from the hands of men taught to think to the hands of untrained demagogues? We ought not to forget that despite the pressure of poverty, and despite the active discouragement and even ridicule of friends, the demand for higher training steadily increases among Negro youth: there were, in the years from 1875 to 1880, 22 Negro graduates from Northern colleges; from 1885 to 1890 there were 43, and from 1895 to 1900, nearly 100 graduates. From Southern Negro colleges there were, in the same three periods, 143, 413, and over 500 graduates. Here, then, *is* the plain thirst for training; by refusing to give this Talented Tenth the key to knowledge, can any sane man imagine that they will lightly lay aside their yearning and contentedly become hewers of wood and drawers of water?

No. The dangerously clear logic of the Negro's position will more and more loudly assert itself in that day when increasing wealth and more intricate social organization preclude the South from being, as it so largely is, simply an armed camp for intimidating black folk. Such waste of energy cannot be spared if the South is to catch up with civilization. And as the black third of the land grows in thrift and skill, unless skilfully guided in its larger philosophy, it must more and more brood over the red past and the creeping, crooked present, until it grasps a gospel of revolt and revenge and throws its new-found energies athwart the current of advance. Even to-day the masses of the Negroes see all too clearly the anomalies of their position and the moral crookedness of yours. You may marshal strong indictments against them, but their counter-cries, lacking though they be in formal logic, have burning truths within them which you may not wholly ignore, O Southern Gentlemen! If you deplore their presence here, they ask, Who brought us? When you cry, Deliver us from the vision of intermarriage, they answer that legal marriage is infinitely better than systematic concubinage and prostitution. And if in just fury you accuse their vagabonds of violating women, they also in fury quite as just may reply: The wrong which your gentlemen have done against helpless black women in defiance of your own laws is written on the foreheads of two millions of mulattoes, and written in ineffaceable blood. And finally, when you fasten crime upon this race as its peculiar trait, they answer that slavery was the arch-crime, and lynching and lawlessness its twin abortion; that color and race are not crimes, and yet they it is which in this land receives most unceasing condemnation, North, East, South, and West.

I will not say such arguments are wholly justified,—I will not insist that there is no other side to the shield; but I do say that of the nine millions of Negroes in this nation, there is scarcely one out of the cradle to whom these arguments do not daily present themselves in the guise of terrible truth. I insist that the question of the future is how best to keep these millions from brooding over the wrongs of the past and the difficulties of the present, so that all their energies may be bent toward a cheerful striving and co-operation with their white neighbors toward a larger, juster, and fuller future. That one wise method of doing this lies in the closer knitting of the Negro to the great industrial possibilities of the South is a great truth. And this the common schools and the manual training and trade schools are working to accomplish. But these alone are not enough. The foundations of knowledge in this race, as in others, must be sunk deep in the college and university if we would build a solid, permanent structure. Internal problems of social advance must inevitably come,—problems of work and wages, of families and homes, of morals and the true valuing of the things of life; and all these and other inevitable problems of civilization the Negro must meet and solve largely for himself, by reason of his isolation; and can there be any possible solution other than by study and thought and an appeal to the rich experience of the past? Is there not, with such a group and in such a crisis, infinitely more danger to be apprehended from half-trained minds and shallow thinking than from over-education and over-refinement? Surely we have wit enough to found a Negro college so manned and equipped as to steer successfully between the *dilettante* and the fool. We shall hardly induce black men to believe that if their stomachs be full, it matters little about their brains. They already dimly perceive that the paths of peace winding between honest toil and dignified manhood call for the guidance of skilled thinkers, the loving, reverent comradeship between the black lowly and the black men emancipated by training and culture.

The function of the Negro college, then, is clear: it must maintain the standards of popular education, it must seek the social regeneration of the Negro, and it must help in the solution of problems of race contact and co-operation. And finally, beyond all this, it must develop men. Above our modern socialism, and out of the worship of the mass, must persist and evolve that higher individualism which the centres of culture protect; there must come a loftier respect for the sovereign human soul that seeks to know itself and the world about; that seeks a freedom for expansion and self-development; that will love and hate and labor in its own way, untrammeled alike by old and new. Such souls aforetime have inspired and guided worlds, and if we be not wholly bewitched by our Rhinegold, they shall again. Herein the longing of black men must have respect: the rich and bitter depth of their experience, the unknown treasures of their inner life, the strange rendings of nature they have seen, may give the world new points of view and make their loving, living, and doing precious to all human hearts. And to themselves in these the days that try their souls, the chance to soar in the dim blue air above the smoke is to their finer spirits boon and guerdon for what they lose on earth by being black. …

5: The Wizard of Oz: Parable on Populism

Henry M. Littlefield

On the deserts of North Africa in 1941 two tough Australian brigades went to battle singing,

> *Have you heard of the wonderful wizard,*
> *The wonderful Wizard of Oz,*
> *And he is a wonderful wizard,*
> *If ever a wizard there was.*[1]

It was a song they had brought with them from Australia and would soon spread to England. Forever afterward it reminded Winston Churchill of those "buoyant days." Churchill's nostalgia is only one symptom of the world-wide delight found in American fairy-tale about a little girl and her odyssey in the strange land of Oz. The song he reflects upon came from a classic 1939 Hollywood production of the story, which introduced millions of people not only to the land of Oz, but to a talented young lady named Judy Garland as well.

Ever since its publication in 1900 Lyman Frank Baum's *The Wonderful Wizard of Oz* has been immensely popular, providing the basis for a profitable musical comedy, three movies and a number of plays. It is an indigenous creation, curiously warm and touching, although no one really knows why. For despite wholehearted acceptance by generations of readers, Baum's tale has been accorded neither critical acclaim, nor extended critical examination. Interested scholars, such as Russell B. Nye and Martin Gardiner, look upon *The Wizard of Oz* as the first in a long and delightful series of Oz stories, and understandably base their appreciation of Baum's talent on the totality of his works.

The Wizard of Oz is an entity unto itself, however, and was not originally written with a sequel in mind. Baum informed his readers in 1904 that he had produced *The Marvelous Land of Oz* reluctantly and only in answer to well over a thousand letters demanding that he create another Oz tale. His original effort remains unique and to some degree separate from the books which follow. But its uniqueness does not rest alone on its peculiar and transcendent popularity.

Professor Nye finds a "strain of moralism" in the Oz books, as well as "a well-developed sense of satire," and Baum stories often include searching parodies on the contradictions in human nature. The second book in the series, *The Marvelous Land of Oz,* is a blatant satire on feminism and the suffragette movement. In

[1]"We're Off to See the Wizard" by Harold Arlen and E. Y. Harburg. Copyright 1938, 1939 (Renewed 1966, 1967) Metro-Goldwyn-Mayer, Inc. Assigned to Leo Feist, Inc. All rights assigned to CBS Catalogue Partnership. All rights controlled and administered by CBS Feist Catalog, Inc. International Copyright Secured. Made in USA. All rights reserved. Used by permission.

it Baum attempted to duplicate the format used so successfully in *The Wizard*, yet no one has noted a similar play on contemporary movements in the latter work. Nevertheless, one does exist, and it reflects to an astonishing degree the world of political reality which surrounded Baum in 1900. In order to understand the relationship of *The Wizard* to turn-of-the-century America, it is necessary first to know something of Baum's background.

Born near Syracuse in 1856, Baum was brought up in a wealthy home and early became interested in the theater. He wrote some plays which enjoyed brief -success and then, with his wife and two sons, journeyed to Aberdeen, South Dakota, in 1887. Aberdeen was a little prairie town and there Baum edited the local weekly until it failed in 1891.

For many years Western farmers had been in a state of loud, though unsuccessful, revolt. While Baum was living in South Dakota not only was the frontier a thing of the past, but the Romantic view of benign nature had disappeared as well. The stark reality of the dry, open plains and the acceptance of man's Darwinian subservience to his environment served to crush Romantic idealism.

Hamlin Garland's visit to Iowa and South Dakota coincided with Baum's arrival. Henry Nash Smith observes,

> *Garland's success* as *a portrayer of hardship and suffering on Northwestern farms was due in part to the fact that his personal experience happened to parallel the shock which the entire West received in the later 1880s from the combined effects of low prices, . . . grasshoppers, drought, the terrible blizzards of the winter of 1886–1887, and the juggling of freight rates. . . .*

As we shall see, Baum's prairie experience was no less deeply etched, although he did not employ naturalism to express it.

Baum's stay in South Dakota also covered the period of the formation of the Populist party which Professor Nye likens to a fanatic "crusade." Western farmers had for a long time sought governmental aid in the form of economic panaceas, but to no avail. The Populist movement symbolized a desperate attempt to use the power of the ballot. In 1891 Baum moved to Chicago where he was surrounded by those dynamic elements of reform which made the city so notable during the 1890s. In Chicago Baum certainly saw the results the frightful depression which had closed down upon the nation in 1893. Moreover, he took part in the pivotal election of 1896, marching in "torch-light parades for William Jennings Bryan."

Martin Gardiner notes besides, that he "consistently voted as a democrat . . . and his sympathies seem always to have been on the side of the laboring classes." No one who marched in even a few such parades could have been unaffected by Bryan's campaign. Putting all the farmers' hopes in a basket labeled "free coinage of silver," Bryan's platform rested mainly on the issue of adding silver to the nation's gold standard. Though he lost, he did at least bring the plight of the little man into national focus.

Between 1896 and 1900, while Baum worked and wrote in Chicago, the great depression faded away and the war with Spain thrust the United States into world prominence. Bryan maintained Midwestern control over the Democratic party, and often spoke out against American policies toward Cuba and the Philippines. By 1900 it was evident that Bryan would run again, although now imperialism and not silver seemed the issue of primary concern. In order to promote greater enthusiasm, however, Bryan felt compelled once more to sound the silver leitmotif in his campaign. Bryan's second futile attempt at the presidency culminated in November 1900. The previous winter Baum had attempted unsuccessfully to sell a rather original volume of children's fantasy, but that April, George M. Hill, a small Chicago publisher, finally agreed to print *The Wonderful Wizard of Oz.*

Baum's allegiance to the cause of Democratic Populism must be balanced against the fact that he was not a political activist. Martin Gardiner finds through all of his writings "a theme of tolerance, with many episodes that poke fun at narrow nationalism and ethnocentrism." Nevertheless, Professor Nye quotes Baum as having a desire to write stories that would "bear the stamp of our times and depict the progressive fairies of today."

The Wizard of Oz has neither the mature religious appeal of a *Pilgrim's Progress,* nor the philosophic depth of a *Candide.* Baum's most thoughtful devotees see in it only a warm, cleverly written fairy tale. Yet the original Oz book conceals an unsuspected depth, and it is the purpose of this study to demonstrate that Baum's immortal American fantasy encompasses more than heretofore believed. For Baum created a children's story with a symbolic allegory implicit within its story line and characterizations. The allegory always remains in a minor key, subordinated to the major theme and readily abandoned whenever it threatens to distort the appeal of the fantasy But through it, in the form of a subtle parable, Baum delineated a Midwesterner's vibrant and ironic portrait of this country as it entered the twentieth century.

We are introduced to both Dorothy and Kansas at the same time:

> *Dorothy lived in the midst of the great Kansas prairies, with Uncle Henry, who was a farmer, and Aunt Em, who was the farmer's wife. Their house was small, for the lumber to build it had to be carried by wagon many miles. There were four walls, a floor and a roof which made one room; and this room contained a rusty-looking cooking stove, a cupboard for the dishes, a table, three or four chairs, and the beds.*
>
> *When Dorothy stood in the doorway and looked around, she could see nothing but the great gray prairie on every side. Not a tree nor a house broke the broad sweep of flat country, that reached to the edge of the sky in all directions. The sun had baked the plowed land into a*

gray mass, with little cracks running through it. Even the grass was not green, for the sun had burned the tops of the long blades until they were the same gray color to be seen everywhere. Once the house had been painted, but the sun blistered the paint and the rains washed it away, and now the house was as *dull and gray* as *everything else.*

When Aunt Em came there to live she was a young, pretty wife. The sun and wind had changed her, too. They had taken the sparkle from her eyes and left them a sober gray; they had taken the red from her cheeks and lips, and they were gray also. She was thin and gaunt, and never smiled now. When Dorothy, who was an orphan, first came to her, Aunt Em had been so startled by the child's laughter that she would scream and press her hand upon her heart whenever Dorothy's merry voice reached her ears; and she still looked at the little girl with wonder that she could find anything to laugh at.

Uncle Henry never laughed. He worked hard from morning till night and did not know what joy was. He was gray also, from his long beard to his rough boots, and he looked stern and solemn, and rarely spoke.

It was Toto that made Dorothy laugh, and saved her from growing as *gray* as *her other surroundings. Toto was not gray; he was a little black dog, with long silky hair and small black eyes that twinkled merrily on either side of his funny, wee nose. Toto played all day long, and Dorothy played with him, and loved him dearly.*

Hector St. John de Crèvecoeur would not have recognized Uncle Henry's farm; it is straight out of Hamlin Garland. On it a deadly environment dominates everyone and everything except Dorothy and her pet. The setting is Old Testament and nature seems grayly impersonal and even angry. Yet it is a fearsome cyclone that lifts Dorothy and Toto in their house and deposits them "very gently—for a cyclone—in the midst of a country of marvelous beauty." We immediately sense the contrast between Oz and Kansas. Here there are "stately trees bearing rich and luscious fruits . . . gorgeous flowers ... and birds with . . . brilliant plumage" sing in the trees. In Oz "a small brook rushing and sparkling along" murmers "in a voice very grateful to a little girl who had lived so long on the dry, gray prairies."

Trouble intrudes. Dorothy's house has come down on the wicked Witch of the East, killing her. Nature, by sheer accident, can provide benefits, for indirectly the cyclone has disposed of one of the two truly bad influences in the Land of Oz. Notice that evil ruled in both the East and the West; after Dorothy's coming it rules only in the West.

The wicked Witch of the East had kept the little Munchkin people "in bondage for many years, making them slave for her night and day." Just what this slavery entailed is not immediately clear, but Baum later gives us a specific example. The Tin Woodman, whom Dorothy meets on her way to the Emerald City, had been put under a spell by the Witch of the East. Once an independent and hard working human being, the Woodman found that each time he swung his axe it clipped off a different part of his body. Knowing no other trade he "worked harder than ever," for luckily in Oz tinsmiths can repair such things. Soon the Woodman was all tin. In this way Eastern witchcraft dehumanized a simple laborer so that the faster and better he worked the more quickly he became a kind of machine. Here is a Populist view of evil Eastern influences on honest labor which could hardly be more pointed.

There is one thing seriously wrong with being made of tin; when it rains rust sets in. Tin Woodman had been standing in the same position for a year without moving before Dorothy came along and oiled his joints. The Tin Woodman's situation has an obvious parallel in the condition of many Eastern workers after the depression of 1893. While Tin Woodman is standing still, rusted solid, he deludes himself into thinking he is no longer capable of that most human of sentiment, love. Hate does not fill the void, a constant lesson in the Oz books, and Tin Woodman feels that only a heart will make him sensitive again. So he accompanies Dorothy to see if the Wizard will give him one.

Oz itself is a magic oasis surrounded by impassable deserts, and the country is divided in a very orderly fashion. In the North and South the people are ruled by good witches, who are not quite as powerful as the wicked ones of the East and West. In the center of the land rises the magnificent Emerald City ruled by the Wizard of Oz, a successful humbug whom even the witches mistakenly feel "is more powerful than all the rest of us together." Despite these forces, the mark of goodness, placed on Dorothy's forehead by the Witch of the North, serves as protection for Dorothy throughout her travels. Goodness and innocence prevail even over the powers of evil and delusion in Oz. Perhaps it is this basic and beautiful optimism that makes Baum's tale so characteristically American—and Midwestern.

Dorothy is Baum's Miss Everyman. She is one of us, levelheaded and human, and she has a real problem. Young readers can understand her quandary as readily as can adults. She is good, not precious, and she thinks quite naturally about others. For all of the attractions of Oz Dorothy desires only to return to the gray plains and Aunt Em and Uncle Henry. She is directed toward the Emerald City by the good Witch of the North, since the Wizard will surely be able to solve the problem of the impassable deserts. Dorothy sets out on the Yellow Brick Road wearing the Witch of the East's magic Silver Shoes. Silver shoes walking on a golden road; henceforth Dorothy becomes the innocent agent of Baum's ironic view of the Silver issue. Remember, neither Dorothy, nor the good Witch of the North, nor the Munchkins understand the power of these shoes. The allegory is abundantly clear. On the next to last page of the book Baum has Glinda, Witch of the South, tell Dorothy, "Your Silver Shoes will carry you over the desert. .. . if you had known their power you could have gone back to your Aunt Em the very first day you came to this country." Glinda explains, "All you have to do is to knock the shoes together three times and command the shoes to carry you wherever you wish to go." William Jennings Bryan never outlined the advantages of the silver standard any more effectively.

Not understanding the magic of the Silver Shoes, Dorothy walks the mundane—and dangerous—Yellow Brick Road. The first person she meets is a Scarecrow. After escaping from his wooden perch, the Scarecrow displays a terrible sense of inferiority and self doubt, for he has determined that he needs real brains to replace the common straw in his head. William Allen White wrote an article in 1896 entitled "What's the Matter with Kansas?" In it he accused Kansas farmers of ignorance, irrationality and general muddle-headedness. What's wrong with Kansas are the people, said Mr. White. Baum's character seems to have read White's angry characterization. But Baum never takes White seriously and so the Scarecrow soon emerges as innately a very shrewd and very capable individual.

The Scarecrow and the Tin Woodman accompany Dorothy along the Yellow Brick Road, one seeking brains, the other a heart. They meet next the Cowardly Lion. As King of Beasts he explains, "I learned that if I roared very loudly every living thing was frightened and got out of my way." Born a coward, he sobs, "Whenever there is danger my heart begins to beat fast" "Perhaps you have heart disease," suggests Tin Woodman, who always worries about hearts. But the Lion desires only courage and so he joins the party to ask help from the Wizard.

The Lion represents Bryan himself. In the election of 1896 Bryan lost the vote of Eastern labor, though he tried hard to gain their support. In Baum's story the Lion, on meeting the little group, "struck at the Tin Woodman will his sharp claws." But, to his surprise, "he could make no impression on the tin, although the Woodman fell over in the road and lay still." Baum here refers to the fact that in 1896 workers were often pressured into voting for McKinley and gold by their employers. Amazed, the Lion says, "he nearly blunted my claws," and he adds even more appropriately, "When they scratched against the tin it made a coldshiver run down my back." The King of Beasts is not after all very cowardly, and Bryan, although a pacifist and an anti-imperialist in a time of national expansion, is not either. The magic Silver Shoes belong to Dorothy, however. Silver's potent charm, which had come to mean so much to so many in the Midwest, could not be entrusted to a political symbol. Baum delivers Dorothy from the world of adventure and fantasy to the real world of heartbreak and desolation through the power of Silver. It represents a real force in a land of illusion, and neither the Cowardly Lion nor Bryan truly needs or understands its use.

All together now the small party moves toward the Emerald City. Coxey's Army of tramps and indigents, marching to ask President Cleveland for work in 1894, appears no more naively innocent than this group of four characters going to see a humbug Wizard, to request favors that only the little girl among them deserves.

Those who enter the Emerald City must wear green glasses. Dorothy later discovers that the greenness of dresses and ribbons disappears on leaving, and everything becomes a bland white. Perhaps the magic of any city is this self imposed. But the Wizard dwells here and so the Emerald City represents the national Capitol. The Wizard, a little bumbling old man, hiding behind a facade of papier mâché and noise, might be any President from Grant to Mckinley. He comes straight from the fair grounds in Omaha, Nebraska, and he symbolizes the American criterion for leadership—he is able to be everything to everybody.

As each of our heroes enters the throne room to ask a favor the Wizard assumes different shapes, representing different views toward national leadership. To Dorothy, he appears as an enormous head, "bigger than the head of the biggest giant." An apt image for a naive and innocent little citizen. To the Scarecrow he appears to be a lovely, gossamer fairy, a most appropriate form for an idealistic Kansas farmer. The Woodman sees a horrible beast, as would any exploited Eastern laborer after the trouble of the 1890s. But the Cowardly Lion, like W. J. Bryan, sees a "Ball of Fire, so fierce and glowing he could scarcely bear to gaze upon it." Baum then provides an additional analogy, for when the lion "tried to go nearer he singed his whiskers and he crept back tremblingly to a spot nearer the door."

The Wizard has asked them all to kill the Witch of the West. The golden road does not go in that direction and so they must follow the sun, as have many pioneers in the past. The land they must now pass through is "rougher and hillier, for there were no farms nor houses in the country of the West and the ground was unfilled." The Witch of the West uses natural forces to achieve her ends; she is Baum's version of sentient and malign nature.

Finding Dorothy and her friends in the West, the Witch sends forty wolves against them, then forty vicious crows and finally a great swarm of black bees. But it is through the power of a magic golden cap that she summons the flying monkeys. They capture the little girl and dispose of her companions. Baum makes these Winged Monkeys into an Oz substitute for the plains Indians. Their leader says, "Once . . . we were a free people, living happily in the great forest, flying from tree to tree, eating nuts and fruit, and doing just as we pleased without calling anybody master." "This," he explains, "was many years ago, long before Oz came out of the clouds to rule over this land." But like many Indian tribes Baum's monkeys are not inherently bad; their actions depend wholly upon the bidding of others. Under the control of an evil influence, they do evil. Under the control of goodness and innocence, as personified by Dorothy, the monkeys are helpful and kind, although unable to take her to Kansas. Says the Monkey King, "We belong to this country alone, and cannot leave it." The same could be said with equal truth of the first Americans.

Dorothy presents a special problem to the Witch. Seeing the mark on Dorothy's forehead and the Silver Shoes on her feet, the Witch begins "to tremble with fear, for she knew what a powerful charm belonged to them." Then "she happened to look into the child's eyes and saw how simple the soul behind them was, and that the little girl did not know of the wonderful power the Silver Shoes gave her." Here Baum again uses the Silver allegory to state the blunt homily that while goodness affords a people ultimate protection against evil, ignorance of their capabilities allows evil to impose itself upon them. The Witch assumes the proportions of a kind of western Mark Hanna or Banker Boss, who, through natural malevolence, manipulates the people and holds them prisoner by cynically taking advantage of their innate innocence.

Enslaved in the West, "Dorothy went to work meekly, with her mind made up to work as hard as she could; for she was glad the Wicked Witch had decided not to kill her." Many Western farmers have held these same grim thoughts in less mystical terms. If the Witch of the West is a diabolical force of Darwinian or Spencerian nature, then another contravening force may be counted upon to dispose of her. Dorothy destroys the evil Witch by angrily dousing her with a bucket of water. Water, that precious commodity which the drought-ridden farmers on the great plains needed so badly, and when if correctly used could create an agricultural paradise, or at least dissolve a wicked witch. Plain water brings an end to malign nature in the West.

When Dorothy and her companions return to the Emerald City they soon discover that the Wizard is really nothing more than "a little man, with a bald head and a wrinkled face." Can this be the ruler of the land?

Our friends looked at him in surprise and dismay.

> *"I thought Oz was a great Head," said Dorothy. . . . "And I thought Oz was a terrible Beast," said the Tin Woodman. "And I thought Oz was a Ball of Fire," exclaimed the Lion. "No; you are all wrong," said the little man meekly. "I have been making believe."*

Dorothy asks if he is truly a great Wizard. He confides, "Not a bit of it, my dear; I'm just a common man." Scarecrow adds, "You're more than that . . . you're a humbug."

The Wizard's deception is of long standing in Oz and even the Witches were taken in. How was it accomplished? "It was a great mistake my ever letting you into the Throne Room," the Wizard complains. "Usually I will not see even my subjects, and so they believe I am something terrible." What a wonderful lesson for youngsters of the decade when Benjamin Harrison, Grover Cleveland and William McKinley were hiding in the White House. Formerly the Wizard was a mimic, a ventriloquist and a circus balloonist. The latter trade involved going "up in a balloon on circus day, so as to draw a crowd of people together and get them to pay to see the circus." Such skills are as admirably adapted to success in late-nineteenth-century politics as they are to the humbug wizardry of Baum's story. A pointed comment on Midwestern political ideals is the fact that our little Wizard comes from Omaha, Nebraska, a center of Populist agitation. "Why that isn't very far from Kansas," cries Dorothy. Nor, indeed, are any of the characters in the wonderful land of Oz.

The Wizard, of course, can provide the objects of self-delusion desired by Tin Woodman, Scarecrow and Lion. But Dorothy's hope of going home fades when the Wizard's balloon leaves too soon. Understand this: Dorothy wishes to leave a green and fabulous land, from which all evil has disappeared, to go back to the gray desolation of the Kansas prairies. Dorothy is an orphan, Aunt Em and Uncle Henry are her only family. Reality is never far from Dorothy's consciousness and in the most heartrending terms she explains her reasoning to the Good Witch Glinda,

> *Aunt Em will surely think something dreadful has happened to me, and that will make her put on mourning; and unless the crops are better this year than they were last I am sure Uncle Henry cannot afford it.*

The Silver Shoes furnish Dorothy with a magic means of travel. But when she arrives back in Kansas she finds, "The Silver Shoes had fallen off in her flight through the air, and were lost forever in the desert." Were the "her" to refer to America in 1900, Baum's statement could hardly be contradicted.

Current historiography tends to criticize the Populist movement for its "delusions, myths and fables," Professor C. Vann Woodward observed recently. Yet *The Wonderful Wizard of Oz* has provided unknowing generations with a gentle and friendly Midwestern critique of the Populist rationale on these very same grounds. Led by naive innocence and protected by good will, the farmer, the laborer and the politician approach the mystic holder of national power to ask for personal fulfillment. Their desires, as well as the Wizard's cleverness in answering them, are all self-delusion. Each of these characters carries within him the solution to his own problem, were he only to view himself objectively. The fearsome Wizard turns out to be nothing more than a common man, capable of shrewd but mundane answers to these self-induced needs. Like any good politician he gives the people what they want. Throughout the story Baum poses a central thought; the American desire for symbols of fulfillment is illusory. Real needs lie elsewhere.

Thus the Wizard cannot help Dorothy, for of all the characters only she has a wish that is selfless, and only she has a direct connection to honest, hopeless human beings. Dorothy supplies real fulfillment when she returns to her aunt and uncle, using the Silver Shoes, and cures some of their misery and heartache. In this way Baum tells us that the Silver crusade at least brought back Dorothy's lovely spirit to the disconsolate plains farmer. Her laughter, love and good will are no small addition to that gray land, although the magic of Silver has been lost forever as a result.

Noteworthy too is Baum's prophetic placement of leadership in Oz after Dorothy's departure. The Scarecrow reigns over the Emerald City, the Tin

Woodman rules in the West and the Lion protects smaller beasts in "a grand old forest." Thereby farm interests achieve national importance, industrialism moves West and Bryan commands only a forest full of lesser politicians.

Baum's fantasy succeeds in bridging the gap between what children want and what they should have. It is an admirable example of the way in which an imaginative writer can teach goodness and morality without producing the almost inevitable side effect of nausea. Today's children's books are either saccharine and empty, or boring and pedantic. Baum's first Oz tale—and those which succeed it—are immortal not so much because the "heart-aches and night-mares are left out" as that "the wonderment and joy" are retained.

Baum declares, "The story of 'the Wonderful Wizard of Oz' was written solely to pleasure children of today." In 1963 there are very few children who have never heard of the Scarecrow, the Tin Woodman or the Cowardly Lion, and whether they know W. W. Denslow's original illustrations of Dorothy, or Judy Garland's whimsical characterization, is immaterial. *The Wizard* has become a genuine piece of American folklore because, knowing his audience, Baum never allowed the consistency of the allegory to take precedence over the theme of youthful entertainment. Yet once discovered, the author's allegorical intent seems clear, and it gives depth and lasting interest even to children who only sense something else beneath the surface of the story. Consider the fun in picturing turn-of-the-century America, a difficult era at best, using these ready-made symbols provided by Baum. The relationships and analogies outlined above are admittedly theoretical, but they are far too consistent to be coincidental, and they furnish a teaching mechanism which is guaranteed to reach any level of student.

The Wizard of Oz says so much about so many things that it is hard not to imagine a satisfied and mischievous gleam in Lyman Frank Baum's eye as he had Dorothy say, "And oh, Aunt Em! I'm so glad to be at home again!"

6. Why Did the United States Fight Spain in 1898?

John Offner

The United States went to war against Spain because of longstanding foreign affairs interests as well as immediate domestic political events. From the early days of the Republic, North American politicians considered Cuba's geographic position as vital to the United States. The island was located ninety miles from Florida and commanded important seaways connecting the Atlantic Ocean with the Gulf of Mexico and the Caribbean Sea. When Spain lost most of its Central and South American colonies, some U.S. leaders worried that Great Britain or France might gain control of Cuba and menace the United States. During the 1850s, some North Americans believed that the United States was destined to annex the island. After the Civil War, these earlier concerns became less important but remained as basic concepts that influenced later affairs.

During the latter part of the nineteenth century, Cuba became an important producer of sugar cane and tobacco. Toward the end of the century, North American investment, particularly in plantations, mills, and mines, rose rapidly in Cuba. By 1895 North American businessmen had invested up to 50 million dollars in Cuba, and by 1893, commerce between the mainland and the island exceeded 100 million dollars. For the United States, Cuba was an important market for industrial goods and a source of raw sugar, tobacco, and various minerals; for Cuba, the United States was the essential importer of over 90 percent of sugar produced on the island.[2]

Despite growing economic ties with Cuba, many North Americans were prejudiced against Spaniards and Cubans. U.S. scholars and textbooks depicted Spain as degenerate, with Catholic inquisition cruelties, a corrupt monarchy, and a backward economy.[3] In addition, many North Americans were prejudiced against people of African descent, and about one third of Cuba's population was African. Another change in Cuba was the emergence of insular nationalism. In 1868 some Cubans began fighting for independence, and at the end of three decades, this goal became an irreconcilable conflict between Cuban nationalists and Spanish imperialists. The final fight for independence broke out in 1895: General Maximo Gómez, head of the Cuban army, lacked sufficient personnel and munitions to wage a conventional war against Spain's larger army. Controlling no seaport, Gómez could not import large amounts of ammunition and

[2]See Louis A. Perez, Jr., *Cuba and the United States: Ties of Singular Intimacy* (Athens: University of Georgia Press, 1990); and Walter La Feber, The New Empire. *An Interpretation of American Expansion, 1860-1898* (Ithaca: Cornell University Press, 1963).

[3]Richard L Kagan, "Prescott's Paradigm: American Historical Scholarship and the Decline of Spain," American Historical Review 101, no. 2 (April 1996): 423-446; Gerald F. Linderman, *The Mirror of War: American Society and the Spanish-American War* (Ann Arbor: University of Michigan Press, 1974).

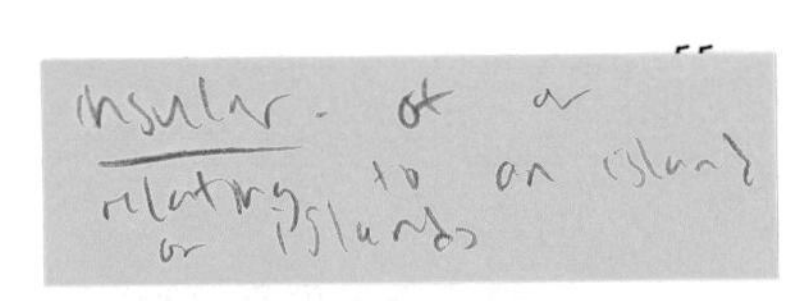

medicine. Therefore, he divided his army into small units and directed them to destroy the island's economy, believing that eventually Spain would grow weary of war and withdraw from the island. Avoiding large Spanish forces and traditional battles, the insurgents instead attacked small Spanish units and outposts, and they burned cane fields and mills. Gómez's forces, based in eastern Cuba, rapidly spread the war to the western shores of Cuba.[4]

Surprised by insurgent successes, the Spanish countered with harsh military repression. Spain sent General Valeriano Weyler Nicolau together with more than two hundred thousand troops to Cuba, while enlisting about eighty thousand local Cuban volunteers. Weyler erected fortifications around the major cities and towns, and controlled two fortified roads running from North to South across the island. The Spanish troops began clearing much of the western third of the island, but they were unable to drive the Cuban insurgents from the central war zone. Because Cuban peasants were aiding the insurgents with food and information, the Spanish relocated several hundred thousand villagers to the defenses of towns and cities. The Spanish then burned the unoccupied homes and fields. Since Spain was not prepared to feed and house the reconcentrated population, tens of thousands of *reconcentrados* eventually starved, sickened, and died. By 1898 both Washington and Madrid believed that some four hundred thousand Cuban civilians had died, about one fourth of the island's population, and, that many more were vulnerable.[5]

In 1897-1898 no one could foresee an early end to the Cuban—Spanish war. Cuban insurgents, about forty thousand strong, controlled the mountainous eastern third of the island and much of the countryside in central Cuba, but lacked the personnel and munitions to mount sustained assaults on Spain's fortified towns and cities. During three years of campaigning, many Spanish soldiers fell ill and died from disease, and only about sixty thousand remained fit for combat. Although supported by thousands of local volunteers, the Spanish forces were inadequate to defeat the widespread insurgency. In addition, Spain's political resolve to send more soldiers to Cuba had nearly come to an end, yet the Spanish government and its military leaders were unwilling to quit the island. Tens of thousands of *reconcentrados* suffered while both Cuban and Spanish soldiers continued to lay waste to the island.

The United States soon felt the 1895 eruption of war, and the events in Cuba and Spain triggered a series of U.S. responses that culminated in military intervention. Initially, commerce collapsed followed by mounting U.S. property claims against Spain. It soon became apparent that many North Americans sympathized with the insurgents and favored Cuban independence. Reliable reports of horrific Cuban civilian suffering increased U.S. public criticism of Spain.

[4]For details of the war, including Cuba, Spain, the United States, and the Philippines, see David F. Trask, *The War with Spain in 1898* (New York: Macmillan, 1981).

[5]A United States Army census of 1899 estimated that 235,000 Cubans died from the insurrection, most of them civilians; that was over one eighth of the island's population

Grover Cleveland, the first president to consider the Cuban war, proclaimed U.S. neutrality, urged Spain to seek a political settlement, and condemned Gómez's scorched earth tactics that destroyed and threatened U.S. investments. In time, the Cleveland administration became convinced that Cuba would fare better under Spanish sovereignty that would provide more safety and stability on the island; moreover, Cleveland did not believe the insurgents had a functional and responsible civilian government. Republican legislators, on the other hand, led the Congress in passing pro Cuban resolutions; these, however, were non-binding on Cleveland's administration. The division between Cleveland, a Democrat, and the Republicans in Congress led to the Republican Party's close identification with Cuban independence. However, the intense competition of the 1896 presidential campaign momentarily diverted national attention from Cuba. After the election, President Cleveland, troubled by a military stalemate in Cuba and alarmed by rising *reconcentrado* deaths, warned Spain that if its military efforts appeared to be futile, then the United States would intervene.[6] Thus, Cleveland established humanitarianism as a justifiable basis for U.S. intervention.

When William McKinley became president in March 1897, his views on Cuba were unknown.[7] Although his political party and many congressional supporters championed Cuban independence, most business leaders who had supported the Republican victory wanted peace with Spain. The new president, unlike Cleveland, soon decided that peace on the island would most likely come from ending Spanish rule in Cuba. A reliable report of terrible Cuban suffering prompted McKinley to demand that Spain follow civilized warfare and adopt sufficient political and economic reforms to bring a quick end to the insurrection.

As tension between the United States and Spain mounted, an assassin murdered the Spanish prime minister. A new Spanish government, headed by Práxedes Sagasta (a critic of the previous regime) initiated many reforms. During the fall of 1897, Sagasta recalled General Weyler, nearly ended the flow of soldiers to Cuba, increased relief for starving Cubans, allowed some *reconcentrados* to return to their homes, and offered autonomy to Cuba. The McKinley administration welcomed Sagasta's reforms.[8]

Sagasta's initiatives, however, encountered major obstacles. The Cuban insurgents flatly rejected autonomy and continued fighting. Many Spanish officers and nationalists also opposed a political settlement; on 12 January 1898 Spanish officers in Havana led rioters in attacks on the offices of newspapers that supported autonomy. Although Spain quickly restored order, the McKinley administration feared that future riots might turn anti-American; moreover, hope for a Spanish-Cuban political settlement had faded. The United States had been

[6]For more on the Cleveland administration, see Gerald G. Eggert, *Richard Olney.-Evolution of a Statesman* (University Park: Pennsylvania State University Press, 1974).

[7]For more on McKinley's presidency, see Lewis L. Gould, *The Presidency of William McKinley* (Lawrence: Regents Press of Kansas, 1980).

[8]For more on diplomacy, see John L. Offner, *An Unwanted War. The Diplomacy of the United States and Spain over Cuba, 1895-1898* (Chapel Hill: University of North Carolina Press, 1992).

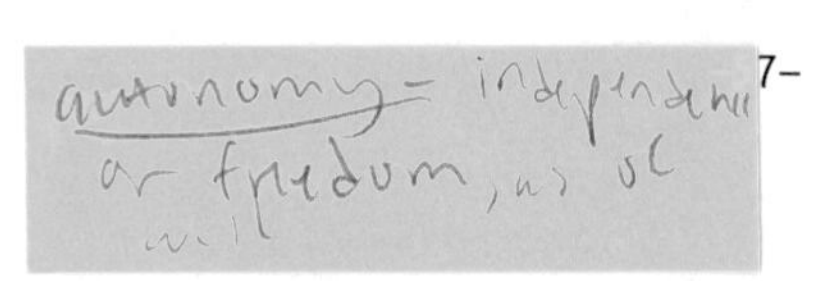

concentrating naval ships in preparation for a possible conflict with Spain, and McKinley decided to send the *Maine* from Key West to Havana Harbor to protect Americans.

Two unexpected events in February greatly increased the likelihood of U.S. intervention. The Spanish minister in Washington, Enrique Dupuy de Lôme, had written a private letter that criticized McKinley and treated Sagasta's reforms as insincere. Publication of the letter resulted in a brief diplomatic storm that ended with the resignation of Dupuy de Lome and an apology from the Spanish government. On 15 February, the *Maine* exploded in Havana harbor with a loss of 266 crew members. The cause of the disaster was unknown; spontaneous combustion in the coal might have ignited the powder magazines, but many Americans suspected Spanish treachery. Sensational journals charged that Spaniards had triggered the explosion.[9] McKinley cautioned the public to reserve judgment until the United States Navy investigated the wrecked ship and determined the cause of its destruction. It took six weeks for the naval board of inquiry to report on the *Maine*. During this time details of the "secret" investigation regularly leaked to the press, and the public quickly learned that the naval inquiry members believed an external explosion, probably a mine, set off an internal explosion of the ship's magazines and caused the disaster. The naval board did not know who was responsible for the external explosion, however.[10]

While the nation waited for the official naval report, both the McKinley administration and the Spanish government sought a diplomatic solution that would prevent war. McKinley considered buying Cuba, but key senators opposed this, and Spain was not interested in a sale; McKinley displayed his condescending attitude toward the Cubans when he never asked them what they thought of a U.S. purchase. A more promising initiative was a proposal for a cease-fire. Spain and the United States explored the possibility of an armistice in the fighting on the island to allow time for Spanish-Cuban peace negotiations, but the proposal failed amid details. Spain wanted the Cubans to ask for a cease-fire, and the Cubans, suspecting Spanish trickery, were unwilling to stop fighting. Spain thought the United States should force the Cubans to end the war; the United States lacked the leverage to persuade the Cubans to lay down their arms, and it refused to join Spain in suppressing the Cubans. McKinley asked the Spanish government to offer an armistice that would provide for six months of Spanish-Cuban negotiations, and if these failed, Spain should accept U.S. arbitration; the

[9]Some historians believe that sensational journalism played a central role in creating U.S. war hysteria. For example, see Marcus W. Wilkerson, *Public Opinion and the Spanish-American War* (Baton Rouge: Louisiana State University Press, 1932). The Cuban facts, however, published in the traditional press and government documents needed no sensational exaggeration to inflame public opinion.

[10]See Hyman G. Rickover, How the *Battleship Maine Was Destroyed* (Washington, D.C.: Department of the Navy, Naval History Division, 1976). Rickover concluded that there was no external mine and that the explosion originated within the *Maine*, probably in the coal bunkers.

Spanish government refused. By the end of March, with fighting continuing and negotiations fruitless, hopes for a diplomatic settlement lapsed.

The final weeks of diplomatic negotiations were accompanied by a rapidly rising demand in the United States for military intervention. On 17 March Senator Redfield Proctor described to the Senate the horrible conditions in Cuba that he had recently observed. His dramatic speech convinced many businessmen and religious leaders that the United States had a humanitarian duty to use military force, if necessary, to end the fighting in Cuba.[11] During the following ten days the official naval report on the *Maine* became public. With large numbers of Americans angry and vengeful, many Republican legislators worried that if the McKinley administration did not act quickly and decisively, Democrats would seize the Cuban issue and win the November elections. These Republican congressmen opposed McKinley's diplomatic plan of an armistice followed by six months of negotiations; this would drag out a Cuban solution until October, and the outcome was uncertain. Thus, Republican legislators wanted the administration to champion the Cuban cause, even if this meant war with Spain. It was widely accepted that a war would be a quick and easy U.S. victory. When McKinley continued to seek an armistice, more than one hundred Republican House members caucused and threatened to join with Democrats in voting for war; dissident Republicans joined by the Democrats would form a House majority.

With diplomatic negotiations going nowhere, Republican House members in rebellion, and public outrage evident, McKinley decided to turn the Cuban issue over to Congress. He still hoped that Spain, faced by an unwinnnable war, would relent, and at the last moment, 9 April, Sagasta's government offered a suspension of hostilities in Cuba. Spain, however, did not offer independence, and the Cuban insurgents quickly rejected Spain's offer. McKinley wanted additional time for negotiations, but several influential Republican congressional leaders refused to delay further. Thus, McKinley reluctantly turned the Cuban problem over to Congress, asking for authority to intervene to end Cuban suffering, to protect U.S. life and property, to restore commerce, and to end the constant threat to peace that agitated the United States.

In the end, diplomacy failed due to internal politics; each party to the negotiation lacked flexibility and the desire to compromise. McKinley lost control of Congress to Republicans who demanded intervention; Sagasta's government faced rigid military officers and threats of civil war that prevented Spain from abandoning Cuba; and the Cuban insurgents would accept nothing less than complete independence from Spain.

When Congress considered the Cuban issue, a difference emerged between McKinley and some influential Senate Republicans over the objectives of war. A Senate majority favored recognizing the Republic of Cuba. McKinley objected for several reasons: he did not want the U.S. Army to come under Cuban sover-

[11]For more on business and religious opinion, see Julius W. Pratt, *Expansionists of 1898. The Acquisition off Hawaii and the Spanish Islands* (Baltimore: Johns Hopkins Press, 1936).

eignty when it invaded the island; he thought that recognition might hurt U.S. claims against Cuba for property the insurgents had destroyed; and most significantly, he lacked confidence in Cuban leaders' ability to restore and maintain peace on the island. During the Senate debate, Senator Henry M. Teller offered an amendment, proposed by Cuban lobbyists, that asserted a U.S. intention to leave Cuba after the war. Teller's amendment did not recognize the Cuban Republic, but it promised Cuban independence; both the Senate and the McKinley administration accepted Teller's formula.[12] Congress then passed a set of resolutions permitting U.S. military intervention in the Spanish-Cuban conflict. As a result, Spain broke diplomatic relations; the United States began a naval blockade of Cuba; and Congress set the official start of the war as 21 April 1898.

The war lasted less than three months, for in nearly every clash, U.S. arms prevailed. On 1 May the United States Navy sank a Spanish fleet in Manila harbor, and on 3 July another fleet off Santiago de Cuba was destroyed. The United States Army invaded Cuba, Luzon, and Puerto Rico, and obtained the surrender of Santiago de Cuba while the navy seized Guam. One day after a peace protocol was signed, the Spanish surrendered Manila to U.S. forces. Holding the military upper hand, the United States dictated the peace. Without consulting the Cubans, Puerto Ricans, or Filipinos about peace terms, the McKinley administration decided to remove Spain from the New World. It required Spain to leave Cuba and demanded Puerto Rico as an indemnity of war. McKinley asked for an island, eventually Guam, in the Ladrones (Marianas). The McKinley administration, however, was undecided about the future of the Philippines, so McKinley asked that the United States Army occupy and control Manila until a peace conference could determine the disposition of the islands. With Spanish military forces in retreat and facing ever greater losses, Spain reluctantly accepted McKinley's terms, and on 15 August the two nations signed a protocol that led to an armistice.

Although fighting stopped between United States, Cuban, and Spanish forces, it continued between Philippine insurgents and the Spanish. Filipino nationalists, led by Emilio Aguinaldo, rapidly took control of Luzon and successfully invaded several islands in the central portion of the archipelago. By the time the United States and Spanish peace commissioners met on 1 October in Paris to negotiate a treaty, Aguinaldo's forces were advancing in the Philippines, and he was forming a permanent government for the entire archipelago; at the same time, there was increasing friction between the Filipino nationalists and the American occupation forces stationed in Manila. Moreover, Germany and Japan had revealed their interest in acquiring some or all of the Philippines, while Great Britain urged Washington to annex the entire archipelago.[13]

[12]Philip S. Foner, *The Spanish-Cuban American War and the Birth of American Imperialism, 1895-1902*, 2 vols. (New York: Monthly Review Press, 1972).

[13]For more on the Philippines, see Ephraim K. Smith, "William McKinley's Enduring Legacy: The Historiographical Debate on the Taking of the Philippine Islands," in *Crucible of Empire:*

Within the United States most Americans expected the McKinley administration to keep Manila and many advocated taking all of the islands. Following a political tour of the Midwest in October, McKinley decided that the public and the Senate would support a treaty securing the entire archipelago. Because the United States had not conquered the Philippines, McKinley offered twenty million dollars for internal improvements that Spain had made in the islands. The final peace treaty consisted of the 15 August protocol provisions and the financial settlement for the Philippine Islands. After a closely contested Senate debate, senators voted fifty-seven to twenty-seven, thereby narrowly providing a two thirds majority for the treaty.

In sum, there were irreconcilable differences between Cuban nationalists and Spanish colonialists that left no room for a negotiated political settlement. The three-year war for independence caused U.S. economic losses and the death and suffering of hundreds of thousands of Cuban people. By the spring of 1898 there was no diplomatic resolution to the conflict and no end in sight to the fighting. Many Americans, prejudiced against Spain and sympathetic to Cuba, were angered over the destruction of the *Maine;* the approaching national election galvanized congressional Republicans to seek military intervention. McKinley, who had long considered U.S. military intervention as a possibility, put the best face on the se of force by justifying it as necessary to secure humanitarian ends and U.S. interests. The president removed Spain from the New World and prepared for a long-term U.S. presence in Cuba that would exclude the European powers.

The Spanish-American War and Its Aftermath, ed. James C. Bradford (Annapolis: Naval Institute Press, 1993).

7. The Anti-Imperialists, the Philippines and the Inequality of Man

Christopher Lasch

The cession of the Philippine Islands to the United States precipitated a great debate on the nature of our foreign policy and our national destiny. Opinion on the wisdom of retaining the Philippines was divided without regard to party or section; indeed, the intrusion of the expansionist issue into the politics of the period tended for a time to obliterate sectionalism. Yet sectional considerations, particularly in the South, were not absent from the debate. Southern Democrats were almost unanimous in condemning "imperialism," on the grounds that Asiatics, like Negroes, were innately inferior to white people and could not be assimilated to American life. Two decades earlier such arguments would have called forth angry rejoinders from the North. That the South's recourse to them at the end of the century did not revive the old controversy over Reconstruction revealed the extent to which Northern liberals had retreated from the implications of their emancipation of the Negro—a retreat the irony of which Southern statesmen never tired of expounding. An examination of the debate over imperialism helps to explain this remarkable change in Northern opinion and thereby enables us to see Southern racialism, so prevalent in the nineties, in a larger perspective. Thus a revaluation of an experience essentially national, not sectional, compels a revaluation of sectional history as well. Just as the corruption of the Reconstruction governments was paralleled by corruption in Northern state governments and in Washington, as historians are beginning to show, so at a somewhat later date illiberalism in the South also had its counterpart in the North. The retreat from idealism was a national, not a local, phenomenon.

That Northerners of the expansionist persuasion made no reply to those who in the course of challenging the annexation of the Philippines challenged some of the fundamental assumptions of American democracy should come as no surprise. The expansionists were in a delicate predicament. Men who favored acquiring the Philippines on the grounds that the natives were unfit for self-government could hardly afford to apply another logic to the Negro problem in the South; Senator Henry Cabot Lodge, among others, might well look back on his recent Force Bill as a youthful indiscretion which it were prudent to forget. But one would not have expected anti-imperialists in the North to share this reluctance to revive the dispute over equality. Because they professed a fervid devotion to the rights of man, the anti-imperialists might have been expected to guide the debate over annexation to higher ground by rejecting outright the leading argument both of the expansionists and of the Southern anti-expansionists, namely that men are created unequal. Most historians have in fact assumed that anti-imperialism was genuinely liberal in inspiration and that the anti-imperialists were voicing objections to colonialism now commonly accepted.

The position of the anti-imperialists does at first appear to have been sensible and straightforward: that is, that imperialism was not only inexpedient but unjust, a departure from the historic principles of the Declaration of Independence. But a closer examination of certain facets of anti-imperialism may require us to see the anti-imperialists in a rather different light. Their argument did not foreshadow the liberalism of the Good Neighbor policy. It was in fact no more liberal than that of the expansionists. Indeed, it resembled the expansionist rationale, against which it appeared to be a protest, far more closely than it does any of the objections we might today raise against a colonial policy, or for that matter than it resembled the theories of Thomas Jefferson. It was a product of the late nineteenth century, not of the eighteenth or twentieth centuries. The anti-imperialists, like the imperialists, saw the world from a pseudo-Darwinian point of view. They accepted the inequality of man—or, to be more precise, of races—as an established fact of life. They did not question the idea that Anglo-Saxons were superior to other people, and some of them would even have agreed that they were destined eventually to conquer the world. They did not quarrel with the idea of "destiny"; they merely refused to believe that destiny required such strenuous exertions of the American people, particularly when they saw in those exertions the menace of militarism and tyranny. There were important differences of opinion, of course, between those who favored and those who opposed the annexation of the Philippines, but for the moment it is perhaps more important to dwell on the matters on which they agreed. Most middle-class Americans of the 1890s agreed in attaching great importance to the concept of race, and it was that agreement which gave the intellectual life of the period its peculiar tone.

It is characteristic of the period that neither side in the debate over the Philippines was content to rest its case on considerations of expediency alone, although the expansionist clique on whom defense of the "large policy" devolved tried to rouse the business community, which was apathetic toward the whole question of expansion, with visions of glittering markets in China. But economic arguments could too easily be attacked as sordid, and the expansionists preferred to stand on higher ground. They appealed to "manifest destiny," an old idea, and to the newer, post-Darwinian idea that it was the manifest *duty* of higher civilizations to displace lower ones, either through outright elimination (as the white man had eliminated the Indian) or through a process of uplift and "Christianization." It was as carriers of civilization, they argued, that the American people were obliged to annex the Philippines, however disagreeable the obligation might appear.

The anti-imperialists, largely ignoring the economic and strategic arguments for annexation, replied with a moral argument of their own. They admitted that our history, as the expansionists were fond of showing, was a record of territorial expansion, but they fixed the limits of our westward destiny at the shores of

the Pacific. The American destiny, they contended, was merely continental, not global. All of the areas previously acquired by the United States had been on the North American continent, and all except Alaska had been contiguous to the old states. Because they were contiguous and because they were thinly populated, they came to be settled by citizens from the older states, by white, Protestant, English-speaking people—by a population, in short, indistinguishable from that of the older states. The new territories, therefore, could be, and were, admitted to statehood. (Alaska, again, was the single exception.)

But to annex distant islands already heavily populated by racial aliens, the anti-imperialists maintained, would be a momentous and disastrous departure from the past. The Filipinos, for any number of reasons, could not become American citizens; they would have to be governed as subjects. But how could a republic have subjects? For the United States to acquire the Philippines without admitting their people to full citizenship would amount to government without the consent of the governed—a flat contradiction of the cardinal principle of American democracy, the principle over which we separated from England, the principle of the Declaration of Independence. Nor was this all. As a result of the initial injustice, others would follow. A large standing army would have to be created in order to defend our new possessions not only against foreign powers but against the natives themselves, who were already in revolt against American rule; and an army called into being for the purpose of crushing freedom abroad would ultimately be used to destroy it at home. The administration had already begun to censor news from the Philippines, in order to create the impression that the hostilities there were purely defensive in character, and the anti-imperialists saw in this an evil omen—proof that if the United States persisted in imperialism, she would eventually go the way of Rome.

The exponents of annexation could offer no satisfactory answer to all this. Instead, they attempted to create a dilemma of their own—to show that there was no satisfactory alternative to annexation. Accordingly they argued that the Filipinos were not "ready" for self-government and if left to themselves would fall into the hands of a native dictator or a foreign conqueror. But not a single expansionist proposed that the privileges of citizenship be extended to the Philippines. They assumed that the Filipinos would have to be governed as second-class citizens, and with that assumption they departed from the natural-rights philosophy of the Declaration of Independence, exactly as their antagonists accused them of doing. Senator Henry M. Teller, an expansionist, confessed that to hold the islanders as subjects would be "rather objectionable in a republic"; but there seemed no choice. Not all the expansionists had similar reservations, but almost all of them recognized and admitted the implications of their policy for the doctrine of natural rights. In effect, they substituted for the Jeffersonian proposition that the right to liberty is "natural"'—hence universal—the proposition that rights depend on environment—on "civilization," of which there were now seen to be many stages of development; on race; even on climate. A pseudo-Darwinian hierarchy of cultural stages, unequal in the capacity for enjoyment of the rights associated with self-government, replaced the simpler and more liberal theory of the Enlightenment, which recognized only the distinction between society and nature. "Rights," as absolutes, lost their meaning by becoming relative to time and place. Rights now depended on a people's "readiness" to enjoy them.

It is not surprising that the anti-imperialists accused the expansionists of abandoning the Declaration of Independence. What is surprising is that their own arguments were no closer to the spirit of that document than the ones they denounced with such fervor. The anti-imperialists were in fact no more Jeffersonian in their essential outlook than Theodore Roosevelt or Henry Cabot Lodge or Alfred T Mahan was, for they did not challenge the central assumption of imperialist thought: the natural inequality of men. The imperialists at least had the merit of consistency; they made no professions of Jeffersonianism. The anti-imperialists, on the other hand, invoked the name of Jefferson at every opportunity.

Some light on the anti-imperialists is shed by the high proportion of Southerners among them. In the Senate, only four of twenty-eight Southern senators favored unconditional ratification of the treaty with Spain, and Southerners led the attack on the treaty in debate. Their arguments against ratification clearly reflected the lingering bitterness of Reconstruction, as well as more recent movements to exclude Negroes from the benefits of citizenship. Annexation of the Philippines, they argued, would merely compound the race problem by introducing into the country what Senator John W. Daniel of Virginia called a "mess of Asiatic pottage." Benjamin R. Tillman of South Carolina was especially active in the anti-imperialist cause, playing ingenious variations on the racial theme. At times he gave it a distinctly Darwinian note: " . . . we [he said, referring to the South] understand and realize what it is to have two races side by side that can not mix or mingle without deterioration and injury to both and the ultimate destruction of the civilization of the higher." At other times he gave it a pro-labor bias: " . . . here are 10,000,000 Asiatics who will have the right as soon as the pending treaty is ratified, to get on the first ship that they can reach and come here and compete in the labor market of the United States." In a more somber mood, he appeared to speak more in sorrow than in anger: " . . . coming . . . as a Senator from . . . South Carolina, with 750,000 colored population and only 500,000 whites, I realize what you are doing, while you don't; and I would save this country from the injection into it of another race question which can only breed bloodshed and a costly war and the *loss* of the lives of our brave soldiers." More often, however, he spoke with biting irony which revealed the Negro, not the Filipino, as the real source of his anxiety and, further, which showed that he was more interested in embarrassing the North—in forcing its senators to admit to a contradiction—than he was in preventing the acquisition of the Philippines. When Knute Nelson of Minnesota, once an abolitionist, declared that the Filipinos were incapable of self-government, Tillman replied: "I want to call the Senator's attention to the fact, however, that he and others who are now contending for a different policy in Hawaii and the Philippines gave the slaves of the South not only self-government, but they forced on the white men of the South, at the point of the bayonet, the rule and domination of those ex-slaves. Why the difference? Why the change? Do you acknowledge that you were wrong in 1868?"

It is unnecessary to insist that such arguments did not spring from deep-seated attachment to the Declaration of Independence. But it would be manifestly unfair to judge the whole anti-imperialist movement on the basis of its Southern wing, particularly when many Northern men of the persuasion were clearly uncomfortable at finding themselves in the company of men like Tillman. An examination of their own arguments, however, discloses no important difference from that of the Southerners, except that Northern anti-imperialists did not dwell on the parallel with the Southern Negro problem—something they were by this time anxious to forget. One is left with the impression that it was not the Southern argument as such that disconcerted the Northerners, but the use to which the South put it. When it came to giving reasons why the Philippines should not be annexed, North and South found themselves in close agreement.

Anti-imperialists contended that the Filipinos, unless they were given their independence, would have to be held in subjection, since they could not be admitted as citizens. What is interesting is the manner in which they arrived at the latter conclusion. A brief study of the process reveals a Darwinism as thoroughgoing as that of the imperialists themselves.

In the first place, the anti-imperialists argued, if the Filipinos became citizens, they would migrate to the United States and compete with American labor—a prospect especially alarming in view of the racial composition of the islands. As Samuel Gompers declared: "If the Philippines are annexed, what is to prevent the Chinese, the Negritos, and the Malays coming to our own country?" This was more than an economic argument. It implied that those people were accustomed to a low standard of living and, what is more, that they were incapable, by virtue of their race, of longing for anything better. It implied that Orientals, in short, would work for low wages because they could not, and never would, appreciate the finer things of life which money alone could buy. This view had already come into vogue on the West Coast, where it was particularly popular with organized labor; it is not surprising, therefore, to find Gompers appealing to it.

If cheap Filipino labor would compete unfairly with American labor, cheap Filipino goods could be expected to compete unfairly with American goods. If we took over the islands, we could neither prevent immigration nor levy protective import duties. Annexation would therefore injure both capital and labor.

But the Filipinos would also be given the vote. Considering, again, the racial composition of the islands, the results would clearly be ruinous. Carl Schurz declared:

If they become states on an equal footing with the other states they will not only be permitted to govern themselves as to their home concerns, but will take part in governing the whole republic, in governing us, by sending senators and representatives into our Congress to help make our laws, and by voting for president and vice-president to give our national government its executive. The prospect of the consequences which would follow the admission of the Spanish creoles and the negroes of the West India islands and of the Malays and Tagals of the Philippines to participation in the conduct of our government is so alarming that you instinctively pause before taking the step.

The same sentiments were expressed by James L. Blair of St. Louis, the son of the old Free Soil leader Francis Preston Blair. "History," Blair said, "shows no instance of a tropical people who have demonstrated a capacity for maintaining an enduring form of Republican government. To admit such a people into a share in the government of the United States would be self-destructive. David Starr Jordan warned his countrymen: "If we govern the Philippines, so in their degree must the Philippines govern us." Or as Champ Clark put it even more forcefully in the House of Representatives: "No matter whether they are fit to govern themselves or not, they are not fit to govern us [applause]."

But if it was undesirable for the Filipinos to come to the United States or to take part in American government, was it not still possible that Americans would emigrate to the Philippines and gradually displace the native culture? The anti-imperialists denied that any such outcome was possible. In the first place, "the two races could never amalgamate"; "the racial differences between the Oriental and Western races are never to be eradicated." But suppose the Filipinos were eliminated by force or herded into reservations, like the American Indians. Even then, the anti-imperialists insisted, annexation would be unwise, for the fact was that neither the "northern" (or "Anglo-Saxon" or "Germanic") race nor democratic institutions could survive in a tropical climate. "Civilization," said Jordan, "is, as it were, suffocated in the tropics." On another occasion he explained that the Philippines "lie in the heart of the torrid zone, Nature's asylum for degenerates.'" "Neither the people nor the institutions of the United States can ever occupy the Philippines," he said. "The American home cannot endure there, the town-meeting cannot exist." Schurz echoed the same refrain:

They are . . . situated in the tropics, where people of the northern races, such as Anglo-Saxons, or generally speaking, people of Germanic blood, have never migrated in mass to stay; and they are more or less

> *densely populated, parts of them* as *densely* as *Massachusetts—their population consisting almost exclusively of races to whom the tropical climate is congenial— . . . Malays, Tagals, Filipinos, Chinese, Japanese, Negritos, and various more or less barbarous tribes... .*

Such arguments clearly showed that the anti-imperialists had abandoned the natural-rights philosophy of the Declaration of Independence for a complicated Darwinian view of the world. According to this view, which appeared to be substantiated by the science of the day and by the writings of historians like Herbert Baxter Adams, geography, race, and political institutions were inextricably intertwined. The temperate zone—specifically the northern part of it—bred the "Germanic" race, from which Americans were descended. Free institutions were associated with the rise of that race; a study of other cultures showed no similar institutions. Because they alone were capable of using liberty wisely, the Germans had already risen to a cultural level far beyond that of any other race and were possibly destined to supplant all others. In view of their inability to survive in the tropics, however, it was not quite clear how this was to be accomplished; and for that reason, perhaps, the anti-imperialists preferred to see the Anglo-Saxons stay at home, in their native habitat. In any case, to mingle their blood with that of Asiatics would be a fatal departure from what Charles Francis Adams, for example, called the "cardinal principle in our policy as a race." He referred to our Indian policy, which he admitted had been harsh; but it had "saved the Anglo-Saxon stock from being a nation of half-breeds." The acquisition of the Philippines would again endanger the purity of the old stock, on which America's very survival depended.

An examination of the arguments against annexation of the Philippines leads to a number of interesting conclusions. In the first place, it is difficult, after having read their writings and speeches, to convince oneself that the anti-imperialists had the better of the argument, as historians have tended to assume. Whatever the merits of the expansionists' contention that the Filipinos were not ready for self-government, the expansionists were at least consistent in the conclusions which they drew from it. If it was true that the Filipinos could not govern themselves, the humane policy (although not necessarily the wisest one) was to govern them ourselves. The anti-imperialists, on the other hand, while sharing the expansionists' basic assumption (an assumption contrary to the spirit of American Democracy), were prefectly willing to leave the Filipinos to their fate—certainly a most un-Christian policy if they were indeed unable to manage their own affairs. So far as the moral argument had any validity at all, the anti-imperialists were on weak ground; and since they insisted on treating the question as a matter of right and wrong, it seems fair to judge them accordingly.

But it is not possible to condemn anti-imperialists for holding certain opinions on race unless one is willing to condemn the entire society of which they were a part. The fact is that the atmosphere of the late nineteenth century was so thoroughly permeated with racist thought (reinforced by Darwinism) that few men managed to escape it. The idea that certain cultures and races were naturally inferior to others was almost universally held by educated, middle-class, respectable Americans—in other words, by the dominant majority. The widespread and almost unconscious adherence to it was unmistakably manifested, in the same period, in the national policy toward minorities more familiar to American experience than the Filipinos, and in particular toward immigrants and Negroes. This was the period of the first serious restrictions on immigration; it was the period of the South's successful re-elimination of the Negro from white society. Men who called themselves liberals—survivors of the antislavery crusade and the battles of the sixties and seventies on behalf of the Negroes: liberal Republicans, mugwumps, "independents—acquiesced in these developments. A study of anti-imperialism makes it a little clearer why they did, for the anti-imperialist movement was dominated by these same men—men like Schurz, Adams, Jordan, and Moorfield Storey. Except for Storey, these men had now receded from their earlier idealism. They continued to speak of their part in the struggle for Negro rights, to refer to it with pride, but by referring to it as *a* fight which had already been won they indicated their indifference to the continuing plight of the Southern Negro. Indeed, they had abandoned him, as they now proposed to abandon the Filipinos. They had no further interest in crusading; the times, it appeared, called for retrenchment.

retrench - to cut down, reduce, or diminish (expenses)

II

The Progressive Era and the Twenties, 1900–1928

8. Progressivism

Robert M. Crunden

Like romanticism or Victorianism progressivism is one of those words people frequently use but rarely define with precision. Both at the time and in subsequent histories, a person seemed progressive who supported one or more reforms popular after the turn of the twentieth century. Any political activity that pretended to make the American economic or political system fairer in some way qualified. Although the term applied most obviously to the short-lived Progressive party of former president Theodore Roosevelt in the 1912 elections, progressivism as a general stance clearly applied to many members of the Republican, Democratic, Socialist, and Prohibition parties as well.

Progressivism in this context was a blanket term for many political movements on the local level, it included efforts to reform the structure of city governments, to grant them home rule, to lower transit fares, to regulate or socialize natural monopolies such as electricity and natural gas, and to rid politics of the stench of the saloon and the open control of politicians by those engaged in dubious business practices. At both state and local levels, progressives argued for the right of citizens to initiate legislation, to nominate candidates in open primary elections, to vote on laws directly, to elect and recall judges, to have secret ballots, and to revise the tax system to spread burdens more justly.

At the national level, progressive movements supported antitrust laws, the establishment of the Federal Reserve System of currency management, lower tariffs, imposition of an income tax, the right of women to vote and of all vote to elect senators directly, and the prohibition of the sale of alcoholic beverages. This list is long but hardly exhaustive.

Scholars have viewed the period in conflicting ways. Some have assumed that progressivism was the form liberalism took for the first fourteen years of the century, a firm if inadequate step toward the welfare legislation of the New Deal. Others have countered this view with the observation that many elements of the movement were reactionary, pointing out the fundamentalist religion, the puritanical legislation in morals, and the nostalgia for a yeoman farmer past clearly evident in so eminent a leader as William Jennings Bryan. They have stressed the middle-class nature of the reformers and the fear many seemed to have that they were losing status in economic and social life to those from untraditional backgrounds. Radicals have argued that because some businessmen were involved in the enactment of reforms and in the machinery of their administration, progressive legislation actually fended off true reform. Social scientists have stressed the way modernization affected the class structure and accelerated the shift from rural to urban living patterns Many analysts have asserted that amid such a tangle of factors, generalization becomes meaningless and clear definition impossible.

The "progressive movement" lingers as a term but should disappear. It is too precise and insistently political, too redolent of Whig assumptions of inevitable progress, to fit the larger picture now available. "Progressivism" fits better, as a climate of creativity, an ethos, a persuasion, making the events of the thirty years between 1889 and 1920 cohere as everyone assumed they did at the time Progressivism in this broader context was political only on its surface. At its core it was religious, an attempt by Americans from all social classes, but chiefly the middle class, to restore the proper balances among Protestant moral values, capitalistic competition, and democratic processes, which the expansion of business in the Gilded Age seemed to have changed in alarming ways. Having lost the literal faith of their ancestors, progressive leaders still wanted religious values to dominate political and economic life; they wanted better and fairer competition; and they wanted every citizen to participate in the polity. Such views could be either reactionary or enlightened, depending on context, and among themselves progressives disagreed on practically every specific proposal. In other words, they agreed on the need to remoralize society, but disagreed about how to accomplish it.

Religious thinkers were prominent in ways they never were again in American history. Conscious that many influential citizens were leaving their churches, both for reasons of belief and reasons of residence in outlying suburbs, clergy in most Protestant faiths began to apply Christian doctrine to policy concerning the poor who often lived close by. Washington Gladden preached largely to his local congregation; George D. Herron taught college students and then spoke across the country; Walter Rauschenbusch redefined the Christian mission from his quiet study in a theological seminary. Gladden's autobiography, Herrons collected speeches, and Rauschenbusch's *Christianity and the Social Crisis* (1907) and *Christianizing the Social Order* (1912) formulated the essential elements of Christian progressivism- work in this world to establish a Kingdom of God with social justice for all.

Progressives were primarily members of a post–Civil War generation that had to master a world very different from that of their parents. They were children of religious homes, and their autobiographies repeat the tales of discipline, of long Sundays with two or three church services, and of the duty everyone had of choosing a calling in which to work. But these children crew up in an age of Darwinism and big business; they did not have the religious fervor of their parents, nor did they have any special desire to grow rich. Farming bored them, the ministry was no longer attractive, and other professional opportunities few Young progressives channeled Protestant energies into the forming of new professions, which they pursued with the same zeal their parents had displayed in converting sinners and fighting slavery. They went to the new graduate schools founded along the lines of Johns Hopkins University; they created modern journalism and social work; they went into teaching and the law; and a few entered politics, finding in statesmanship the best outlet for Christian stewardship. Jews and Roman Catholics occasionally worked on the edges of progressivism, but those who set the tone and wrote the manifestos were Protestants

Considered on this broad scale, progressivism began with the founding of Hull-House by Jane Addams and Ellen Gates Starr in the fall of 1889 These pioneers of social work in Chicago soon became role models for young men and women in other cities, attracting such figures as John Dewey and George Herbert Mead to study what they were doing and to work their insights into a pragmatic philosophy that would solve the problems of democracy. A new breed of journalists soon appeared, often referred to as muckrakers who publicized the problems social workers faced and illuminated the business and political conditions that made social work important in the modern city. No one spoke of "networking" in the years around 1900, but social workers, intellectuals, and journalists all quickly came to know of each other. Journalists such as Lincoln Steffens and Ida Tarbell, social scientists such as Richard Ely and Woodrow Wilson, and politicians such as Brand Whitlock and Robert La Follette were soon in touch through letters and occasional meetings. With the inauguration of President Theodore Roosevelt in 1901, they had a national hero capable of dramatizing issues and providing leadership insofar as he was willing.

Progressivism produced three presidents, and their achievements comprise the most important legacy in the eyes of many analysts. Roosevelt moved against the trusts and backed railway regulation, pure food and drug laws, and the conservation of natural resources. William Howard Taft compromised on several issues, such as the tariff and conservation, but pursued a policy of vigorous judicial progressivism in his efforts to break up trusts, strengthen the Interstate Commerce Commission, and facilitate the workings of the courts. Woodrow Wilson lowered the tariff, reformed the currency, and toughened the trust laws yet again. He then carried progressive ideals into World War I, seeing it as a fight for democracy; at Versailles, however, he failed to work out a treaty capable of maintaining a free and peaceful world. Progressivism died twice: at Versailles itself, where Wilson compromised his position repeatedly in the face of European pressures, and in the US. Senate, which refused to ratify the treaty or permit American participation in the League of Nations.

But politics was only one discipline in which progressivism flourished; even the inclusion of journalism and social work in no way exhausts the scope of its influence. In literature, many novelists wrote about prison conditions, political corruption, prostitution, and other evils; the best-known volume is *The Jungle* (1906), Upton Sinclair's socialist examination of Chicago's Packingtown, its savage working conditions and unsanitary products. Painters entered the slums, the sporting halls, and the circuses to produce the Ashcan school of realistic portrayal that, in many cases, held manifest political content: Robert Henri was an anarchist, for example, and John Sloan a socialist. The poetry of Vachel Lindsay recalled William Jennings Bryan and William Booth, founder of the Salvation Army, and that of Carl Sandburg celebrated Chicago. Charles Beard and

Frederick Jackson Turner wrote progressive histories, reinterpreting the past so it would be "useful" and "relevant" to democratic citizens and legislators. John Dewey's pragmatism entered the public schools and dominated pedagogy for three generations, making progressive education" perhaps the most enduring, both for better and for worse, of the achievements of those years.

The two most eminent of the creative personalities whom progressivism produced, ironically and untypically, were in the fine arts. In music, Charles Ives looked back at the transcendentalists to create an aesthetic of innovative nostalgia; by trying to recapture the lost paths of Emerson and Thoreau, the romances of Hawthorne, and the antiabolitionist riots of his forebears, he made so many experiments in dissonance, polytonality, and polyrhythm that he emerged after World War II as the most important pioneer in American musical history. Architect Frank Lloyd Wright exceeded even Ives's achievements. Sharing an affection for the organic ideas of the American Renaissance before the Civil War and asserting that form and function were one, Wright developed the Prairie school of architecture, which sought to integrate the design of housing and the land it used and forced Americans to think more carefully about rapid urbanization. In terms of impact abroad, perhaps the most useful yardstick of achievement, Wright's work still influences architects and city planners.

For a climate that began with optimism, progressivism ended with extreme pessimism. President Wilson's foreign policy lay in rubble, and few politicians or publicists dared to recommend intervention in world affairs for the next generation, thus preventing Franklin D. Roosevelt from taking proper steps against the Japanese and the Germans in the 1930s. The political reforms worked no miracles. Women used their new right to vote to help elect Presidents Warren G. Harding, Calvin Coolidge, and Herbert Hoover and did little to purify the political process. Race relations, never a progressive priority, went from bad to worse. The initiative, referendum, and recall had only minor impact. Only in financial matters did any important legacy remain: the Federal Reserve System, despite changes, remained at the heart of the economy, and the income tax paid many of the bills for important welfare measures and the fighting of World War II. Surviving progressives themselves often grew disillusioned, and a majority opposed the more significant New Deal measures. The largest exception to this generalization was the group that identified with social settlement work: from Jane Addams to Eleanor Roosevelt, these progressives supported the New Deal and helped usher the welfare state into the American system.

Robert M. Crunden, *Ministers of Reform: The Progressives' Achievement in American Civilization, 1889 1920* (1982); Richard Hofstadter, *The Age of Reform (1955).*

ROBERT M. CRUNDEN

See also Ashcan School; Beard, Charles A., and Beard, Mary R, Dewey, John; Ives, Charles; Jungle, The; Muckrakers; Progressive Parties: 1912, 1924, 1948; Roosevelt, Theodore; Settlement Houses; Taft, William Howard; Turner, Frederick Jackson; Wilson, Woodrow.

9. Divorce in the Progressive Era

William L. O'Neill

An important aspect of the Progressive Movement was the attempt by middle class whites to impose their morality through legislative and moral suasion upon all Americans. The most famous example of this was the Prohibition movement, which sought to eliminate the production and consumption of intoxicating liquors from American life. The movement won tremendous support in rural America and fed upon the fear that urbanizaton and immigration were combining to weaken the moral fiber of the nation. Other crusades attacked prize fighting and prostitution, two activities also associated in the public's mind with immigrants and cities.

In the following essay historian William L. O'Neill evaluates the reaction of Americans to the upswing in the divorce rate. Like the Prohibition Movement, the antidivorce crusade won the support of Americans who feared the changes caused by a more urban society. They attributed the failure of marriages—one in nine in 1916—to a general decline in American morality. In fact, the problem was less one of declining morality than of expanding opportunities. Women were beginning to rebel against the expectations of traditional moral leaders. Many demanded more educational and employment opportunities, as well as an end to a marital system based simply on the physical beauty of the woman. The failure of the antidivorce movement clearly marked the beginning of a more free American society. The price of freedom, however, was often dear.

During the Progressive years the divorce rate, which had been rising steadily since the Civil War, attained critical dimensions. Consequently, Americans of this period took a graver view of the problem than any subsequent generation. Their varied responses proved to be decisive as far as the future of divorce itself was concerned, and they illuminate aspects of the Progressive Era which have received little attention from historians.

The precipitate growth of the divorce rate can be easily demonstrated. In 1880 there was one divorce for every twenty-one marriages; in 1900 there was one divorce for every twelve marriages; in 1909 the ratio dropped to one in ten, and by 1916 it stood at one in nine. Naturally this dramatic increase in the divorce rate stimulated public alarm.

In 1881 the New England Divorce Reform League was established to conduct research on family problems, educate the public and lobby for more effective legislative curbs on divorce. Under the leadership of Samuel Dike, a Congregational minister, the league enjoyed a long and useful life, but Dike's reluctance to advance legislative solutions to the divorce problem failed to deter others from resorting to politics.

Efforts to arrest the spread of divorce by legal means took two forms. State campaigns were waged to amend local divorce laws, and repeated attempts were made to achieve uniform marriage and divorce laws either through a constitutional amendment or through the voluntary enactment of uniform codes by the several states. Typical of the many local fights to alter state divorce laws was the successful battle in 1893 to end South Dakota's status as a divorce colony. After their admission to the Union in 1889 North and South Dakota retained Dakota Territory's generous ninety-day residence requirement.

Sioux City, largest and most accessible town in the two states, soon developed a substantial divorce trade and gained national fame as a divorce colony. The resulting notoriety provoked local resentment which was mobilized by the return from Japan of the popular Episcopal Bishop William Hobart Hare, who in 1893 led Protestants, Catholics and Populists in an attack on the ninety-day residence requirement. The state legislature was successfully petitioned to extend the residence requirement to six months and the migratory divorce trade was diverted to North Dakota.

The South Dakota campaign conformed to what was already an established pattern. It was led by conservative clergymen, supported by women's groups, and met little apparent opposition. Although these local campaigns did not succeed anywhere in abolishing divorce, they were part of a widespread tendency toward stricter divorce legislation. When such local crusades failed, it was usually because of public apathy, sometimes coupled with undercover resistance from commercial and legal interests which profited from the divorce trade.

Serious attempts to secure uniform marriage and divorce legislation through a constitutional amendment began in 1892 when James Kyle, the Populist Senator from out Dakota, introduced a joint resolution which read in full: "The Congress shall have the exclusive power to regulate marriage and divorce in the several states, Territories, and the District of Columbia." Senator Kyle's resolution died in committee as did all later resolutions, presumably because of a disinclination on the part of Congress to increase the power of the Federal government at the expense of the states.

More popular, if equally unsuccessful, was the movement to secure voluntary uniformity through the drafting of model statutes which were to be enacted by the states. The most persistent of the organizations dedicated to this goal was the National Conference of Commissioners on Uniform State Laws, which met annually in connection with the American Bar Association. It was established by the Bar Association in 1889 to frame model codes on a wide range of subjects. The Commissioners were usually appointed by their state governors, and over the years drafted seven model statutes concerning marriage and divorce. However, few of the states demonstrated an interest in these models, and by 1916 the Commissioners were forced to admit that their approach had been a failure.

If the experience of the National Conference of Commissioners on Uniform State Laws to 1906 had not been conclusive, the fate of the National Divorce Congress in that year was. A national meeting to draft uniform legislation had been talked about for years on the grounds that it would attract sufficient attention to succeed where the more diffident Commissioners had failed. In 1906 President Roosevelt was persuaded to request a new census study of marriage and divorce, and the interest aroused by this led Governor Pennypacker of Pennsylvania to call a national conference to draft model uniform legislation on these subjects. The Congress met twice, once in Washington to appoint committees, and again in Philadelphia to ratify the proposed statutes. The first meeting was attended by delegates from 42 of the 45 states and consisted largely of clergymen and lawyers, many of the latter having also been members of the NCCUSL. Despite the widespread approval which met their efforts, few states adopted their model statutes.

The antidivorce forces were also active within the established Protestant churches. During the Progressive Era repeated efforts were made in almost all the great Protestant denominations to stiffen their positions on divorce. The Episcopal Church, traditionally more hostile to divorce than most Protestant bodies, was in the van of this movement, thanks principally to William Croswell Doane, Bishop of Albany, New York. Doane was perhaps the most vocal and consistent enemy of divorce in the whole country. He favored prohibiting divorce altogether, and his activities within the Episcopal Church were directed at the canon which allowed the innocent party in an adultery suit to remarry. This canon was only slightly less severe than the refusal of the Roman Catholic Church to allow any divorced person to remarry, but it seemed dangerously lax to Doane and he regularly introduced an amendment which would have denied the sacraments to all divorced persons without exception.

In 1898 the House of Bishops, usually more conservative than the lower House, which included laymen, at the policy-making Triennial Convention, rejected Doane's amendment 31 to 24. In 1901 his amendment was defeated by a narrower margin, but in 1904 it passed the House of Bishops only to fail in the House of Deputies, whose members felt that it was too far removed from the spirit of the country. Thereafter enthusiasm within the Episcopal church for the Doane amendment declined, and while it was re-introduced at later conventions, it failed to pass even in the House of Bishops. Similar efforts were made in the other Protestant denominations with what proved to be an equal lack of success.

American attitudes toward marriage and divorce during the Progressive years must be seen in terms of the widespread fear of divorce demonstrated by these examples. It is not too much to say that there was a national crisis generated by divorce. It *was* a crisis to begin with because people believed it was. As Daniel Bell has demonstrated in his *The End of Ideology,* it is not necessary for activities seen to be antisocial actually to increase in order to create a crisis atmosphere—it is enough if people simply believe that such activities are increasing.

An even better example perhaps was the white slave panic of 1912–13. If anything, prostitution was declining, but irrespective of the facts, widespread public alarm over this presumed social evil was triggered by local investigations and newspaper publicity.

However, divorce actually was increasing by leaps and bounds. When one marriage in twelve ended in divorce, there were legitimate grounds for concern. These were crucial years for divorce, finally, because the Progressive period was the last time when public opinion could reasonably have been expected to support genuinely repressive action. With the 1902s and the advent of the revolution in morals the opportunity to abolish or seriously restrict divorce was lost forever. Some of the antidivorce leaders sensed that time was running out for them, and this awareness gave their strictures art urgent tone which became more shrill with the years.

Although divorce had political, psychological and other dimensions, the increase of divorce was usually seen as a moral and social problem. It is difficult, if indeed not actually pointless, to try to determine which of these two aspects alarmed critics of divorce the most. The enemies of divorce invariably regarded it as both immoral and antisocial. Since most opponents of divorce were either clergymen or strongly religious people, it seems fair to assume that the moral side of the divorce question was what first engaged their attention, but having once declared divorce to be immoral, there is little more one can say in that direction, and most of the serious attacks on divorce emphasized its antisocial character.

The attack on divorce hinged on the common belief that divorce destroyed the family, which was the foundation of society and civilization. Theodore Schmauk, editor of the *Lutheran Church Review,* President of the Lutheran General Council and a leading theologian, characterized the family as "the great and fundamental institution in social life." *The Catholic World* in an attack on H. G. Wells' view of divorce felt that it had demolished his position when it observed that Wells failed to see that the family "was the cradle of civil society." Lyman Abbott, an influential Progressive editor and associate of Theodore Roosevelt, once charged a prominent divorcee with being "the worst type of anarchist" because divorce, like anarchy, threatened to destroy society altogether. President Roosevelt, in addressing Congress on the need for uniform legislation, described marriage as being "at the very foundation of our social organization.... Marriage and the family are, of course, quite different institutions, but the critics of divorce did not usually distinguish between them.

Felix Adler took this contention a step further when he insisted that divorce menaced "the physical and spiritual existence of the human race..." Adler was in some ways a surprising figure to find on this side of the divorce question. The founder of Ethical Culture and a leading advocate of liberal religion, he consistently attacked dogma and orthodoxy and supported a wide variety of social reforms. He had earlier supported divorce, but by 1915 had changed his mind and accepted the point, usually advanced by the theologically orthodox, that divorce had to be suppressed as a matter of social survival. His conversion showed how this argument operated independently of its conservative religious base, and helps to explain why some enemies of divorce attached such importance to their campaign. One could hardly play for higher stakes.

A related theme which engaged the attention of divorce critics was the role of woman. It was generally believed that the family was woman's special responsibility and its protection her primary concern. Moreover women were thought to be more active than men in securing divorces (and they probably were since about two-thirds of all divorces were awarded to women). *The North American Review* reflected this point of view when it entitled one of its divorce symposiums. "Are Women to Blame?" The *Review's* female panelists charged women with responsibility for the divorce rate, and accused them of being spoiled romantic, impatient, jealous of men and usurpers of the male's time-honored functions. Many of these women were successful writers, as was Anna B. Rogers, a popular essayist, who repeated the same charges in her book, *Why American Marriages Fail* nineteen years later.

While the critics of divorce, especially the men, were inclined to argue that women were really happier when they stayed at home and held the family together, the more tough-minded accepted the fact that the woman's traditional role was often painful and difficult. Few had a clearer picture of what was involved than the respected novelist Margaret Deland. Mrs. Deland was a warm supporter of many Progressive causes and a woman with courage enough to defend the rights of unwed mothers in Victorian Boston. But she believed that civilization "rests on the permanence of marriage." For this reason women dared not turn to divorce, for it would mean the end of everything. "If we let the flame of idealism be quenched in the darkness of the senses," she cried, "our civilization must go upon the rocks." Even adultery was no excuse for giving up the fight, she continued, because men were instinctively promiscuous and their lapses from grace had to be tolerated for the sake of the greater good.

Implicit in these arguments was the belief that the individual was less important than the group. Most opponents of divorce agreed that divorce was part of an unwholesome tendency toward a "dangerous individualism." Margaret Deland bewailed the absence of team-play among women and Professor Lawton called frankly for the "suppression of the individual in favor of the community." Samuel Dike in his Cook Lecture attributed divorce to the rising tide of individualism menacing all progressive societies, while Felix Adler as early as 1890 was tracing the whole ugly business back to Rousseau's "false democratic ideals." Although, as we shall see, most leading sociologists believed in divorce, Charles A. Ellwood did not. This future president of the American Sociological Society, despite his Progressive sympathies, also attributed divorce to excessive individualism. Francis Peabody, an eminent theologian and student of the Higher Criticism, believed that the family's major enemies were scientific socialism and "the reactionary force of self-interested individualism.

The opponents of divorce were more varied and had much more to say than I have been able to indicate, but the foregoing gives at least some idea of who they were and what they thought. The defenders of divorce, by way of contrast, were fewer in number and easier to locate. Opinion against divorce was so widespread and diffuse that it cannot be attributed to a handful of groups, but the sentiment favoring divorce was largely confined to sociology liberal clergymen and feminists. The defenders of divorce, like its enemies, viewed the problem primarily in moral and social terms. But unlike the critics of divorce, its supporters, who were with few exceptions liberals, were much more interested in the morality of divorce and more inclined to see its moral and social dimensions as too interrelated for separate discussion and analysis.

The case for divorce gained initial momentum in the 1880s and 1890s when a trickle of protest against Victorian marriage began to make itself heard. The plays of Henrik Ibsen, especially *A Doll's House* (1879) and *Ghosts* (1881), were affecting English audiences in the late 1880s and American opinion somewhat later. By the 1890s a number of English men were attacking marriage and the views of Mona Caird and Grant Allen became well known in the United States through their own writings, and through the publicity given their ideas by the American press. Mona Caird was a feminist whose essays appeared for the most part in high-quality limited circulation periodicals. Her most controversial proposal was an attempt to substitute for divorce short-term marriage contracts whose expiration would leave both parties free to separate or to negotiate a new contract.

Grant Allen's best-known statement on the question was a sensational novel boosting feminism and free love entitled *The Woman Who Did*. Allen was really calling for an end to marriage altogether, but his polemics against the institution supported divorce as much as free love. Within a few years the radical attack on marriage enlisted such big guns as H. G. Wells who in a characteristically exuberant preview of the future in 1901, announced hat monogamy was dissolving and sexual standards relaxing to the point where in a hundred years the present moral code "would remain nominally operative in sentiment and practice, while being practically disregarded..." Marriage was also under fire from the new moralists like the mystical Edward Carpenter, Havelock Ellis and his wife Edith, and the South African feminist Olive Schreiner, among others.

The effect of this stream of marriage propaganda was to invigorate and inspire those Americans who believed in the right to divorce. Few respectable Americans were prepared to go as far as new moralists like Wells and Carpenter, but a substantial number of liberals were beginning to feel that traditional marriage was needlessly tyrannical and repressive, that it discriminated against women, and that divorce was not only an escape hatch for abused women, but offered real opportunities for a reform of the whole marriage system. At the bottom of most, if not all, of this sentiment was the feminist impulse, for most divorce liberals were acutely conscious of the usefulness of divorce as an instrument for the emancipation of women.

Unlike the new moralists whose feminism was concerned with freeing women for a fuller sex life, the American feminist was inclined to defend divorce because it freed women from sex. Benjamin O. Flower, who edited the populistic *Arena,* called for easier divorce laws as a way of protecting women from the excessive sexual appetites of their husbands. He argued that the common prostitute was "far freer than the wife who is nightly the victim of the unholy passion of her master..." By 1914 this argument had become so familiar that it was thought fit for the respectable readers of the cautious *Good Housekeeping* magazine. In that year Jesse Lynch Williams, feminist and playwright, asked rhetorically, "is allowing herself to be owned body and soul by a man she loathes doing right?" before going on to delicately suggest "that seems rather like a dishonorable institution more ancient than marriage."

Many feminists contended that not only did traditional marriage make women the sexual victims of their husbands, but it also exaggerated the importance of sex by denying women the chance to develop their other traits of character through work and education, and by forcing them to compete in the marriage market largely on the basis of their sexual attractions. The most desirable women had the best marital opportunities and so, through a kind of natural selection, sexuality prospered at the expense of other attributes. Divorce, along with expanded opportunities for education and employment, was a way of combatting this pernicious tendency.

If the impulse to defend divorce came first from feminists who agreed with Elizabeth Cady Stanton on the need for a "larger freedom in the marriage relation," social scientists performed a crucial service in coping with the public's fear of the social consequences of divorce. The first man of stature to defend divorce was Carrol Wright, U.S. Commissioner of Labor Statistics and a self-trained social scientist, who at the national Unitarian convention in 1891 boldly declared himself for liberal divorce laws. A few years later he wrote:

> *The pressure for divorce finds its impetus outside of laws, outside of our institutions, outside of our theology; it springs from the rebellion of the human heart against that slavery which binds in the cruelest bonds human beings who have by their haste, their want of wisdom, or the intervention of friends, missed the divine purpose* as *well* as *the civil purpose of marriage.*

But it was not until 1904 that a leading professionally trained social scientist joined the fight. In his massive *A History of Matrimonial Institutions* and subsequent writings George E. Howard an eminent historian and sociologist tried to show how the divorce rate was the product of forces which were dramatically improving American society. He argued that industrialization urbanization and the other pressures which were breaking up the old patriarchal family produced not only more divorces but a new kind of marriage marked by higher spiritual standards and greater freedom. Closing with the problem of individualism which so alarmed the enemies of divorce, he declared that the growing power of the state was tending to make the individual and not the family the functional unit of society and that this process not only freed the individual from familial authoritarianism but elevated the family by abolishing its coercive power and transforming it into a "spiritual and psychic association of parent and child based on persuasion."

Within a few years Wright and Howard were joined by a host of social scientists including most of the leading men in the field. The weight of sociological opinion was solidly on the side of divorce by 1908 when the American Sociological Society devoted its third annual meeting to the family. President William G. Sumner, the crusty, aging president of the society who had done so much to establish sociology as an academic discipline, opened the proceedings by observing gloomily that "the family has to a great extent lost its position as a conservative institution and has become a field for social change." The program of the convention confirmed Sumner's fears for virtually every paper described the changes affecting the family, called for more changes, or did both. Charlotte P. Gilman read a paper summarizing her *Women and Economics*, and a group of papers dealt with the damage inflicted on the family by urban, industrial life.

The high point of the meeting was George Howard's "Is the Freer Granting of Divorce an Evil?" Howard repeated his now familiar views and touched off a controversy which showed the drift of professional opinion. He was attacked by Samuel Dike, who insisted that divorce was produced by a dangerous individualism and the decline of ideals, and by Walter George Smith. Smith was a prominent Catholic lawyer who had advocated stricter divorce laws for many years and was a leader in the campaign for uniform divorce legislation. His criticisms stressed divorce's incompatibility with orthodox religion and he accused Howard of condoning a social revolution that destroyed the divinely constituted order of things. Nothing, he declared, could alter the fact of feminine inferiority. Howard replied that marriage was a purely social institution "to be freely dealt with by men according to human needs."

Despite this unusually spirited clash, Smith and his friends were making an illusory show of strength. The moralistic flavor of their language, so different in tone from Howard's, revealed their professional isolation. Theirs was the faintly anachronistic rhetoric of a discredited tradition of social criticism. The opponents of Howard's position were, moreover, all laymen with the exception of President Sumner and Albion Small, while on his side were ranged most of the speakers, including E. A. Ross, James Lichtenberger and other leading scientists. As a profession then, sociology was committed to a positive view of divorce at a time when virtually every other organized group in the country was opposed to it. But although heavily outnumbered, the sociologists were the only people who could claim to speak on the problem with expert authority, and in the Progressive Era expertise was coming to be highly valued. As experts, the social scientists conferred respectability on the cause of free divorce at the same time as they did much to allay public anxiety over its effects.

A final problem that remained for the divorce liberals was finding some way to weaken the general conviction that divorce was forbidden by the Bible, and to diminish the impact of the clergy's opposition to divorce. It was here that the handful of liberal ministers who supported divorce performed a signal, and indeed indispensable, service. Simply by saying that divorce was a morally acceptable device, the liberal ministers endowed it with a certain degree of legitimacy. If supporting divorce with their moral prestige was the more important function performed by the liberal ministers, some went beyond this and effectively disputed the traditional charge that the Bible specifically prohibited divorce.

One of the most impressive statements of the liberal position was delivered by William G. Ballentine, classicist, Bible scholar, onetime president of Oberlin College and for twenty years editor of the *Bibliotheca Sacra.* Ballentine argued that "even if all thoughtful Christian men were today united in a resolute purpose of conformity to the letter of Scripture the path of duty would be far from plain." He pointed out that a Biblical injunction against divorce cited by Bishop Doane in a recent magazine article appeared in the same passage as the admonition to resist evil. How, he asked, were Christians to know which commandment to obey and which to ignore? Ballentine described the life of Jesus as a struggle against Talmudic literalism:

> *During His whole life, He fought against the tyranny of mere words, and for the lordship of the present living spiritual man. In his discourse He suggested great truths by parables, by questions, by metaphors, by paradoxes, by hyperboles, by every device that could elude the semblance of fixed judicial formulas. It is the irony of history that such language should be seized upon for statute law.*

Other scholars, theologians and Higher Critics attacked the presumed Biblical sanctions against divorce in different ways, but the effect of their work was to undercut the general belief that the Bible clearly forbade divorce.

On a more popular level the Rev. Minot J. Savage declared that as love was the essence of marriage two people who no longer loved each other had every reason to get divorced. This same conviction informed the writings of John H. Holmes, a great civil libertarian and advocate of liberal Christianity, who believed that the passing of love destroyed marriage in fact if not in name.

Gradually the climate of opinion began to change. As noted earlier there was a substantial organized opposition to divorce during the Progressive period, but despite local victories, the movement to retard divorce by legal and political means was resoundingly unsuccessful. There were other signs which demonstrated that attitudes were being modified. Samuel Dike died in 1913 and his League expired shortly thereafter. It was essentially a one-man operation, but it was supported by the enemies of divorce, whose financial contributions had declined sharply even before his death, to the point where receipts after 1910 were about half of what they had been in the 1890s. The Committee on the Family which *was* routinely formed by the Federal Council of Churches in 1911 was singularly inactive, and in 1919 it was dropped altogether.

At the same time the solid wall of opposition to divorce maintained by the nation's press was repeatedly breached. Before 1900 no important American magazine defended the right to divorce except the radical *Arena.* Articles favorable to divorce were very rare in the general press. After about 1900, however, a few bold magazines like the *Independent* endorsed the right of divorce editorially, and many more began to print occasional articles defending divorce. The *North American Review,* which was more interested in the problem than any other major periodical, began the new century with a rousing attack on the opponents of divorce by the aging but still magnificent Elizabeth Cady Stanton. Other magazines, too numerous to mention, also began to print articles favoring divorce.

Even the uncompromisingly hostile *Outlook* unbent to this extent, and in 1910 it conceded editorially that there were times when divorce was permissible. This shift influenced popular as well as serious magazines. In 1910 the slick monthly *World's Work* announced that "The True View of Increasing Divorce" was that the divorce rate was not alarming, and that divorces should not be subject to excessive restrictions.

Obviously the changes in public opinion which these articles represented did not constitute a general recognition of the desirability of divorce. Although a few journals accepted the liberal argument that divorce was a therapeutic social mechanism, most did not. In many cases nothing more was involved than the admission that there were probably two sides to the question. This of itself, however, was a form of moral relativism on the issue which would have been unthinkable in the 1890s. This new tolerance of divorce coincided with the eruption of a number of curious phenomena like the dance craze and the white slave panic which marked the onset of the revolution in morals.

Divorce was a part of the complex transformation of moral values and sexual customs which was to help give the 1920s their bizarre flavor. It was not only the most visible result of this vast social upheaval, but in many ways it was the most compatible with traditional modes of thought. It was, on the whole, an orderly, public and institutionalized process which took due account of the formal difference between right and wrong, guilt and innocence. It had the blessings of the highest sociological authorities, and it was recommended by many feminists as a cure for the brutalizing sexual indignities known to occur in some marriages. Conservatives could, therefore, more easily resign themselves to divorce than to other, more extravagant, demonstrations of the changing moral order.

Although divorce has today assumed proportions undreamed of in the Progressive Era, the nature of the American response to mass divorce was determined at that time. Between 1905, when the magnitude of divorce as a social problem had become fully apparent, and 1917, when the movement to limit or direct the spread of divorce had clearly failed, something of importance for American social history had occurred. This was the recognition by moral conservatives that they could not prevent the revolution in morals represented by mass divorce. Their failure of morale in the immediate prewar period paved the way for the spectacular changes which took place after the war.

platitude - a dull remark as though it was profound

10. Theodore Roosevelt, President

Edmund Morris

Let us dispose, in short order, with Theodore Roosevelt's faults. He was an incorrigible preacher of platitudes; or to use Elting E. Morison's delicious phrase, he had "a recognition, too frequently and precisely stated, of the less recondite facts of life." He significantly reduced the wildlife population of some three continents. He piled his dessert plate with so many peaches that the cream spilled over the sides. And he used to make rude faces out of the presidential carriage at small boys in the streets of Washington.

Now those last two faults are forgivable if we accept British diplomat Cecil Spring-Rice's advice, "You must always remember the President is about six." The first fault—his preachiness—is excused by the fact that the American electorate dearly loves a moralist. As to the second and most significant fault—Theodore Roosevelt's genuine blood-lust and desire to destroy his adversaries, whether they be rhinoceroses or members of the United States Senate—it is paradoxically so much a part of his virtues, both as a man and a politician, that I will come back to it in more detail later.

One of the minor irritations I have to contend with as a biographer is that whenever I go to the library to look for books about Roosevelt, Theodore, they infallibly are mixed up with books about Roosevelt, Franklin—and I guess FDR scholars have the same problem in reverse. Time was when the single word "Roosevelt" meant only Theodore; FDR himself frequently had to insist, in the early thirties, that he was not TR's son. He was merely a fifth cousin, and what was even more distant, a Democrat to boot. In time, of course, Franklin succeeded in preempting the early meaning of the word "Roosevelt," to the point that TR's public image, which once loomed as large as Washington's and Lincoln's, began to fade like a Cheshire cat from popular memory. By the time of FDR's own death in 1945, little was left but the ghost of a toothy grin.

Only a few veterans of the earlier Roosevelt era survived to testify that if Franklin was the greater politician, it was only by a hairsbreadth, and as far as sheer personality was concerned, Theodore's superiority could be measured in spades. They pointed out that FDR himself declared, late in life, that his "cousin Ted" was the greatest man he ever knew.

Presently the veterans too died. But that ghostly grin continued to float in the national consciousness, as if to indicate that its owner was meditating a reappearance. I first became aware of the power behind the grin in Washington, in February of 1976. The National Theater was trying out an ill-fated musical by Alan Lerner and Leonard Bernstein, *1600 Pennsylvania Avenue.* For two and a half hours Ken Howard worked his way through a chronological series of impersonations of historic Presidents. The audience sat on its hands, stiff with boredom, until the very end, when Mr. Howard clamped on a pair of pince-nez and a false mustache, and bared all his teeth in a grin. The entire theater burst into delighted applause.

What intrigued me was the fact that few people there could have known much about TR beyond the obvious cliches of San Juan Hill and the Big Stick. Yet somehow, subconsciously, they realized that here for once was a positive President, warm and tough and authoritative and funny, who believed in America and who, to quote Owen Wister, "grasped his optimism tight lest it escape him."

In the last year or so Theodore Roosevelt has made his long-promised comeback. He has been the subject of a *Newsweek* cover story on American heroes; Russell Baker has called him a cinch to carry all fifty states if he were running for the White House today; he's starring on Broadway in *Tintypes,* on television in *Bully,* and you'll soon see him on the big screen in *Ragtime.* Every season brings a new crop of reassessments in the university presses, and as for the pulp mills, he figures largely in the latest installment of John Jakes's Kent Chronicles. No time like the present, therefore, to study that giant personality in color and fine detail.

When referring to Theodore Roosevelt I do not use the word "giant" loosely. "Every inch of him," said William Allen White, "was over-engined." Lyman Gage likened him, mentally and physically, to two strong men combined; Gifford Pinchot said that his normal appetite was enough for four people, Charles J. Bonaparte estimated that his mind moved ten times faster than average, and TR himself, not wanting to get into double figures, modestly remarked, "I have enjoyed as much of life as any nine men I know." John Morley made a famous comparison in 1904 between Theodore Roosevelt and the Niagara Falls, "both great wonders of nature." John Burroughs wrote that TR's mere proximity made him nervous. "There was always something imminent about him, like an avalanche that the sound of your voice might loosen." Ida Tarbell, sitting next to him at a musicale, had a sudden hallucination that the President was about to burst. "I felt his clothes might not contain him, he was so steamed up, so ready to go, to attack anything, anywhere."

Reading all these remarks it comes as a surprise to discover that TR's chest measured a normal forty-two inches, and that he stood only five feet nine in his size seven shoes. Yet unquestionably his initial impact was physical, and it was overwhelming. I have amused myself over the years with collecting the metaphors that contemporaries used to describe this Rooseveltian "presence." Here's a random selection. Edith Wharton thought him radioactive; Archie Butt and others used phrases to do with electricity, high-voltage wires, generators, and dynamos; Lawrence Abbott compared him to an electromagnetic nimbus; John Burroughs to "a kind of electric bombshell, if there can be such a thing"; James E. Watson was reminded of TNT; and Senator Joseph Foraker, in an excess of imagination, called TR "a steam-engine in trousers." There are countless other steam-engine metaphors, from Henry Adams' "swift and awful Chicago express" to Henry James's "verily, a wonderful little machine: destined to be overstrained, perhaps, but not as yet, truly, betraying the least creak." Lastly we have Owen Wister comparing TR to a solar conflagration that cast no shadow, only radiance.

These metaphors sound fulsome, but they refer only to TR's physical effect, which was felt with equal power by friends and enemies. People actually tingled in his company; there was something sensually stimulating about it. They came out of the presidential office flushed, short-breathed, energized, as if they had been treated to a sniff of white powder. He had, as Oscar Straus once said, "the quality of vitalizing things." His youthfulness (he was not yet forty-three at the beginning of his first term, and barely fifty at the end of his second), his air of glossy good health, his powerful handshake—all these things combined to give an impression of irresistible force and personal impetus.

But TR was not just a physical phenomenon. In many ways the quality of his personality was more remarkable than its quantity. Here again, I have discovered recurrences of the same words in contemporary descriptions. One of the more frequent images is that of sweetness. "He was as sweet a man," wrote Henry Watterson, "as ever scuttled a ship or cut a throat." But most comments are kinder than that. "There is a sweetness about him that is very compelling," sighed Woodrow Wilson. "You can't resist the man." Robert Livingstone, a journalist, wrote after TR's death: "He had the double gifts of a sweet nature that came out in every hand-touch and tone . . . and a sincerely powerful personality that left the uneffaceable impression that whatever he said was right. Such a combination was simply irresistible." Livingstone's final verdict was that Theodore Roosevelt had "unquestionably the greatest gift of personal magnetism ever by an American."

That may or may not be true, but certainly there are very few recorded examples of anybody, even TR's bitterest political critics, being able to resist him in person. Brand Whitlock, Mark Twain, John Jay Chapman, William Jennings Bryan, and Henry James were all seduced by his charm, if only temporarily. Peevish little Henry Adams spent much of the period from 1901 to 1909 penning a series of magnificent insults to the President's reputation. But this did not prevent him from accepting frequent invitations to dine at the White House and basking gloomily in TR's effulgence. By the time the Roosevelt era came to an end, Adams was inconsolable. "My last vision of fun and gaiety will vanish when my Theodore goes . . . never can we replace him."

It's a pity that the two men never had a public slanging match over the table, because when it came to personal invective, TR could give as good as he got. There was the rather slow British ambassador whom he accused of having "a mind that functions at six guinea-pig power." There was the State Supreme Court Justice he called "an amiable old fuzzy-wuzzy with sweetbread brains." There was that "unspeakably villainous little monkey," President Castro of Venezuela, and President Marroquín of Colombia, whom he described in one word as a "Pithecanthropoid." Woodrow Wilson was "a Byzantine logothete" (even Wilson had to go to the dictionary for that one); John Wanamaker was "an ill-constitutioned creature, oily, with bristles sticking up through the oil," and poor Senator Warren Pfeffer never quite recovered from being called "a pin-headed anarchistic crank, of hirsute and slabsided aspect." TR did not use bad language—the nearest to it I've found is his description of Charles Evans Hughes as "a psalm-singing son of a bitch!" but then Charles Evans Hughes tended to invite such descriptions. Moreover, TR usually took the sting out of his insults by collapsing into laughter as he uttered them. Booth Tarkington detected "an undertone of Homeric chuckling" even when Roosevelt seemed to be seriously castigating someone—"as if, after all, he loved the fun of hating, rather than the hating itself."

Humor, indeed, was always TR's saving grace. A reporter who spent a week with him in the White House calculated that he laughed, on average, a hundred times a day—and what was more, laughed heartily. "He laughs like an irresponsible schoolboy on a lark, his face flushing ruddy, his eyes nearly closed, his utterance choked with merriment, his speech abandoned for a weird falsetto. . . . The President is a joker, and (what many jokers are not) a humorist as well."

If there were nothing more to Theodore Roosevelt's personality than physical exuberance, humor, and charm, he would indeed have been what he sometimes is misperceived to be: a simple-minded, amiable bully. Actually he was an exceedingly complex man, a polygon (to use Brander Matthews' word) of so many political, intellectual, and social facets that the closer one gets to him, the less one is able to see him in the round. Consider merely this random list of attributes and achievements:

He graduated *magna cum laude* from Harvard University. He was the author of a four-volume history of the winning of the West which was considered definitive in his lifetime, and a history of the naval war of 1812 which remains definitive to this day. He also wrote biographies of Thomas Hart Benton, Gouverneur Morris, and Oliver Cromwell, and some fourteen other volumes of history, natural history, literary criticism, autobiography, political philosophy, and military memoirs, not to mention countless articles and approximately seventy-five thousand letters. He spent nearly three years of his life in Europe and the Levant, and had a wide circle of intellectual correspondents on both sides of the Atlantic. He habitually read one to three books a day, on subjects ranging from architecture to zoology, averaging two or three pages a minute and effortlessly memorizing the paragraphs that interested him. He could recite poetry by the hour in English, German, and French. He married two women and fathered six children. He was a boxing championship finalist, a Fifth Avenue socialite, a New York State Assemblyman, a Dakota cowboy, a deputy sheriff, a president of the Little Missouri Stockmen's Association, United States Civil Service Commissioner, Police Commissioner of New York City, Assistant Secretary of the Navy, Colonel of the Rough Riders, Governor of New York, Vice-President, and finally

President of the United States. He was a founding member of the National Institute of Arts and Letters and a fellow of the American Historical Society. He was accepted by Washington's scientific community as a skilled ornithologist, paleontologist, and taxidermist (during the White House years, specimens that confused experts at the Smithsonian were occasionally sent to TR for identification), and he was recognized as the world authority on big-game mammals of North America.

Now all these achievements predate his assumption of the Presidency—in other words, he packed them into his first forty-three years. I will spare you another list of the things he packed into his last ten, after leaving the White House in 1909, except to say that the total of books rose to thirty-eight, the total of letters to 150,000, and the catalogue of careers expanded to include world statesman, big-game collector for the Smithsonian, magazine columnist, and South American explorer.

If it were possible to take a cross section of TR's personality, as geologists, say, ponder a chunk of continent, you would be presented with a picture of seismic richness and confusion. The most order I have been able to make of it is to isolate four major character seams. They might be traced back to childhood. Each seam stood out bright and clear in youth and early middle age, but they began to merge about the time he was forty. Indeed the white heat of the Presidency soon fused them all into solid metal. But so long as they were distinct they may be identified as aggression, righteousness, pride, and militarism. Before suggesting how they affected his performance as President, I'd like to explain how they originated.

The most fundamental characteristic of Theodore Roosevelt was his aggression—conquest being, to him, synonymous with growth. From the moment he first dragged breath into his asthmatic lungs, the sickly little boy fought for a larger share of the world. He could never get enough air; disease had to be destroyed; he had to fight his way through big, heavy books to gain a man's knowledge. Just as the struggle for wind made him stretch his chest, so did the difficulty of relating to abnormally contrasting parents extend his imagination. Theodore Senior was the epitome of hard, thrusting Northern manhood; Mittie Roosevelt was the quintessence of soft, yielding Southern femininity. The Civil War—the first political phenomenon little Teedie was ever aware of—symbolically opposed one to the other. There was no question as to which side, and which parent, the child preferred. He naughtily prayed God, in Mittie's presence, to "grind the Southern troops to powder," and the victory of Union arms reinforced his belief in the superiority of Strength over Weakness, Right over Wrong, Realism over Romance.

Teedie's youthful "ofserv-a-tions" in natural history gave him further proof of the laws of natural selection, long before he fully understood Darwin and Herbert Spencer. For weeks he watched in fascination while a tiny shrew successively devoured a mass of beetles, then a mouse twice her size, then a snake so large it whipped her from side to side of the cage as she was gnawing through its neck. From then on the rule of tooth and claw, aided by superior intelligence, was a persistent theme in Theodore Roosevelt's writings.

Blood sports, which he took up as a result of his shooting for specimens, enabled him to feel the "strong eager pleasure" of the shrew in vanquishing ever larger foes; his exuberant dancing and whooping after killing a particularly dangerous animal struck more than one observer as macabre. From among his own kind, at college, he selected the fairest and most unobtainable mate—"See that girl? I'm going to marry her. She won't have me, but I am going to have her."—and he ferociously hunted her down. That was Alice Lee Roosevelt, mother of the late Alice Longworth.

During his first years in politics, in the New York State Assembly, he won power through constant attack. The death of Alice Lee, coming as it did just after the birth of his first child—at the moment of fruition of his manhood—only intensified his will to fight. He hurried West, to where the battle for life was fiercest. The West did not welcome him; it had to be won, like everything else he lusted for. Win it he did, by dint of the greatest physical and mental stretchings out he had yet made. In doing so he built up the magnificent body that became such an inspiration to the American people (one frail little boy who vowed to follow the President's example was the future world heavyweight champion, Gene Tunney). And by living on equal terms with the likes of Hashknife Simpson, Bat Masterson, Modesty Carter, Bronco Charlie Miller, and Hell-Roaring Bill Jones, he added another mental frontier to those he already had inherited at birth. Theodore Roosevelt, Eastern son of a Northern father and a Southern mother, could now call himself a Westerner also.

TR's second governing impulse was his personal righteousness. As one reviewer of his books remarked, "He seems to have been born with his mind made up." No violent shocks disturbed his tranquil prosperous childhood in New York City. Privately educated, he suffered none of the traumas of school. Thanks to the security of his home, the strong leadership of his father, and the adoration of his brother and sisters, Teedie entered adolescence with no sexual or psychological doubts whatsoever. Or if he had any, he simply reasoned them out, according to the Judeo-Christian principles Theodore Senior had taught him, reached the proper moral decision, and that was that. "Thank heaven!" he wrote in his diary after falling in love with Alice Lee, "I am perfectly pure."

His three great bereavements (the death of his father in 1878, and the deaths of his mother and wife in the same house and on the same day in 1884) came too late in his development to do him any permanent emotional damage. They only served to convince him more that he must be strong, honest, clean-living, and industrious. "At least I can live," he wrote, "so as not to dishonor the memory of the dead whom I so loved," and never was a cliché more heartfelt. Experiment after experiment proved the correctness of his instincts—in graduating *magna cum laude* from Harvard, in marrying successfully, in defying the doctors who ordered him to live a sedentary life, in winning international acclaim as writer and politician long before he was thirty. (He received his first nomination for the Presidency, by the *Baltimore American*, when he was only twenty-eight; it had to be pointed out to the newspaper's editors that he was constitutionally debarred from that honor for the next seven years.)

In wild Dakota Territory, he proceeded to knock down insolent cowboys, establish the foundations of federal government, pursue boat thieves in the name of the law, and preach the gospel of responsible citizenship. One of the first things he did after Benjamin Harrison appointed him Civil Service Commissioner was call for the prosecution of Postmaster General William Wallace of Indianapolis—who just happened to be the President's best friend. "That young man," Harrison growled, "wants to put the whole world right between sunrise and sunset."

TR's egotistic moralizing as a reform Police Commissioner of New York City was so insufferable that the *Herald* published a transcript of one of his speeches with the personal pronoun emphasized in heavy type. The effect in a column of gray newsprint, was of buckshot at close range. This did not stop TR from using the personal pronoun thirteen times in the first four sentences of his account of the Spanish-American War. In fact, a story went around that halfway through the typesetting, Scribner's had to send for an extra supply of capital *I's*.

The third characteristic of Theodore Roosevelt's personality was his sense of pride, both as *an* aristocrat and as an American. From birth servants and tradespeople deferred to him. Men and women of high quality came to visit his parents and treated him as one of their number. He accepted his status without question, as he did the charitable responsibilities it entailed. At a very early age he was required to accompany his father on Sunday excursions to a lodging house for Irish newsboys and a night school for little Italians. It cannot have escaped his attention that certain immigrant groups lacked the intellectual and social graces of others. Extended tours of Europe and the Levant as *a* child, teen-ager, and young man soon taught him that this was not due to ethnic inferiority so much as to centuries of economic and political deprivation. Prosperous, independent countries like England and Germany were relatively free of slums and disease; but in Italy women and children scrabbled like chickens for scraps of his cake, and in Ireland people lay down in the road from sheer hunger. From what he read, things were no better in the Slavic countries.

Only in America, with its limitless economic opportunities and freedom from political bondage, might these peasants begin to improve their stock. And only in America could they revitalize their racial characteristics. His own extremely mixed ancestry proved that a generation or two of life in the New World was enough to blend all kinds of European blood into a new, dynamic American breed. (As President, he had a habit when shaking hands with ethnic groups of saying, "Congratulations, I'm German too!" and "Dee-lighted! I'm also Scotch-

Irish, you know!" Newspapermen privately referred to him as "Old Fifty-seven Varieties.")

TR knew the value of an ethnic vote as well as the next man. There is a famous—alas, probably apocryphal—story of his appointment of Oscar Straus as the first Jewish Cabinet officer in American history. At a banquet to celebrate the appointment, TR made a passionate speech full of phrases like "regardless of race, color, or creed" and then turned to Jacob Schiff, the New York Jewish leader, and said, "Isn't that so, Mr. Schiff?" But Schiff, who was very deaf and had heard little of the speech, replied, "Dot's right, Mr. President, you came to me and said, 'Chake, who is der best Choo I can put in de Cabinet?'"

TR realized, of course, that the gap between himself and Joe Murray—the Irish ward-heeler who got him into the New York Assembly—was unbridgeable outside of politics. But in America a low-born man had the opportunity—the duty—to fight his way up from the gutter, as Joe had done. He might then merit an invitation to lunch at Sagamore Hill, or at least tea, assuming he wore a clean shirt and observed decent proprieties.

Here I must emphasize that TR was not a snob in the trivial sense. He had nothing but contempt for the Newport set and the more languid members of the Four Hundred. When he said, at twenty-one, that he wanted to be a member of "the governing class," he was aware that it was socially beneath his own. At Albany, and in the Bad Lands, and as Colonel of the Rough Riders, he preferred to work with men who were coarse but efficient, rather than those who were polished and weak. He believed, he said, in "the aristocracy of worth," and cherished the revolution that had allowed such an elite to rise to the top in government. On the other hand (to use his favorite phrase) the historian John Blum has noted that he rarely appointed impoverished or unlettered men to responsible positions. He made great political capital, as President, of the fact that his sons attended the village school at Oyster Bay, along with the sons of his servants, of whom at least one was black; but as soon as the boys reached puberty he whisked them off to Groton.

Only the very young or very old dared call him "Teddy" to his face. Roosevelt was a patrician to the tips of his tapering fingers, yet he maintained till death what one correspondent called an "almost unnatural" identity with the masses. "I don't see how you understand the common people so well, Theodore," complained Henry Cabot Lodge. "No, Cabot, you never will," said TR, grinning triumphantly, "because I am one of them, and you are not." TR deluded himself. His plebeian strength was due to understanding, not empathy.

The fourth and final major trait of Theodore Roosevelt's character was his militarism. I will not deal with it in much detail because it is a familiar aspect of him, and in any case did not manifest itself much during his Presidency. There is no doubt that in youth, and again in old age, he was in love with war; but oddly enough, of all our great Presidents, he remains the only one not primarily associated with war (indeed, he won the Nobel Peace Prize in 1906).

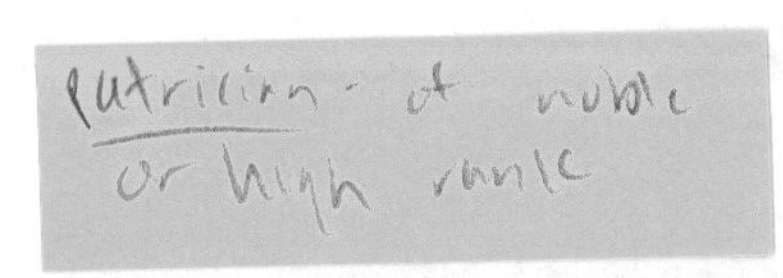

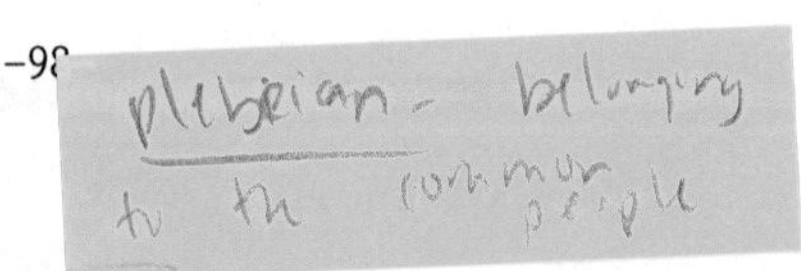

He did not lack for military influences as a child; four of his Georgian ancestors had been military men, and stories of their exploits were told him by his mother. Two of his uncles served with distinction in the Confederate navy—a fact of which he proudly boasts in his *Autobiography,* while making no reference to his father's civilian status. (The *Autobiography,* by the way, is one of history's great examples of literary amnesia. You would not guess, from its pages, that Theodore Senior ever hired a substitute soldier, that Alice Lee ever lived or died, that TR was blind in one eye as President, that anything called the Brownsville Affair ever occurred, or that Elihu Root ever sat at his Cabinet table. As James Bryce once said, "Roosevelt wouldn't always look at a thing, you know.")

When TR learned to read, he reveled in stories "about the soldiers of Valley Forge, and Morgan's riflemen," and confessed, "I had a great desire to be like them." In his senior year at Harvard, he suddenly developed an interest in strategy and tactics and began to write *The Naval War of 1812;* within eighteen months he was the world expert on that subject. As soon as he left college he joined the National Guard and quickly became a captain, which stood him in good stead when he was called upon to lead a cavalry regiment in 1898. Throughout his literary years he made a study of classical and modern campaigns, and he would wage the great battles of history with knives and forks and spoons on his tablecloth. No doubt much of this fascination with things military related to his natural aggression, but there was an intellectual attraction too: he read abstract tomes on armaments, navigation, ballistics, strategy, and service administration as greedily as swashbuckling memoirs. Nothing is more remarkable about *The Naval War of 1812* than its cold impartiality, its use of figures and diagrams to destroy patriotic myths. Roosevelt understood that great battles are fought by thinking men, that mental courage is superior to physical bravado. Nobody thrilled more to the tramp of marching boots than he, but he believed that men must march for honorable reasons, in obedience to the written orders of a democratically elected Commander in Chief. In that respect, at least, the pen was mightier than the sword.

Now how much did these four character traits—aggression, righteousness, pride, and militarism—affect TR's performance as President of the United States? The answer is, strongly, as befits a strong character and a strong Chief Executive. The way he arrived at this "personal equation" is interesting, because he was actually in a weak position at the beginning of his first administration.

When TR took the oath of office on September 14, 1901, he was the youngest man ever to do so—a Vice-President, elevated by assassination, confronted by a nervous Cabinet and a hostile Senate. Yet from the moment he raised his hand in that little parlor in Buffalo, it was apparent that he intended to translate his personal power into presidential power. The hand did not stop at the shoulder; he raised it high above his head, and held it there, "steady as if carved out of marble." His right foot pawed the floor. *Aggression.* He repeated the words of the oath confidently, adding an extra phrase, not called for in the Constitution, at the end: "And so I swear." *Righteousness.* His two senior Cabinet officers, John Hay and Lyman Gage, were not present at the ceremony, but TR announced that they had telegraphed promises of loyalty to him. Actually they had not; they were both considering resignation, but TR knew any such resignations would be construed as votes of no confidence in him, and he was determined to forestall them. By announcing that Hay and Gage would stay, out of loyalty to the memory of the dead President, he made it morally impossible for them to quit. *Pride.*

As for *militarism,* TR was seen much in the company of the New York State Adjutant General the next few days, and an armed escort of cavalrymen accompanied him wherever he went. This was perhaps understandable, in view of the fact that a President had just been assassinated, but it is a matter of record that more and more uniforms were seen glittering around TR as the months and years went on. Toward the end of his second administration, *Harper's Weekly* complained that "there has been witnessed under President Roosevelt an exclusiveness, a rigor of etiquette, and a display of swords and gold braid such as none of his predecessors ever dreamed of."

As the theatrical gestures at TR's Inauguration make plain, he was one of the most flagrant showmen ever to tread the Washington boards. He had a genius for dramatic entrances—and always was sure the spotlight was trained his way before he made one. The first thing he asked at Buffalo was, "Where are all the newspapermen?" Only three reporters were present. His secretary explained that there was no room for more. Ignoring him, TR sent out for the rest of the press corps. Two dozen scribes came joyfully crowding in, and the subsequent proceedings were reported to the nation with a wealth of detail.

Here again we see a pattern of presidential performance developing. The exaggerated concern for the rights of reporters, the carefully staged gestures (so easy to write up, such fun to read about!)—it was as if he sensed right away that a tame press, and an infatuated public, were his surest guarantees of political security. To win election in his own right in 1904—his overriding ambition for the next three years—he would have to awake these two sleeping giants and enlist their aid in moral warfare against his political opponents, notably Senator Mark Hanna. (Hanna was chairman of the Republican National Committee and the obvious choice to take over McKinley's government after "that damned cowboy," as he called TR, had filled in as interim caretaker.)

The new President accordingly took his case straight to the press and the public. Both instantly fell in love with him. Neither seemed to notice that administratively and legislatively he accomplished virtually nothing in his first year in office. As David S. Barry of the *Sun* wrote, "Roosevelt's personality was so fascinating, so appealing to the popular fancy, so overpowering, so alive, and altogether so unique that . . . It overshadowed his public acts; that is, the public was more interested in him, and the way he did things . . . than they were about what he did."

This does not mean that TR managed, or even tried, to please all the people all the time. He was quite ready to antagonize a large minority in order to win the approval of a small majority. The sods had hardly stopped rattling on the top of McKinley's coffin when the following press release was issued: "Mr. Booker T. Washington of Tuskegee, Alabama, dined with the President last evening." Now this release, arguably the shortest and most explosive ever put out by the White House, has always been assumed to be a reluctant confirmation of the discovery of a reporter combing TR's guest book. Actually the President himself issued it, at two o'clock in the morning—that is, just in time for maximum exposure in the first edition of the newspapers. By breakfast time white supremacists all over the South were gagging over their grits at such headlines as ROOSEVELT DINES A NIGGER, and PRESIDENT PROPOSES TO CODDLE THE SONS OF HAM. This was the first time that a President had ever entertained a black man in the first house of the land. The public outcry was deafening—horror in the South, acclamation in the North—but overnight 9,000,000 African-Americans, hitherto loyal to Senator Hanna, trooped into the Rooseveltian camp. TR never felt the need to dine a black man again.

Although we may have no doubt he had the redistribution of Southern patronage in mind when he sent his invitation to Washington, another motive was simply to stamp a bright, clear, first impression of himself upon the public imagination. "I," he seemed to be saying, "am a man *aggressive* enough to challenge a hundred-year prejudice, *righteous* enough to do so for moral reasons, and *proud* enough to advertise the fact."

Again and again during the next seven years, he reinforced these perceptions of his personality. He aggressively prosecuted J. P. Morgan, Edward H. Harriman, and John D. Rockefeller (the holy trinity of American capitalism) in the Northern Securities antitrust case, threw the Monroe Doctrine at Kaiser Wilhelm's feet like a token of war in the Caribbean, rooted out corruption in his own administration, and crushed Hanna's 1904 presidential challenge by publicly humiliating the Senator when he was running for re-election in 1903. He righteously took the side of the American worker and the American consumer against big business in the great anthracite strike, proclaimed the vanity of muckrake journalists, forced higher ethical standards upon the food and drug industry, ordered the dishonorable discharge of 160 African-American soldiers after the Brownsville Affair (on his own willful reading of the evidence, or lack thereof), and to quote Mark Twain, "dug so many tunnels under the Constitution that the transportation facilities enjoyed by that document are rivalled only by the City of New York."

For example, when the anthracite strike began to drag into the freezing fall of 1902, TR's obvious sympathy for the miners, and for millions of Americans who could not afford the rise in fuel prices, began to worry conservative members of Congress. One day Representative James E. Watson was horrified to hear that the President had decided to send federal troops in to reopen the anthracite mines on grounds of general hardship. Watson rushed round to the White House. "What about the Constitution of the United States?" he pleaded.

"What about seizing private property for public purposes without due processes of law?"

TR wheeled around, shook Watson by the shoulder, and roared, *"To hell with the Constitution when the people want coal!'* Remarks like that caused old Joe Cannon to sigh, "Roosevelt's got no more respect for the Constitution than a tomcat has for a marriage license."

Pride, both in himself and his office, was particularly noticeable in TR's second term, the so-called imperial years, when Henry James complained, "Theodore Rex is distinctly tending—or trying to make a court." But this accusation was not true. Although the Roosevelts entertained much more elaborately than any of their predecessors, they confined their pomp and protocol to occasions of state. At times, indeed, they were remarkable for the all-American variety of their guests. On any given day one might find a Rough Rider, a poet, a British viscount, a wolf hunter, and a Roman Catholic cardinal at the White House table, each being treated with the gentlemanly naturalness which was one of TR's most endearing traits. His pride manifested itself in things like his refusal to address foreign monarchs as "Your Majesty," in his offer to mediate the Russo-Japanese War (no American President had yet had such global presumptions), and, when he won the Nobel Peace Prize for successfully bringing the war to a conclusion, in refusing to keep a penny of the forty-thousand-dollar prize money. This was by no means an easy decision, because TR could have used the funds: he spent all his presidential salary on official functions and was not himself a wealthy man. He confessed he was tempted to put the Nobel money into a trust for his children, but decided it belonged to the United States.

Pride and patriotism were inseparable in Theodore Roosevelt's character; indeed, if we accept Lord Morely's axiom that he "was" America, they may be considered as complementary characteristics. And neither of them was false. just as he was always willing to lose a political battle in order to win a political war, so in diplomatic negotiations was he sedulous to allow his opponents the chance to save face—take all the glory of settlement if need be—as long as the essential victory was his.

As I have noted earlier, TR's militarism did not loom large during his Presidency. The organizational structure of the U.S. Army was revamped in such a way as to strengthen the powers of the Commander in Chief, but Secretary of War Elihu Root takes credit for that. TR can certainly take the credit for expanding the American Navy from fifth to second place in the world during his seven and a half years of power—an amazing achievement, but quite in keeping with his policy, inherited from Washington, that "to be prepared for war is the most effectual means to promote peace." The gunboat TR sent to Panama in 1903 was the only example of him shaking a naked mailed fist in the face of a weaker power; for the rest of the time he kept that fist sheathed in a velvet glove. The metaphor of velvet on iron, incidentally, was TR's own; it makes a refreshing change from the Big Stick.

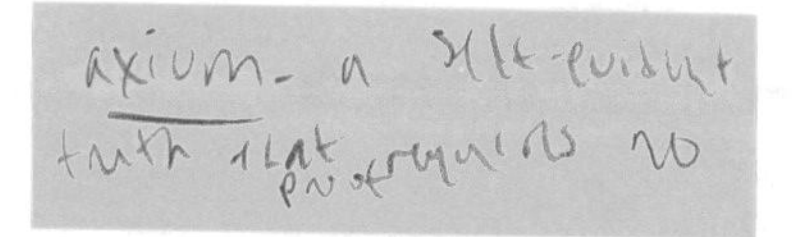

If I may be permitted a final metaphor of my own, I would like to quote one from *The Rise of Theodore Roosevelt* in an attempt to explain why, on the whole, TR's character shows to better advantage as President than in his years out of power. "The man's personality was cyclonic, in that he tended to become unstable in times of low pressure. The slightest rise in the barometer outside, and his turbulence smoothed into a whir of coordinated activity, while a core of stillness developed within. Under maximum pressure Roosevelt was sunny, calm, and unnaturally clear." This explains why the first Roosevelt era was a period of fair weather. Power became Theodore Roosevelt, and absolute power became him best of all. He loved being President and was so good at his job that the American people loved him for loving it. TR genuinely dreaded having to leave the White House, and let us remember that a third term was his for the asking in 1908. But his knowledge that power corrupts even the man who most deserves it, his reverence for the Washingtonian principle that power must punctually revert to those whose gift it is, persuaded him to make this supreme sacrifice in his prime. The time would come, not many years hence, when fatal insolence tempted him to renege on his decision. That is another story. But the self-denial that he exercised in 1908 gives us one more reason to admire Old-Fifty-seven Varieties.

June 1981

11. Woodrow Wilson Wouldn't Yield

Thomas A. Bailey

The story of America's rejection of the League of Nations revolves largely around the personality and character of Thomas Woodrow Wilson.

Born in Virginia and reared in Yankee-gutted Georgia and the Carolinas, Wilson early developed a burning hatred of war and a passionate attachment to the Confederate-embraced principle of self-determination for minority peoples. From the writings of Thomas Jefferson he derived much of his democratic idealism and his invincible faith in the judgment of the masses, if properly informed. From his stiff-backed Scotch-Presbyterian forebears, he inherited a high degree of inflexibility; from his father, a dedicated Presbyterian minister, he learned a stern moral code that would tolerate no compromise with wrong, as defined by Woodrow Wilson.

As a leading academician who had first failed at law, he betrayed a contempt for "money-grubbing" lawyers, many of whom sat in the Senate, and an arrogance toward lesser intellects, including those of the "pygmy-minded" senators. As a devout Christian keenly aware of the wickedness of this world, he emerged as a fighting reformer, whether as president of Princeton, governor of New Jersey, or President of the United States.

As a war leader, Wilson was superb. Holding aloft the torch of idealism in one hand and the flaming sword of righteousness in the other, he aroused the masses to a holy crusade. We would fight a war to end wars; we would make the world safe for democracy. The phrase was not a mockery then. The American people, with an amazing display of self-sacrifice, supported the war effort unswervingly.

The noblest expression of Wilson's idealism was his Fourteen Points address to Congress in January, 1918. It compressed his war aims into punchy, placard-like paragraphs, expressly designed for propaganda purposes. It appealed tremendously to oppressed peoples everywhere by promising such goals as the end of secret treaties, freedom of the seas, the removal of economic barriers, a reduction of arms burdens, a fair adjustment of colonial claims, and self-determination for oppressed minorities. In Poland university men would meet on the streets of Warsaw, clasp hands, and soulfully utter one word, "Wilson." In remote regions of Italy peasants burned candles before poster portraits of the mighty new prophet arisen in the West.

The fourteenth and capstone point was a league of nations, designed to avert future wars. The basic idea was not original with Wilson; numerous thinkers, including Frenchmen and Britons, had been working on the concept long before he embraced it. Even Henry Cabot Lodge, the Republican senator from Massachusetts, had already spoken publicly in favor of a league of nations. But the more he heard about the Wilsonian League of Nations, the more critical of it he became.

A knowledge of the Wilson-Lodge feud is basic to an understanding of the tragedy that unfolded. Tall, slender, aristocratically bewhiskered, Dr. Henry Cabot Lodge (Ph.D., Harvard), had published a number of books and had been known as the scholar in politics before the appearance of Dr. Woodrow Wilson (Ph.D., Johns Hopkins). The Presbyterian professor had gone further in both scholarship and politics than the Boston Brahmin, whose mind was once described as resembling the soil of his native New England: "naturally barren but highly cultivated." Wilson and Lodge, two icy men, developed a mutual antipathy, which soon turned into freezing hatred.

The German armies, reeling under the blows of the Allies, were ready to give in by November, 1918. The formal armistice terms stipulated that Germany was to be guaranteed a peace based on the Fourteen Points, with two reservations concerning freedom of the seas and reparations.

Meanwhile the American people had keyed themselves up to the long-awaited march on Berlin; eager voices clamored to hang the Kaiser. Thus the sudden end of the shooting left inflamed patriots with a sense of frustration and letdown that boded ill for Wilson's policies. The red-faced Theodore Roosevelt, Lodge's intimate of long standing, cried that peace should be dictated by the chatter of machine guns and not the clicking of typewriters.

Wilson now towered at the dizzy pinnacle of his popularity and power. He had emerged as the moral arbiter of the world and the hope of all peoples for a better tomorrow. But regrettably his wartime sureness of touch began to desert him, and he made a series of costly fumbles. He was so preoccupied with reordering the world, someone has said, that he reminded one of the baseball player who knocks the ball into the bleachers and then forgets to touch home plate.

First came his brutally direct appeal for a Democratic Congress in October, 1918. The voters trooped to the polls the next month and, by a narrow margin, returned a Republican Congress. Wilson had not only goaded his partisan foes to fresh outbursts of fury, but he had unnecessarily staked his prestige on the outcome—and lost. When the Allied leaders met at the Paris peace table, he was the only one not entitled to be there, at least on the European basis of a parliamentary majority.

Wilson next announced that he was sailing for France, presumably to use his still enormous prestige to fashion an enduring peace. At that time no President had ever gone abroad, and Republicans condemned the decision as evidence of a dangerous Messiah complex—of a desire, as former President Taft put it, "to hog the whole show."

The naming of the remaining five men to the peace delegation caused partisans further anguish. Only one, Henry White, was a Republican, and he was a minor figure at that. The Republicans, now the majority party, complained that they had been good enough to die on the battlefield; they ought to have at least an equal voice at the peace table. Nor were any United States senators included, even though they would have a final whack at the treaty. Wilson did not have much respect for the "bungalow-minded" senators, and if he took one, the logical choice would be Henry Cabot Lodge. There were already enough feuds brewing at Paris without taking one along.

Doubtless some of the Big Business Republicans were out to "get" the President who had been responsible for the hated reformist legislation of 1913–14. If he managed to put over the League of Nations, his prestige would soar to new heights. He might even arrange—unspeakable thought!—to be elected again and again and again. Much of the partisan smog that finally suffocated the League would have been cleared away if Wilson had publicly declared, as he was urged to do, that in no circumstances would he run again. But he spurned such counsel, partly because he was actually receptive to the idea of a third term.

The American President, hysterically hailed by European crowds as "Voovro Veelson," came to the Paris peace table in January, 1919, to meet with Lloyd George of Britain, Clemenceau of France, and Orlando of Italy. To his dismay, he soon discovered that they were far more interested in imperialism than in idealism. When they sought to carve up the territorial booty without regard for the colonials, contrary to the Fourteen Points, the stern-jawed Presbyterian moralist interposed a ringing veto. The end result was the mandate system—a compromise between idealism and imperialism that turned out to be more imperialistic than idealistic.

Wilson's overriding concern was the League of Nations. He feared that if he did not get it completed and embedded in the treaty, the imperialistic powers might sidetrack it. Working at an incredible pace after hours, Wilson headed the commission that drafted the League Covenant in ten meetings and some thirty hours. He then persuaded the conference not only to approve the hastily constructed Covenant but to incorporate it bodily in the peace treaty. In support of his adopted brain child he spoke so movingly on one occasion that even the hard-boiled reporters forgot to take notes.

Wilson now had to return hurriedly to the United States to sign bills and take care of other pressing business. Shortly after his arrival the mounting Republican opposition in the Senate flared up angrily. On March 4, 1919, 39 senators or senators-elect—more than enough to defeat the treaty—published a round robin to the effect that they would not approve the League in its existing form. This meant that Wilson had to return to Paris, hat in hand, and there weaken his position by having to seek modifications.

Stung to the quick, he struck back at his senatorial foes in an indiscreet speech in New York just before his departure. He boasted that when he brought the treaty back from Paris, the League Covenant would not only be tied in but so thoroughly tied in that it could not be cut out without killing the entire pact. The Senate, he assumed, would not dare to kill the treaty of peace outright.

At Paris the battle was now joined in deadly earnest. Clemenceau, the French realist, had little use for Wilson, the American idealist. "God gave us the ten commandments and we broke them," he reportedly sneered. "Wilson gave us the Fourteen Points—we shall see." Clemenceau's most disruptive demand was for the German Rhineland; but Wilson, the champion of self-determination, would never consent to handing several million Germans over to the tender mercies of the French. After a furious struggle, during which Wilson was stricken with influenza, Clemenceau was finally persuaded to yield the Rhineland and other demands in return for a security treaty. Under it, Britain and America agreed to come to the aid of France in the event of another unprovoked aggression. The United States Senate shortsightedly pigeonholed the pact, and France was left with neither the Rhineland nor security.

Two other deadlocks almost broke up the conference. Italy claimed the Adriatic port of Fiume, an area inhabited chiefly by Yugoslays. In his battle for self-determination, Wilson dramatically appealed over the head of the Italian delegation to the Italian people, whereupon the delegates went home in a huff to receive popular endorsement. The final adjustment was a hollow victory for self-determination.

The politely bowing Japanese now stepped forward to press their economic claims to China's Shantung, which they had captured from the Germans early in the War. But to submit 30,000,000 Chinese to the influence of the Japanese would be another glaring violation of self-determination. The Japanese threatened to bolt the conference, as the Italians had already done, with consequent jeopardy to the League. In the end, Wilson reluctantly consented to a compromise that left the Japanese temporarily in possession of Shantung.

The Treaty of Versailles, as finally signed in June, 1919, included only about four of the original Fourteen Points. The Germans, with considerable justification, gave vent to loud cries of betrayal. But the iron hand of circumstance had forced Wilson to compromise away many of his points in order to salvage his fourteenth point, the League of Nations, which he hoped would iron out the injustices that had crept into the treaty. He was like the mother who throws her younger children to the pursuing wolves in order to save her sturdy first-born son. Bitter opposition to the completed treaty had already begun to form in America. Tens of thousands of homesick and disillusioned soldiers were pouring home, determined to let Europe "stew in its own juice." The wartime idealism, inevitably doomed to slump, was now plunging to alarming depths. The beloved Allies had apparently turned out to be greedy imperialists. The war to make the world safe for democracy had obviously fallen dismally short of the goal. And at the end of the war to end wars there were about twenty conflicts of varying intensity being waged all over the globe.

The critics increased their clamor. Various foreign groups, including the Irish-Americans and the Italian-Americans, were complaining that the interests of the old country had been neglected. Professional liberals, for example the editors of the *New Republic,* were denouncing the treaty as too harsh. The illiberals, far more numerous, were denouncing it as not harsh enough. The Britain-haters, like the buzz-saw Senator James Reed of Missouri and the acid-penned William R. Hearst, were proclaiming that England had emerged with undue influence. Such ultranationalists as the isolationist Senator William E. Borah of Idaho were insisting that the flag of no superstate should be hoisted above the glorious Stars and Stripes.

When the treaty came back from Paris, with the League firmly riveted in, Senator Lodge despaired of stopping it.

"What are you going to do? It's hopeless," he complained to Borah. "All the newspapers in my state are for it," The best that he could hope for was to add a few reservations. The Republicans had been given little opportunity to help write the treaty in Paris; they now felt that they were entitled to do a little rewriting in Washington.

Lodge deliberately adopted the technique of delay. As chairman of the powerful Senate Committee on Foreign Relations, he consumed two weeks by reading aloud the entire pact of 264 pages, even though it had already been printed. He then held time-consuming public hearings, during which persons with unpronounceable foreign names aired their grievances against the pact.

Lodge finally adopted the strategy of tacking reservations onto the treaty, and he was able to achieve his goal because of the peculiar composition of the Senate. There were 49 Republicans and 47 Democrats. The Republicans consisted of about twenty "strong reservationists" like Lodge, about twelve "mild reservationists" like future Secretary of State Kellogg, and about a dozen "irreconcilables." This last group was headed by Senator Borah and the no less isolationist Senator Hiram Johnson of California, a fiery spellbinder.

The Lodge reservations finally broke the back of the treaty, They were all added by a simple majority vote, even though the entire pact would have to be approved by a two-thirds vote. The dozen or so Republican mild reservationists were not happy over the strong Lodge reservations and if Wilson had deferred sufficiently to these men, he might have persuaded them to vote with the Democrats. Had they done so, the Lodge reservations could have all been voted down, and a milder version, perhaps acceptable to Wilson, could have been substituted.

As the hot summer of 1919 wore on, Wilson became increasingly impatient with the deadlock in the Senate. Finally he decided to take his case to the country, as he had so often done in response to his ingrained "appeal habit." He had never been robust, and his friends urged him not to risk breaking himself down in a strenuous barnstorming campaign. But Wilson, having made up his mind, was unyielding. He had sent American boys into battle in a war to end wars; why should he not risk his life in a battle for a League to end wars?

Wilson's spectacular tour met with limited enthusiasm in the Middle West, the home of several million German-Americans. After him, like baying bloodhounds, trailed Senators Borah and Johnson, sometimes speaking in the same halls a day or so later, to the accompaniment of cries, of "Impeach him, impeach him!" But on the Pacific Coast and in the Rocky Mountain area the enthusiasm for Wilson and the League was overwhelming. The high point—and the breaking point—of the trip came at Pueblo, Colorado, where Wilson, with tears streaming down his cheeks, pleaded for his beloved League of Nations.

That night Wilson's weary body rebelled. He was whisked back to Washington, where he suffered a stroke that paralyzed the left side of his body. For weeks he lay in bed, a desperately sick man. The Democrats, who had no first-rate leader in the Senate, were left rudderless. With the wisdom of hindsight, we may say that Wilson might better have stayed in Washington, providing the necessary leadership and compromising with the opposition, insofar as compromise was possible. A good deal of compromise had already gone into the treaty, and a little more might have saved it.

Senator Lodge, cold and decisive, was now in the driver's seat. His Fourteen Reservations, a sardonic parallel to Wilson's Fourteen Points, had been whipped into shape. Most of them now seem either irrelevant, inconsequential, or unnecessary; some of them merely reaffirmed principles and policies, including the Monroe Doctrine, already guaranteed by the treaty or by the Constitution.

But Wilson, who hated the sound of Lodge's name, would have no part of the Lodge reservations. They would, he insisted, emasculate the entire treaty. Yet the curious fact is that he had privately worked out his own set of reservations with the Democratic leader in the Senate, Gilbert M. Hitchcock, and these differed only in slight degree from those of Senator Lodge.

As the hour approached for the crucial vote in the Senate, it appeared that public opinion had veered a little. Although confused by the angry debate, it still favored the treaty—but with some safeguarding reservations. A stubborn Wilson was unwilling to accept this disheartening fact, or perhaps he was not made aware of it. Mrs. Wilson, backed by the President's personal physician, Dr. Cary Grayson, kept vigil at his bedside to warn the few visitors that disagreeable news might shock the invalid into a relapse.

In this highly unfavorable atmosphere, Senator Hitchcock had two conferences with Wilson on the eve of the Senate voting. He suggested compromise on a certain point, but Wilson shot back, "Let Lodge compromise" Hitchcock conceded that the Senator would have to give ground but suggested that the White House might also hold out the olive branch. "Let Lodge hold out the olive branch," came the stern reply. On this inflexible note, and with Mrs. Wilson's anxiety mounting, the interview ended.

The Senate was ready for final action on November 19, 1919. At the critical moment Wilson sent a fateful letter to the Democratic minority in the Senate, urging them to vote down the treaty with the hated Lodge reservations so that a true ratification could be achieved. The Democrats, with more than the necessary one-third veto, heeded the voice of their crippled leader and rejected the treaty with reservations. The Republicans, with more than the necessary one-third veto, rejected the treaty without reservations.

The country was shocked by this exhibition of legislative paralysis. About four-fifths of the senators professed to favor the treaty in some form, yet they were unable to agree on anything. An aroused public opinion forced the Senate to reconsider, and Lodge secretly entered into negotiations with the Democrats in an effort to work out acceptable reservations. He was making promising progress when Senator Borah got wind of his maneuvers through an anonymous telephone call. The leading irreconcilables hastily summoned a council of war, hauled Lodge before them, and bluntly accused him of treachery. Deeply disturbed, the Massachusetts Senator said: "Well, I suppose I'll have to resign as majority leader."

"No, by God!" burst out Borah. "You won't have a chance to resign! On Monday, I'll move for the election of a new majority leader and give the reasons for my action." Faced with an upheaval within his party such as had insured Wilson's election in 1912, Lodge agreed to drop his backstage negotiations.

The second-chance vote in the Senate came on March 19, 1920. Wilson again directed his loyal Democratic following to reject the treaty, disfigured as it was by the hateful Lodge reservations. But by this time there was no other form in which the pact could possibly be ratified. Twenty-one realistic Democrats turned their backs on Wilson and voted Yea; 23 loyal Democrats, mostly from the rock-ribbed South, joined with the irreconcilables to do the bidding of the White House. The treaty, though commanding a simple majority this time of 49 Yeas to 35 Nays, failed of the necessary two-thirds vote.

Wilson, struggling desperately against the Lodge reservation trap, had already summoned the nation in "solemn referendum" to give him a vote in favor of the League in the forthcoming presidential election of 1920. His hope was that he could then get the treaty approved without reservations. But this course was plainly futile. Even if all the anti-League senators up for re-election in 1920 had been replaced by the pro-League senators, Wilson would still have lacked the necessary two-thirds majority for an unreserved treaty.

The American people were never given a chance to express their views directly on the League of Nations. All they could do was vote either for the weak Democratic candidate, Cox, who stood for the League, and the stuffed-shirt Republican candidate, Harding, who wobbled all over the map of the League arguments. If the electorate had been given an opportunity to express itself, a powerful majority probably would have favored the world organization, with at least some reservations. But wearied of Wilsonism, idealism, and self-denial, and confused by the wordy fight over the treaty, the voters rose up and swept Harding into the White House on a tidal wave of votes. The winner had been more anti-League than pro-League, and his prodigious plurality of 7,000,000 votes condemned the League to death in America.

What caused this costly failure of American statesmanship?

Wilson's physical collapse intensified his native stubbornness. A judicious compromise here and there no doubt would have secured Senate approval of the treaty, though of course with modifications. Wilson believed that in any event the Allies would reject the Lodge reservations. The probabilities are that the Allies would have worked out some kind of acceptance, so dire was their need of America's economic support, but Wilson never gave them a chance to act.

Senator Lodge was also inflexible, but prior to the second rejection he was evidently trying to get the treaty through—on his own terms. As majority leader of the Republicans, his primary task was to avoid another fatal split in his party. Wilson's primary task was to get the pact approved. From a purely political point of view, the Republicans had little to gain by engineering ratification of a Democratic treaty.

The two-thirds rule in the Senate, often singled out as the culprit, is of little relevance. Wilson almost certainly would have pigeonholed the treaty if it had passed with the Lodge reservations appended.

Wilson's insistence that the League be wedded to the treaty actually contributed to the final defeat of both. Either would have had a better chance if it had not been burdened by the enemies of the other. The United Nations, one should note, was set up in 1945 independently of any peace treaty.

Finally, American public opinion in 1919-20 was not yet ready for the onerous new world responsibilities that had suddenly been forced upon it. The isolationist tradition was still potent, and it was fortified by postwar disillusionment. If the sovereign voters had spoken out for the League with one voice, they almost certainly would have had their way. A treaty without reservations, or with a few reservations acceptable to Wilson, doubtless would have slipped through the Senate. But the American people were one war short of accepting leadership in a world organization for peace.

June 1957

III

Depression and War, 1929–1945

12 . American Individualism

Herbert Hoover

In the decade after the first World War, Herbert Hoover (1874-1964) was one of the most famous and highly regarded men in the entire world. Following a phenomenally successful career as a mining engineer, Hoover distinguished himself as an administrator and humanitarian through his work as head of the Committee for Relief in Belgium and then as United States Food Administrator. After service at the Versailles Peace Conference, he became Secretary of Commerce under Presidents Harding and Coolidge before winning the Presidency itself in 1928.

American Individualism

We have witnessed in this last eight years the spread of revolution over one-third of the world. The causes of these explosions lie at far greater depths than the failure of governments in war. The war itself in its last stages was a conflict of social philosophies — but beyond this the causes of social explosion lay in the great inequalities and injustices of centuries flogged beyond endurance by the conflict and freed from restraint by the destruction of war. The urgent forces which drive human society have been plunged into a terrible furnace. Great theories spun by dreamers to remedy the pressing human ills have come to the front of men's minds. Great formulas came into life that promised to dissolve all trouble. Great masses of people have flocked to their banners in hopes born of misery and suffering. Nor has this great social ferment been confined to those nations that have burned with revolutions.

Now, as the storm of war, of revolution and of emotion subsides there is left even with us of the United States much unrest, much discontent with the surer forces of human advancement. To all of us, out of this crucible of actual, poignant, individual experience has come a deal of new understanding, and it is for all of us to ponder these new currents if we are to shape our future with intelligence.

Even those parts of the world that suffered less from the war have been partly infected by these ideas. Beyond this, however, many have had high hopes of civilization suddenly purified and ennobled by the sacrifices and services of the war; they had thought the fine unity of purpose gained in war would be carried into great unity of action in remedy of the faults of civilization in peace. But from concentration of every spiritual and material energy upon the single purpose of war the scene changed to the immense complexity and the many purposes of peace.

Thus there loom up certain definite underlying forces in our national life that need to be stripped of the imaginary — the transitory — and a definition should be given to the actual permanent and persistent motivation of our civilization. In contemplation of these questions we must go far deeper than the superficials of our political and economic structure, for these are but the products of our social philosophy — the machinery of our social system.

Nor is it ever amiss to review the political, economic, and spiritual principles through which our country has steadily grown in usefulness and greatness, not only to preserve them from being fouled by false notions, but more importantly that we may guide ourselves in the road of progress.

Five or six great social philosophies are at struggle in the world for ascendancy. There is the Individualism of America. There is the Individualism of the more democratic states of Europe with its careful reservations of castes and classes. There are Communism, Socialism, Syndicalism, Capitalism, and finally there is Autocracy — whether by birth, by possessions, militarism, or divine right of kings. Even the Divine Right still lingers on although our lifetime has seen fully two-thirds of the earth's population, including Germany, Austria, Russia, and China, arrive at a state of angry disgust with this type of social motive power and throw it on the scrap heap.

All these thoughts are in ferment today in every country in the world. They fluctuate in ascendancy with times and places. They compromise with each other in daily reaction on governments and peoples. Some of these ideas are perhaps more adapted to one race than another. Some are false, some are true. 'What we are interested in is their challenge to the physical and spiritual forces of America.

The partisans of some of these other brands of social schemes challenge us to comparison; and some of their parties even among our own people are increasing in their agitation that we adopt one or another or parts of their devices in place of our tried individualism. They insist that our social foundations are exhausted, that like feudalism and autocracy America's plan has served its purpose — that it must be abandoned.

There are those who have been left in sober doubt of our institutions or are confounded by bewildering catchwords of vivid phrases. For in this welter of discussions there is much attempt to glorify or defame social and economic forces with phrases. Nor indeed should we disregard the potency of some of these phrases in their stir to action — "The dictatorship of the Proletariat," "Capitalistic nations," "Germany over all," and a score of others. We need only to review those that have jumped to horseback during the last ten years in order that we may be properly awed by the great social and political havoc that can be worked where the bestial instincts of hate, murder, and destruction are clothed by the demagogue in the fine terms of political idealism.

For myself, let me say at the very outset that my faith in the essential truth, strength, and vitality of the developing creed by which we have hitherto lived in this country of ours has been confirmed and deepened by the searching experiences of seven years of service in the backwash and misery of war. Seven years of contending with economic degeneration, with social disintegration, with incessant political dislocation, with all of its seething and ferment of individual and class conflict, could but impress me with the primary motivation of social forces, and the necessity for broader thought upon their great issues to humanity. And from it all I emerge an individualist — an unashamed individualist. But let me say also that I am an American individualist. For America has been steadily developing the ideals that constitute progressive individualism.

No doubt, individualism run riot, with no tempering principle, would provide a long category of inequalities, of tyrannies, dominations, and injustices. America, however, has tempered the whole conception of individualism by the injection of a definite principle, and from this principle it follows that attempts at domination, whether in government or in the processes of industry and commerce, are under an insistent curb. If we would have the values of individualism, their stimulation to initiative, to the development of hand and intellect, to the high development of thought and spirituality, they must be tempered with that firm and fixed ideal of American individualism — *an equality of opportunity.* If we would have these values we must soften its hardness and stimulate progress through the sense of service that lies in our people.

Therefore, it is not the individualism of other countries for which I would speak, but the individualism of America. Our individualism differs from all others because it embraces these great ideals: *that while we build our society upon the attainment of the individual, we shall safeguard to every individual an equality of opportunity to take that position in the community to which his intelligence, character, ability and ambition entitle him; that we keep the social solution free from frozen strata of classes; that we shall stimulate effort of each individual to achievement; that through an enlarging sense of responsibility and understanding we shall assist him to this attainment; while he in turn must stand up to the emery wheel of competition.*

Individualism cannot be maintained as the foundation of a society if it looks to only legalistic justice based upon contracts, property, and political equality. Such legalistic safeguards are themselves not enough. In our individualism we have long since abandoned the laissez faire of the 18th Century — the notion that it is "every man for himself and the devil take the hindmost." We abandoned that when we adopted the ideal of equality of opportunity — the fair chance of Abraham Lincoln. We have confirmed its abandonment in terms of legislation, of social and economic justice, — in part because we have learned that social injustice is the destruction of justice itself. We have learned that the impulse to production can only be maintained at a high pitch if there is a fair division of the product. We have also learned that fair division can only be obtained by certain restrictions on the strong and the dominant...

The will-o'-the-wisp of all breeds of socialism is that they contemplate a motivation of human animals by altruism alone. It necessitates a bureaucracy of the entire population, in which, having obliterated the economic stipulation of each member, the fine gradations of character and ability are to be arranged in relative authority by ballot or more likely by a Tammany Hall or a Bolshevist party, or some other form of tyranny. The proof of the futility of these ideas as *a* stimulation to the development and activity of the individual does not lie alone in the ghastly failure of Russia, but it also lies in our own failure in attempts at nationalized industry.

Likewise the basic foundations of autocracy, whether it be class government or capitalism in the sense that a few men through unrestrained control of property determine the welfare of great numbers, is as far apart from the rightful expression of American individualism as the two poles. The will-o'-the-wisp of autocracy in any form is that it supposes that the good Lord endowed a special few with all the divine attributes. It contemplates one human animal dealing to the other human animals his just share of earth, of glory, and of immortality. The proof of the futility of these ideas in the development of the world does not lie alone in the grim failure of Germany, but it lies in the damage to our moral and social fabric from those who have sought economic domination in America, whether employer or employee.

We in America have had too much experience of life to fool ourselves into pretending that all men are equal in ability, in character, in intelligence, in ambition. That was part of the claptrap of the French Revolution. We have grown to understand that all we can hope to assure to the individual through government is liberty, justice, intellectual welfare, equality of opportunity, and stimulation to service.

It is in maintenance of a society fluid to these human qualities that our individualism departs from the individualism of Europe. There can be no rise for the individual through the frozen strata of classes, or of castes, and no stratification can take place in a mass livened by the free stir of its particles. This guarding of our individualism against stratification insists not only in preserving in the social solution an equal opportunity for the able and ambitious to rise from the bottom; it also insists that the sons of the successful shall not by any mere right of birth or favor continue to occupy their fathers' places of power against the rise of a new generation in process of coming up from the bottom. The pioneers of our American individualism had the good sense not to reward Washington and Jefferson and Hamilton with hereditary dukedoms and fixtures in landed estates, as Great Britain rewarded Marlborough and Nelson. Otherwise our American fields of opportunity would have been clogged with long generations inheriting their fathers' privileges without their fathers' capacity for service.

That our system has avoided the establishment and domination of class has a significant proof in the present Administration in Washington. Of the twelve men comprising the President, Vice-President, and Cabinet, nine have earned their own way in life without economic inheritance, and eight of them started with manual labor.

If we examine the impulses that carry us forward, none is so potent for progress as the yearning for individual self-expression, the desire for creation of something. Perhaps the greatest human happiness flows from personal achievement. Here lies the great urge of the constructive instinct of mankind. But it can only thrive in a society where the individual has liberty and stimulation to achievement. Nor does the community progress except through its participation in these multitudes of achievements.

Furthermore, the maintenance of productivity and the advancement of the things of the spirit depend upon the ever-renewed supply from the mass of those who can rise to leadership. Our social, economic, and intellectual progress is almost solely dependent upon the creative minds of those individuals with imaginative and administrative intelligence who create or who carry discoveries to widespread application. No race possesses more than a small percentage of these minds in a single generation. But little thought has ever been given to our racial dependency upon them. Nor that our progress is in so large a measure due to the fact that with our increased means of communication these rare individuals are today able to spread their influence over so enlarged a number of lesser capable minds as to have increased their potency a million-fold. In truth, the vastly greater productivity of the world with actually less physical labor is due to the wider spread of their influence through the discovery of these facilities. And they can arise solely through the selection that comes from the free-running mills of competition. They must be free to rise from the mass; they must be given the attraction of premiums to effort.

Leadership is a quality of the individual. It is the individual alone who can function in the world of intellect and in the field of leadership. If democracy is to secure its authorities in morals, religion, and statesmanship, it must stimulate leadership from its own mass. Human leadership cannot be replenished by selection like queen bees, by divine right or bureaucracies, but by the free rise of ability, character, and intelligence.

Even so, leadership cannot, no matter how brilliant, carry progress far ahead of the average of the mass of individual units. Progress of the nation is the sum of progress in its individuals. Acts and ideas that lead to progress are born out of the womb of the individual mind, not out of the mind of the crowd. The crowd only feels: it has no mind of its own which can plan. The crowd is credulous, it destroys, it consumes, it hates, and it dreams—but it never builds. It is one of the most profound and important of exact psychological truths that man in the mass does not think but only feels. The mob functions only in a world of emotion. The demagogue feeds on the mob emotions and his leadership is the leadership of emotion, not the leadership of intellect and progress. Popular desires are no criteria to the real need; they can be determine only by deliberative consideration, by education, by constructive leadership...

Economic Phases

That high and increasing standards of living and comfort should be the first of considerations in public mind and in government needs no apology. We have long since realized that the basis of an advancing civilization must be a high and growing standard of living for all the people, not for a single class; that education, food, clothing, housing, and the spreading use of what we so often term non-essentials, are the real fertilizers of the soil from which spring the finer flowers of life. The economic development of the past fifty years has lifted the general standard of comfort far beyond the dreams of our forefathers. The only road to further advance in the standard of living is by greater invention, greater elimination of waste, greater production and better distribution of commodities and services, for by increasing their ratio to our numbers and dividing them justly we each will have more of them.

The superlative value of individualism through its impulse to production, its stimulation to invention has, so far as I know, never been denied. Criticism of it has lain in its wastes but more importantly in its failures of equitable sharing of the product. In our country these contentions are mainly over the division to each of his share of the comforts and luxuries, for none of us is either hungry or cold or without a place to lay his head—and we have much besides. In less than four decades we have added electric lights, plumbing, telephones, gramophones, automobiles, and what not in wide diffusion to our standards of living. Each in turn began as a luxury, each in turn has become so commonplace that seventy or eighty percent of our people participate in them.

To all practical souls there is little use in quarreling over the share of each of us until we have something to divide. So long as we maintain our individualism we will have increasing quantities to share and we shall have time and leisure and taxes with which to fight out proper sharing of the "surplus." The income tax returns show that this surplus is a minor part of our total production after taxes are paid. Some of this "surplus" must be set aside for rewards to saving for stimulation of proper effort to skill, to leadership and invention — therefore the dispute is in reality over much less than the total of such "surplus." While there should be no minimizing of a certain fringe of injustices in sharing the results of production or in the wasteful use made by some of their share, yet there is vastly wider field for gains to all of us through cheapening the costs of production and distribution through the eliminating of their wastes, from increasing the volume of product by each and every one doing his utmost, than will ever come to use even if we can think out a method of abstract justice in sharing which did not stifle production of the total product . . .

But those are utterly wrong who say that individualism has as its only end the acquisition and preservation of private property — the selfish snatching and boarding of the common product. Our American individualism, indeed, is only in part an economic creed. It aims to provide opportunity for self-expression, not merely economically, but spirituality as well. Private property is not a fetich in America. The crushing of the liquor trade without a cent of compensation, which scarcely even a discussion of it, does not bear our the notion that we give property rights any headway over human rights. Our development of individualism shows an increasing tendency to regard right of property not as an object in itself, but in the light of a useful and necessary instrument in stimulation of initiative to the individual; not only stimulation to him that he may gain personal comfort, security in life, protection to his family, but also because individual accumulation and ownership is a basis of selection to leadership in administration of the tools of industry and commerce. It is where dominant private property is assembled in the hands of the groups who control the state that the individual begins to feel capital as an oppressor. Our American demand for equality of opportunity is a constant militant check upon capital becoming a thing to be feared. Out of fear we sometimes even go too far an stifle the reproductive use of capital by crushing the initiative that makes for its creation...

The domination by arbitrary individual ownership is disappearing because the works of today are steadily growing more and more beyond the resources of any one individual, and steadily taxation will reduce relatively excessive individual accumulations. The number of persons in partnership through division of ownership among stockholders is steadily increasing—thus 100,000 to 200,000 partners in a single concern are not uncommon. The overwhelmingly largest portion of our mobile capital is that of our banks, insurance companies, building and loan associations, and the vast majority of all of this is the aggregated small savings of our people. Thus large capital is steadily becoming more and more a mobilization of the savings of the small holder – the actual people themselves –and its administration becomes at once more sensitive to the moral opinions of the people in order to attract their support. The directors and managers of large concerns, themselves employees of these great groups of individual stockholders, or policy holders, reflect a spirit of community responsibility.

Large masses of capital can only find their market for service or production to great numbers of the same kind of people that they employ and they must therefore maintain confidence in their public responsibilities in order to retain their customers. In times when the products of manufacture were mostly luxuries to the average of the people, the condition of their employees was of no such interest to their customers as when they cater to employees in general. Of this latter, no greater proofs need exist than the efforts of many large concerns directly dependent upon public good will to restrain prices in scarcity – and the very general desire to yield a measure of service with the goods sold. Another phase of this same development in administration of capital is the growth of a sort of institutional sense in many large business enterprises. The encouragement of solidarity in all grades of their employees in the common service and common success, the sense of mutuality with the prosperity of the community are both vital developments in individualism...

A great test of the soundness of a social system must be its ability to evolve within itself those orderly shifts in its administration that enable it to apply the new tools of social, economic, and intellectual progress, and to eliminate the malign forces that may grow in the application of these tools. When we were almost wholly an agricultural people our form of organization and administration, both in the governmental and economic fields, could be simple. With the enormous shift in growth to industry and commerce we have erected organisms that each generation has denounced as Frankensteins, yet the succeeding generation proves them to be controllable and useful. The growth of corporate organizations, of our banking systems, of our railways, of our electrical power, of our farm cooperatives, of our trade unions, of our trade associations, and of a hundred other indeed develops both beneficent and malign forces. The timid become frightened. But our basic social ideas march through the new things in the end. Our demagogues, of both radical and standpat breed, thrive on demands for the destruction of one or another of these organizations as the only solution for their defects, yet progress requires only a guardianship of the vital principles of our individualism with its safeguard of true equality of opportunity in them.

Political Phases

It is not the primary purpose of this essay to discuss our political organization. Democracy is merely the mechanism which individualism invented as a device that would carry on the necessary political work of its social organization. Democracy arises out of individualism and prospers through it alone.

Without question, there exists, almost all over the world, unprecedented disquietude at the functioning of government itself. It is in part the dreamy social ferment of war emotion. It is in part the aftermath of a period when the Government was everything and the individual nothing, from which there is much stimulation to two schools of thought: one that all human ills can be cured by governmental regulation, and the other that all regulation is a sin.

During the war, the mobilization of every effort, the destruction of the normal demand and the normal avenues of distribution, required a vast excursion over the deadline of individualism in order that we might secure immediate results. Its continuation would have destroyed the initiative of our people and undermined all real progress. We are slowly getting back, but many still aspire to these supposed short cuts to the millennium.

Much of discontent takes the form of resentment against the inequalities in the distribution of the sacrifices of war. Both silently and vocally there is complaint that while some died, others ran no risk, and yet others profited. For these complaints there is adequate justification. The facts are patent. However, no conceivable human intelligence would be able to manage the conduct of war so as to see that all sacrifices and burdens should be distributed equitably. War is destruction, and we should blame war for its injustices, not a social system whose object is construction. The submergence of the individual, however, in the struggle of the race could be but temporary — its continuance through the crushing of individual action and its equities would, if for no other reason, destroy the foundations of our civilization.

Looked at as the umpire in our social system, our Government has maintained an equality before the law and a development of legal justice and an authority in restraint of evil instincts that support this social system and its ideals so far as the imperfections of developing human institutions permit. It has gone the greatest distance of any government toward maintaining an equality of franchise; an equality of entrance to public office, and government by the majority. It has succeeded far beyond all others in those safeguards of equality of opportunity through education, public information, and the open channels of free speech and free press. It is, however, much easier to chart the course of progress to government in dealing with the abstract problems of order, political liberty, and stimulation to intellectual and moral advancement than it is to chart its relations to the economic seas. These seas are new and only partly discovered or explored.

Our Government's greatest troubles and failures are in the economic field. Forty years ago the contact of the individual with the Government had its largest expression in the sheriff or policeman, and in debates over political equality. In those happy days the Government offered but small interference with the economic life of the citizen. But with the vast development of industry and the train of regulating functions of the national and municipal government that followed from it; with the recent vast increase in taxation due to the war; – the Government has become through its relations to economic life the most potent force for maintenance or destruction of our American individualism.

The entrance of the Government began strongly three decades ago, when our industrial organization began to move powerfully in the direction of consolidation of enterprise. We found in the course of this development that equality of opportunity and its corollary, individual initiative, was being throttled by the concentration of control of industry and service, and thus an economic domination of groups builded over the nation. At this time, particularly, we were threatened with a form of autocracy of economic power. Our mass of regulation of public utilities and our legislation against restraint of trade is the monument to our intent to preserve an equality of opportunity. This regulation is itself proof that we have gone a long way toward the abandonment of the "capitalism" of Adam Smith.

Day by day we learn more as to the practical application of restrictions against economic and political domination. We sometimes lag behind in the correction of those forces that would override liberty, justice, and equality of opportunity, but the principle is so strong within us that domination of the few will not be tolerated. These restraints must keep pace with the growing complexity of our economic organization, but they need tuning, to our social system if they would not take us into great dangers. As we build up our powers of production through the advancing application of science we create new forces with which men may dominate – railway, power, oil, and what not. They may produce temporary blockades upon equality of opportunity.

To curb the forces in business which would destroy equality of opportunity and yet to maintain the initiative and creative faculties of our people are the twin objects we must attain. To preserve the former we must regulate that type of activity that would dominate. To preserve the latter, the Government must keep out of production and distribution of commodities and services. This is the deadline between our system and socialism. Regulation to prevent domination and unfair practices, yet preserving rightful initiative, are in keeping with our social foundations. Nationalization of industry or business is their negation.

When we come to the practical problems of government in relation to these economic questions the test lies in two directions: Does this act safeguard an equality of opportunity? Does it maintain the initiative of our people? For in the first must lie the deadline against domination, and in the second the deadline in preservation of individualism against socialism...

There are malign social forces other than our failures that would destroy our progress. There are the equal dangers both of reaction and radicalism. The perpetual howl of radicalism is that it is the sole voice of liberalism — that devotion to social progress is its field alone. These men would assume that all reform and human advance must come through government. They have forgotten that progress must come from the steady lift of the individual and that the measure of national idealism and progress is the quality of idealism in the individual. The most trying support of radicalism comes from the timid or dishonest minds that shrink from facing the result of radicalism itself but are devoted to defense of radicalism as proof of a liberal mind...

The primary safeguard of American individualism is an understanding of it; of faith that it is the most precious possession of American civilization, and a willingness courageously to test every process of national life upon the touchstone of this basic social premise. Development of the human institutions and of science and of industry have been long chains of trial and error. Our public relations to them and to other phases of our national life can be advanced in no other way than by a willingness to experiment in the remedy of our social faults. The failures and unsolved problems of economic and social life can be corrected; they can be solved within our social theme and under no other system. The solution is a matter of will to find solution; of a sense of duty as well as of a sense of right and citizenship. No one who buys "bootleg" whiskey can complain of gunmen and hooliganism.

13. FDR and the Kingfish

William E. Leuchtenburg

In this selection, historian William E. Leuchtenburg describes the rivalry between two politically ambitious men, Franklin D. Roosevelt and Huey Long. No political rival in the 1930s caused so much concern for Roosevelt as *the colorful Long. Although he cultivated a public image of the proverbial buffoon, Long was far from being an ignoramus. The promises in his "Share Our Wealth" program may have been considered impractical by economic experts, but they seemed simple and understandable to many of the nation's unemployed, who saw no end in sight to the Great Depression. FDR and his advisors feared that a third party headed by Long, and supported by Dr. Francis Townsend and Father Coughlin, presented a real threat to the president's reelection in 1936 Leuchtenburg's article leaves several questions for the reader to ponder. Was Long merely a demagogue who exploited popular discontent for the sake of gaining power, or was he a democrat (with a small "d") who genuinely wanted to bring about long needed reforms? Did Long have dictatorial inclinations? Did FDR "steal Huey's thunder" by adopting parts of Long's program? Given the fate of third parties in American politics, was Long really a threat to Roosevelt in 1936?*

In May 1932 Louisiana's flamboyant senator, Huey Pierce Long, told a throng of newspapermen to prepare for a headline-making announcement. After months of temporizing, he was finally ready to reveal whom he would support for his party's presidential nomination at the upcoming Democratic national convention: his choice was the patrician governor of New York, Franklin Delano Roosevelt. They were an odd couple, and the decision was not one the Kingfish—a nickname borrowed from the popular "Amos 'n Andy" radio show—had come to easily. Five months earlier he had said of FDR, "He ran too poorly with Cox in 1920, and he would be certain to be beat." Even now he told a pro-Roosevelt senator, "I didn't like your son of a bitch, but I'll be for him." In this unpromising fashion began an improbable alliance that would soon be transformed into the stormiest political rivalry of the decade: the conflict between FDR and the Kingfish.

By 1932 Long had already established himself as a figure of national consequence, though he had only arrived in Washington at the start of the year. It had been a debut, however, that the capital was still talking about. There is a well-established rule that not only are freshman senators supposed to be silent, they are supposed to be invisible. But on his first day in the Senate, Huey bounced onto the Senate floor, slapped one distinguished senator on the back, poked an Old Guard Republican in the ribs, and ran around the chamber telling everyone the Kingfish had arrived—all the while puffing on a big cigar, in violation of Senate rules. By the end of the week, Long had attracted more attention than had been accorded a freshman senator in many, many years.

Some of this attention simply resulted from Huey's remarkable flair for focusing the spotlight on himself by deliberately flouting propriety. But he drew attention, too, because at a time in the Great Depression when twelve million people were unemployed, he was the best-known advocate of an ancient panacea: sharing the wealth. A few weeks after he took his Senate seat, he introduced a resolution to limit fortunes to one hundred million dollars—and divide up the residue.

But perhaps the most important reason reporters crowded around Long was that he would control Louisiana's votes at the 1932 Democratic national convention and have a lot to say about the ballots of neighboring Mississippi as well. Once Huey decided to back FDR, he went all the way, and a number of observers credit him with playing a crucial role. "There is no question in my mind," the Bronx County boss, Edward J. Flynn, later declared, "but that without Long's work Roosevelt might not have been nominated."

Long's performance at the convention proved to be the high point of his association with Roosevelt; it was downhill from there. Imbued with a sense of his own importance, he was determined to shape FDR's policies. He even wanted a whole campaign train for himself, in part to promote views that conflicted with Roosevelt's. But the Democratic campaign manager, Jim Farley, shuttled him off to the Great Plains, where he could do little harm (and actually did some good), and Roosevelt kept him at arm's length.

Angry at his inability to win the kinds of commitments he sought, Huey made no secret of his displeasure with Roosevelt's behavior. On one occasion, shortly after the convention, he was heard shouting over a phone: "Goddamn it, Frank, don't you know who nominated you? Why do you have . . . all those Wall Street blankety blanks up there to see you? How do you think it looks to the country? How can I explain it to my people?" A short time afterward, Long reported: "When I talk to him, he says, 'Fine! Fine! Fine!' But [Sen.] Joe Robinson goes to see him the next day, and again he says, 'Fine! Fine! Fine!' Maybe he says 'Fine!' to everybody."

The climactic encounter took place at the end of the first Hundred Days of 1933. Throughout that early springtime of the New Deal, Long had noised his objections to a good number of Roosevelt's proposals and not a few of his appointees. When he visited the White House, he was in a cocky, even insolent, mood. He wore a sailor straw hat that he kept on his head, except when he used it to tap the President on the knee or the elbow to make a point. Roosevelt never blinked. But by the close of the interview it was clear to the senator that none of the vast federal patronage destined for Louisiana was to go to him.

After that, Long and Roosevelt parted ways. Some thought they separated because the Kingfish was disappointed in patronage. Long said it was because he disagreed with FDR's policies. The real reason for the break, though, was surely more complex.

Few rivalries of the 1930s cut so deeply as the conflict between Roosevelt and Long. Each held or was bidding for national power at a time when, in much of the world, totalitarianism was coming to seem the wave of the future. Roosevelt was one of many who feared that unless certain social changes were made peacefully, they would ultimately be made violently and democracy might not survive. For the President and his circle, the threat to democracy came from two sources: the Old Guard conservatives who resisted change and the men like Huey Long who would exploit popular discontent if change was not achieved.

Roosevelt and Long each sensed that there was not room enough in Washington for both of them. One political commentator wrote of Long: "Obviously he cannot succeed while the country still has hopes of the success of the New Deal and trusts the President. Huey's chances depend on those sands of hope and trust running out." FDR, in turn, was aware that if he stumbled, the Kingfish would be there to gobble up the pieces. "It's all very well for us to laugh over Huey," he told an aide, "but actually we have to remember all the time that he really is one of the two most dangerous men in the country. (Asked if he had Father Coughlin in mind as the second dangerous man, the President said, "Oh no. The other is Douglas MacArthur.")

To the New Dealers, Long's Louisiana served as a model for the kind of despotism the country might experience if they did not succeed, for in that state Huey was unabashedly creating a personal dictatorship. He bullied the legislature, intimidated the courts to the point at which their independence all but vanished, and kept a squad of tough—and sometimes savage—bodyguards around him at all times.

Even Long's most sympathetic biographer, T. Harry Williams, has conceded: "He wanted to do good, but for that he had to have power. So he took power and then to do more good seized still more power, and finally the means and the end became so entwined in his mind that he could not distinguish between them, could not tell whether he wanted power as a method or for its own sake. He gave increasing attention to building his power structure, and as he built it, he did strange, ruthless, and cynical things."

"This is my university," Long said of Louisiana State University. "I can fire a thousand of these students and get ten thousand in place of them any time I feel like it." When he learned that a student newspaper planned to carry a letter critical of him, he ordered the presses stopped and the letter deleted. He sent a squad of state troopers to see that the edict was carried out. The university suspended the editor and five members of the staff. Huey explained, "I like students, but this state is puttin' up the money for that college, and I ain't payin' anybody to criticize me."

Long made a point of showing his contempt for the democratic process. When asked how the Kingfish had built his majority in the legislature, one Long leader explained, "They all didn't come for free." Huey, who said of one member of the legislature, "We got that guy so cheap we thought we stole him," boasted openly that his legislature was the "finest collection of lawmakers money can buy." (Years later, his brother Earl, who also became a memorable governor of Louisiana, remarked: "Huey used to buy the legislature like a sack of potatoes. Hell, I never bought one in my life. I just rent 'em. It's cheaper that way.") Huey's legislators voted like automatons. While U.S. senator, Long handed one session of the legislature forty-four bills. In little more than two hours the legislature adopted all forty-four.

One commentator wrote in July 1935, "Unlike the German intelligentsia, who could not judge from experience what Hitler might do, Americans may turn the pages of Louisiana's recent history for . . . insight into the sort of country we would have if Long became our Hitler."

A number of historians have protested applying the term *fascist* to Long, and with good reason. He had elaborated no antidemocratic ideology, no conception of a corporate state. "Long's political fantasies," Arthur Schlesinger, Jr., observes, "had no tensions, no conflicts, except of the most banal kind, no heroism or sacrifice, no compelling myths of class or race or nation." And unlike other Southern demagogues, Long did not rise to power by racist rhetoric against blacks. Though there were serious incidents of suppression of civil liberties in Louisiana, to the end of his life Long was openly attacked by most of the newspapers of his state. Long's political beliefs, a number of writers have stressed, were native to American soil, the culmination of a time-honored line of agrarian dissent.

Yet it is also true that Long—far more than has sometimes been acknowledged—did represent a threat to democracy. His hostility to voluntaristic organizations—from labor unions to bar associations—suggested a totalitarian mentality. His contempt for legislatures, his vengeful, even sadistic, politics, and, most of all, his overwhelming ambition constituted a distinct menace. That Long's ideas were in the American tradition of protest made him more rather than less ominous. In truth, political analysts have always found Long's ideas hard to categorize. They have been puzzled in particular by such questions as whether Long was to the left or to the right of Roosevelt. Huey himself viewed all the efforts to pigeonhole him with droll detachment. When pressed on the matter he once told reporters, "Oh, hell, say that I'm *sui generis* and let it go at that." FDR himself had a simpler view—that his struggle with Long represented a contest between democracy and dictatorship. And so it did. But it was something else, too—a conflict between two rival traditions of reform.

Though Roosevelt has sometimes been thought of as a descendant of Populist reformers, it is, rather, Long who is in the Populist tradition; FDR is better understood as a foe of the heirs of Populism. Long came from Winn Parish, the birthplace of Populism in Louisiana. His slogan, Every Man a King, derived from a line in William Jennings Bryan's "Cross of Gold" speech: "Every man a king, but no man wears a crown." While Roosevelt's approach to politics reflected the outlook of an Eastern-seaboard patrician, Huey's voiced the aspirations of a rural class that had known bitter deprivation.

Long had come to power by challenging the rule of an upperclass oligarchy that was probably the most reactionary and most corrupt of any state in the country. It had three elements: the planters, the corporations (especially oil), and a New Orleans ring headed by the urban boss Martin Behrman. (It was Behrman who, on one occasion, rejected a proposal for a new civic auditorium in the style of a classic Greek theater with the comment, "There aren't enough Greeks living here to make it worthwhile.") This alliance cared for little save its own interests. In literacy, a crucial index of the social health of any political system, Louisiana ranked last in the nation, with an illiteracy rate many times higher than that of neighboring Mississippi. Anyone who came to power by overturning such a system would inevitably carry with him attitudes toward the Establishment vastly different from those of a man like Roosevelt.

In his classic study of Southern politics, the political scientist V. O. Key wrote: "As good a supposition as any is that the longer the period of unrestrained exploitation, the more violent will be the reaction when it comes. Louisiana's rulers controlled without check for a long period. . . . [it] was a case of arrested political development. Its Populism was repressed with a violence unparalleled in the South, and its neo-Populism was smothered by a potent ruling oligarchy."

When Long overturned the old order in Louisiana, he did more than just win an election; he triggered a political revolution. He gave lower-class rural whites from the forks of the creek, for the first time, their day in the sun. In 1928 fifteen thousand people—sunbonneted women and gallused men—swarmed into Baton Rouge to see one of their own elevated to the governorship. Long's election ushered in a "fantastic vengeance upon the Sodom and Gomorrah that was called New Orleans," as the newspaperman Hodding Carter noted. "A squaring of accounts with the big shots, the Standard Oil and the bankers, the big planters, the entrenched interests everywhere." Long's strength, said the novelist Sherwood Anderson, came from "the terrible South ... the beaten, ignorant, Bible-ridden, white South. Faulkner occasionally really touches it. It has yet to be paid for."

Franklin Roosevelt derived from a quite different tradition of reform. He felt kinship with those post-Populist reformers, the Progressives, the followers of Theodore Roosevelt and Woodrow Wilson who feared and despised Populism as an uprising of the ignorant, the suspicious, the envious, the unsuccessful. Theodore Roosevelt and Woodrow Wilson had sought to rescue the reform movement from the rural fundamentalists and direct it in channels of respectability that the urban middle class would accept. It was this tradition—the reform impulse of the Establishment—of which Franklin Roosevelt, like TR and Wilson, was a part. This tradition could find no space for the ambitions of a Huey Long.

FDR held an aristocratic view of the reformer-statesman as the paladin of the lowly. In the novels of Roosevelt's youth—in the political romances of such writers as the American novelist Winston Churchill—the hero is typically a well-born Galahad who battles the machine, purifies the corrupt legislature, and routs the evil combine, all the while wooing a heroine who breathlessly admires his daring in entering the political arena. in the final scene, hero and heroine ride off in their coach to live happily forever after—on their inherited income.

Huey shared no such fantasies. His idols came from the pages of Ridpath's history of the world—kings, conquerors, rulers; and it was unadorned power, the power of an Alexander, that made the greatest appeal. Long's model was Frederick the Great: "'You can't take Vienna, Your Majesty. The world won't stand for it,' his nitwit ambassadors said. 'The hell I can't,' said old Fred. 'My soldiers will take Vienna and my professors at Heidelberg will explain the reasons why!'" Unlike FDR, Long had an antiromantic perception of the state. While Roosevelt took pride in his service as assistant secretary of the Navy during World War I and genuinely regretted he had not been in combat, Long deliberately evaded participation in the war. He even sought deferment on the grounds that he was a notary public. Asked why he had not fought for his country, Huey explained, "I was not mad at anybody over there."

From men such as Endicott Peabody, the headmaster of Groton, Roosevelt learned to conceive of public life as a duty the wellborn owed to their country. To be sure, FDR could never conceal the gusto with which he took to politics nor his ardor for social changes many in the Establishment found appalling, but he accepted the gentlemanly precept that the office seeks the man, not the man the office. Huey made no such disclaimer. Politics, for him and for his followers, represented an opportunity for advancement and rewards. Long was admitted to the bar at the age of twenty-one, and said, "I came out of that courtroom running for office."

Implied in the Endicott Peabody tradition was a high seriousness about politics, and it was against the pretensions of this tradition of reform that Huey turned the weapon of humor. He jeered at claims that Roosevelt and the New Dealers were disinterested public servants. They, like him, Huey insisted, wanted power.

His behavior brings to mind Shakespeare's *Henry IV*, in which Falstaff presides over his circle of followers just as Henry does over his court. Henry celebrates such martial, aristocratic virtues as courage in battle, while Falstaff jeers that it is better to live ignobly than to die, especially to die for impersonal principle. The values of the prince must stand the test of Falstaff's scorn. Long played Falstaff to FDR's Henry.

Long insinuated that Roosevelt and his circle, no less than the Louisiana planters and the oilmen, were part of the Establishment, with a stake in the system. The New Dealers, he sensed, were most vulnerable to the charge that they did not really represent a new order but actually sustained the old one.

An episode in Washington early in 1933 revealed Huey's approach. Shortly before FDR's inauguration Long kicked open the door of one of the Brain Trusters at the Mayflower Hotel and barged into the room. He grabbed an apple, took a big bite, and walked up to Norman Davis, a dignified international diplomat close to both Roosevelt and the house of Morgan. Tapping Davis's stark-white shirtfront with the half-bitten apple, he shouted, "I don't like you and your god-damned banker friends!"

Often Long's barbs seemed to be fired at random, but they were all aimed at making a single point—that he, not Roosevelt, should be the country's leader. His posthumously published *My First Days in the White House* made that contention explicit by effecting, however good-naturedly, a reversal of roles. In that slim literary effort, Huey pictures himself as President and, after naming Herbert Hoover secretary of commerce, demotes FDR to secretary of the Navy.

Though Huey deliberately played the role of clown, he was no fool. His briefs before the Supreme Court were praised by both Chief Justice William Taft and Justice Louis Brandeis. The Washington correspondent of the *New York Times* recalled: "His speech in behalf of the legality of his delegates in '32 was the finest legal argument that anybody has ever heard—or that I ever heard—at a national convention. He dropped all the clowning. He dropped the hillbilly stuff. Huey wasn't the rustic he pretended to be. He was a brilliant man and a very fine lawyer."

However, it served Long's purposes to play the buffoon. By parodying the New Deal, he drew national attention away from Roosevelt and softened the impression of himself as a Louisiana autocrat. Instead of appearing as a would-be dictator, Huey created a picture of himself as a lovable, amiable, harmless soul, an affable country philosopher. At one point he even stirred up a national controversy between dunkers and crumblers of corn pone and got Emily Post to render a when-in-Rome-do-as-the-Romans-do verdict.

But if Long had been nothing more than a jester, he would only have been a seven-day wonder. He got as far as he did because his achievements in Louisiana commanded attention, especially from people who were disenchanted with the New Deal. Unlike many other demagogues, Huey was an innovator and a lawgiver. He was even called "the first Southerner since Calhoun to have an original idea." With a vivid sense of the iconography of politics, Long dismantled the structure of the old regime to make way for a new era in Louisiana. He built a modern skyscraper capitol that symbolized the new commonwealth he was creating on the ruins of the old. (Mark Twain said of the old capitol: "That comes from too much Sir Walter Scott.") He also tore down the antiquated governor's mansion and built a new Executive Mansion in Baton Rouge on the model of the White House, in order, he explained, to be "used to it when he got there."

But these actions were only symbolic. Long did a great deal more. He sponsored Louisiana's first income tax law, eliminated the poll tax, revamped the barbarous state institutions for the insane, considerably expanded public health facilities, and initiated the greatest road-building program of any state in the union. When he took office, Louisiana had less than three hundred miles of concrete roads and only three major bridges; seven years later, there were over thirty-seven hundred miles of paved highways and forty major bridges. He distributed free textbooks to students and got the legislature to tax the oil companies to pay for them. (Huey insisted, "When these fellows suck an oil well dry we want a new schoolhouse somewhere. . . . ") He instituted night schools to cope with the state's illiteracy, and by the time he left for the U.S. Senate in 1932, one hundred thousand people had been taught to read, write, and cipher.

With so much achievement, it was not always easy to recognize that Long's programs had shortcomings too, especially when contrasted to FDR's emerging welfare state. Long opposed minimum-wage legislation; failed to further the Child Labor Amendment (though children in Louisiana toiled for as little as six cents an hour); showed small understanding of the aspirations of the union movement; and did not do much for either the urban unemployed or the sharecropper. Unlike other reform governors, Huey left no shelf of social legislation. Yet Long's reign, deficient, undemocratic, and shamelessly corrupt, nonetheless brought unprecedented change to Louisiana.

At election time the Kingfish could declare: "They tell you that you've got to tear up Longism in this state. All right, my friends, get you a bomb or some dynamite and blow up that new state capitol. Then go out and tear up the concrete roads I've built. Get your spades and your shovels and scrape the gravel off them roads we graveled and let a rain come in on 'em. That'll put 'em back like they was before I come. Tear down all the new buildings I've built at the university. And when your child starts to school tomorrow morning snatch the free textbooks out of his hands. Then, my friends, you'll be rid of Longism in this state, and not before."

With that record of performance in Louisiana, Long was able to mount an effective attack on the New Deal. He questioned whether Roosevelt was concerned with the welfare of the poor (after all, FDR had never known the hardships of Winn Parish), and he denied that the administration had found the road to recovery. Long's assault came at a particularly embarrassing time: after the upturn of the first Hundred Days of 1933, the economy had come to a standstill. At precisely that point, in January 1934, Huey made his bid for national power by establishing a national political organization with an arresting slogan: Share Our Wealth. He named as national organizer Gerald L. K. Smith, a fifth-generation minister of the Disciples of Christ and a stump speaker of unrivaled power who, it has been said, was a combination of Savonarola and Elmer Gantry.

Although the details of Long's program shifted from time to time, the main features remained constant. Huey proposed to liquidate all personal fortunes above a certain amount; from the fund the government would accumulate, every family would get enough to buy a home, an automobile, and a radio; old-age pensions would be paid; and worthy boys would receive a college education. Though it was far from clear how he proposed to do so, Huey would redistribute not only cash but also real property and securities. "No, sir, money is not all of it by a jugful," he explained. "We are going to redistribute in kind so the poor devil who needs a house can get one from some rich bird who has too many houses; so the man who needs a bedstead can get one from the man who has more than he will ever need.... " In vain did critics point out that the economic assumptions behind Huey's proposal were riddled with error. In a period when FDR was involved in such complicated schemes as gold buying, code authorities, and deficit finance, the promises of the Share Our Wealth campaign seemed more specific and understandable than anything the President was offering.

By 1934 Long, who three years earlier had not even been a sectional leader, was winning national and even international notice. The French journal *L'Europe Nouvelle* published an article titled "Huey Long contre Roosevelt," and H. G. Wells sailed across the Atlantic to interview the senator. After talking to the Kingfish, Wells reported that he was "like a Winston Churchill who has never been at Harrow. He abounds in promises. . . . " For a moment, it even seemed that the Kingfish might eclipse the President.

Roosevelt responded to Long's challenge in a variety of ways, including encouraging the Treasury to look into well-founded rumors of tax evasion in Louisiana. In short order thirty-two Treasury agents were installed at the Monteleone Hotel in New Orleans to investigate the finances of the Long crowd. By April 1935, one of Huey's men in the legislature had been sentenced to eighteen months in prison for income tax evasion, and federal revenue agents were dogging the footsteps of Long's closest associates. There is even some evidence that the government contemplated prosecuting the senator himself.

The President also stepped up his use of patronage against Long. Early in February 1935 Roosevelt scolded cabinet officers and other key officials for awarding patronage to foes of the administration. Some people, he said, should be fired on principle. "In a delicate situation like Louisiana we may have to ask your advice," Secretary Wallace interposed. "You won't have to do that," the President replied forcefully. "Don't put anybody in and don't keep anybody that is working for Huey Long or his crowd! That is a hundred percent! . . . Anybody working for Huey Long is not working for us."

Roosevelt and his appointees also hit out at Long by denying Louisiana a share of New Deal spending. In April 1935, when the senator attempted to supervise the distribution of federal funds in his state, he met his match in the public works administrator Harold Ickes. Secretary Ickes announced that "no public works money is going to build up any Share-the-Wealth political machine," and he threatened to cut off the state's grant. Huey answered, "We are doing the United States government a compliment when we let them do business with us." To which Ickes replied, "The emperor of Louisiana has halitosis of the intellect." Ickes, who could play as rough as Long, then withdrew a substantial amount of federal money that had been destined for Louisiana.

It has often been suggested that the most important response to Long came in the New Deal legislation of the second Hundred Days of 1935. Some writers believe that Roosevelt advanced reforms that year with the deliberate purpose of "stealing Huey's thunder." Two acts in particular are said to show Long's influence. The first was FDR's allocation of fifty million dollars to the National Youth

Administration, an agency that, by giving part-time employment to students, offset the appeal of Long's plank for free college education. In June the President took another step that seemed to indicate a much more conspicuous response to Long: his tax message, asking Congress for a new law based on the idea of redistributing the wealth. "For the time being," wrote the *Los Angeles Times,* "he has silenced Huey and taken him into camp. However hard it comes, the Kingfish must perforce applaud."

Yet it is by no means certain that Roosevelt's ventures in the second Hundred Days were undertaken either as *a* rejoinder to Long or that they significantly diminished Huey's strength. Though it is often said that Roosevelt, like other shrewd statesmen, undercut rivals like Long by sponsoring reforms that alleviated the discontent on which these men fed, that is too simple a perception of political movements. Long won allegiance not simply by advocating specific programs but by appealing to a whole constellation of loyalties and resentments that FDR could not, or would not, embody.

The vast following Long had acquired posed a serious threat to Roosevelt in itself, and if the Kingfish could align behind him the supporters of the radio priest Father Coughlin, the old-age pension advocate Dr. Francis Townsend, and the farm leader Milo Reno, he would be more powerful still.

The Share Our Wealth organization provided Long not merely with backing for his scheme but with a countrywide political organization that might shape the outcome of the 1936 elections, and Share Our Wealth was sweeping the country like a prairie fire. Raymond Moley, Roosevelt's former adviser, wrote that the administration came to fed that Long "could make himself political master of the whole, vast Lower Mississippi Valley—perhaps even of great hunks of the West. Who knew where Huey . . . would end?"

Maybe the Democrats worried too much. The subsequent fiasco of the Union party in 1936, a third party that attempted to unite the Long, Coughlin, and Townsend followers, demonstrated what Roosevelt had earlier foreseen. "There is no question that it is all a dangerous situation," the President had confided to Colonel House in 1935. "But when it comes to Show-down these fellows cannot all lie in the same bed and will fight among themselves with almost absolute certainty."

Yet in 1935 Huey was still only forty-two, and his ambitions were boundless; so, many believed, were his prospects. Roosevelt had a long way to go to get the country out of the Depression. And there was no mistaking Long's intent. "I'll tell you here and now," he informed newspaper reporters late in the summer of 1935, "that Franklin Roosevelt will not be the next President of the United States. If the Democrats nominate Roosevelt and the Republicans nominate Hoover, Huey Long will be your next President."

"As God is my judge," Gerald L. K. Smith cried in 1935, "the only way they will keep Huey Long from the White House is to kill him." At least as early as 1934 Long's opponents were talking openly of violence as the only way of ridding the state of the senator and his cronies. In the spring of 1935 one of the few remaining Long opponents in Baton Rouge warned: "I am not gifted with second sight. . .. But I can see blood on the polished floor of this Capitol. For if you ride this thing through, you will travel with the white horse of death."

On the night of September 8, 1935, the Louisiana legislature was meeting in special session to adopt a series of recommendations, some of which stunned even Huey's disciples. One proposed to terminate the career of a Long opponent, Judge Benjamin Pavy; another portended a constitutional crisis by providing for the imprisonment of federal officials. Huey wandered around the legislative chamber that evening in his usual manner—as though he owned it—and then walked out into the corridor of the state capitol. At 9:20 P.M., a white-clad, bespectacled figure stepped out of the shadows from behind a pillar, approached Huey, and fired a small pistol. Long's bodyguards and capitol policemen emptied their guns into the assassin, whose bullet-ridden body was subsequently identified as that of Judge Pavy's son-in-law, Dr. Carl Austin Weiss, who had resented Long's vendetta against his family. Mortally wounded, Huey reeled down the stairs and into a car in the parking lot. Two days later he died.

The assassination of Long ended the only potentially serious political threat to FDR in the 1930s. The Share Our Wealth movement quickly disintegrated. Gerald L. K. Smith tried to seize control of the organization, but Long's henchmen in Louisiana would have none of him. They had no interest in sharing the wealth, no thirst for national power, merely a desire for plunder. As a Louisiana governor later explained, "I swore to uphold the constitutions of Louisiana and the United States, but I didn't take any vow of poverty."

The Long machine had only one concern: to persuade Washington to abandon the tax prosecutions. In return it was willing to throw its support to the President. The details of what happened subsequently are murky. The Roosevelt administration was accused of reaching an accommodation with Long's heirs—what one columnist called the Second Louisiana Purchase. Perhaps it did, but the evidence is not clearcut. (Some years later, both the governor of Louisiana and the president of LSU would go to the penitentiary) However, one thing is certain: at the 1936 Democratic convention, Long's lieutenants waved FDR banners and paraded the aisles for the great and good Franklin Delano Roosevelt.

The administration greeted Long's death with ill-concealed relief. A few weeks afterward, the Democratic national chairman, Jim Farley, remarked, "I always laughed Huey off, but I did not feel that way about him," and then went on to list a number of states that FDR would have lost if the Louisiana senator had run for President. In his lengthy memoir and biography, Rexford Tugwell has reflected "When he was gone it seemed that a beneficent peace had fallen on the land. Father Coughlin, Reno, Townsend, *et al.*, were after all pygmies compared with Huey. He had been a major phenomenon."

Tugwell, one of the original members of the Brain Trust, has captured better than anyone Roosevelt's own response to the death of his most troublesome rival:

"I think he had really given Franklin concern for a bit. . . . It was not a happy circumstance that one of the most effective demagogues the country had ever known should be attacking with spectacular effect every move and every measure devised to meet the situation. It did get on Franklin's nerves. He must have regarded Huey's removal as something of a providential occurrence—one more sign that he himself moved under a star."

14. The Innocent Bystander

Robert A. Divine

"The only thing we have to fear is fear itself," declared Franklin D. Roosevelt in his first inaugural address on March 4, 1933. The fear that the new President sought to assuage was a very real one. That morning the governors of New York and Illinois had closed the banks in their states, and the country's financial life virtually ceased. The nation was at the moment of deepest crisis in the great depression, and the American people waited anxiously for Roosevelt to take decisive action. Focusing on the domestic emergency, the President barely mentioned foreign affairs in his speech. "In the field of world policy I would dedicate this Nation to the policy of the good neighbor—the neighbor who resolutely respects himself and, because he does so, respects the rights of others."[1] Thus, with one generality, Roosevelt dismissed his country's role in world affairs.

Eight years later, fear again spread through the United States. German armies had swept over Europe, driving France into lightning defeat and forcing the British off the Continent. In the summer of 1941, Nazi forces were advancing on Leningrad and Moscow, and military commentators were predicting the fall of Russia by the end of the year. The threat in the Far East was even more awesome. Japan had gained control of the most valuable provinces of China and was moving into Southeast Asia, threatening the British in Malaya, the Dutch in the East Indies, and the American outpost of the Philippines. At home, Roosevelt had carried out his New Deal program, but now both he and the American people had to face a new challenge. The "good neighbor" phrase of the 1930s, made meaningful in Latin American policy, resounded irrationally in a world of bad neighbors who threatened the security of the United States. The challenge of aggression was a fact most Americans learned slowly in the depression decade. But their teachers, Hitler, Mussolini, and the Japanese militarists, provided the dramatic instruction that gradually destroyed the isolationist mood of the 1930's and led to American entry into the Second World War.

I

When the new administration took office in the early spring of 1933, many observers believed that it would make sweeping changes in American foreign policy. Under the Republican Presidents of the 1920s, the United States had held itself aloof from the world, engaging in many diplomatic conferences, tightening the stranglehold on the world's economy the nation had achieved during the

[1]Samuel Rosenman, ed., *The Public Papers and Addresses of Franklin D. Roosevelt* (13 vols.; New York, 1938–1950), II, 11,14.

First World War, but refusing to take responsibility for the peace of the world. After rejection of the Treaty of Versailles and the League of Nations by the Senate in 1919-20, the United States dedicated itself to a nationalistic foreign policy. Tariffs were raised, payment of war debts demanded, and political guarantees and commitments adamantly avoided. Taking as their motto, what is good for the United States is good for the world, the American people supported a foreign policy of self-indulgence that reflected the hedonistic mood of the 1920s. When challenged by foreign critics, Americans could point to the Kellogg-Briand Pact—the treaty which outlawed war except in self-defense.

The election of Franklin D. Roosevelt marked the return to power of the party of Woodrow Wilson, and thus seemed to promise a break with the nationalism of the 1920s. Roosevelt had been a loyal Wilsonian, serving as Assistant Secretary of the Navy and later running as Vice-Presidental candidate in 1920 on a pro-League platform. In the 1920s Roosevelt continued to champion the League and internationalism, playing a leading role in the creation of the Woodrow Wilson Foundation, which sought to perpetuate Wilson's ideals in foreign policy. As an aspiring politician, he gradually shifted with the prevailing nationalist sentiment. In 1922 he wrote his former running mate, James Cox, "I am not wholly convinced that the country is quite ready for a definite stand on our part in favor of immediate entry into the League of Nations."[2] Later in the decade, when he was developing more serious ambitions for the White House, Roosevelt wrote an article for the periodical *Foreign Affairs* in which he endorsed the principle of international cooperation in glowing terms but carefully avoided making any specific commitments. In 1932 political expediency led Roosevelt to repudiate the League of Nations; he stated that it, was no longer the organization that Wilson had struggled to achieve.

Despite Roosevelt's drift away from internationalism, those who hoped to resurrect the Wilsonian ideals rejoiced at his election. They were encouraged by the selection of Cordell Hull as Secretary of State. Hull, a Tennessee Senator who had served in the House during the Wilson years, was a dedicated exponent of international cooperation, particularly the liberalization of trade barriers. Endowed with a salty vocabulary, a rigid code of honor, and a gift for political infighting which enabled him to survive for eleven years in the Roosevelt cabinet, Hull viewed world issues in terms of moral principles. To Hull diplomacy was the art of preaching, not of negotiation. His closest confidant and adviser was Norman H. Davis, a fellow Tennessean who had made a fortune in Cuban sugar and banking. Davis had served as a financial adviser to Wilson at Paris, but had been passed over for the post of Secretary of State by Roosevelt because of his close association with the House of Morgan. He possessed the skill at diplomatic bargaining which Hull lacked, and he was a fervent believer in collective security.

[2]Frank Freidel, *Franklin D. Roosevelt: The Ordeal* (Boston, 1954), p. 122.

The State Department was slanted toward internationalism, but there were some strong balances. Raymond Moley, the Columbia professor who had organized Roosevelt's "brain trust" during the 1932 campaign, became an Assistant Secretary of State much to the disgust of Hull. Moley was an intense economic nationalist who believed that the depression must be beaten at home by government action which would preclude any effort at international currency stabilization or tariff reduction. Moley's views were shared by many key New Dealers in other departments of the government, and the more general belief that foreign policy must play a secondary role until the domestic crisis was eased pervaded the Roosevelt administration. The strength of this sentiment became apparent in June 1933 when Roosevelt, going even beyond Moley's position, undermined the World Economic Conference at London by refusing to agree to currency stabilization. On the economic front the United States was pledged to a nationalist effort to overcome the depression without regard to the rest of the world. The following year Roosevelt finally did accept Hull's proposal for reciprocal tariff reduction, but though many such treaties were signed in the 1930s, the breakdown of world trade had progressed so far in the depression years that little advance was made toward restoring an international economy.

The most serious diplomatic problems facing the new administration came in the Far East. Japan had succeeded in destroying the American Open Door Policy by her conquest of Manchuria in 1931 and 1932. Although Secretary of State Henry L. Stimson protested vigorously against the Japanese aggression, President Herbert Hoover refused to permit any policy stronger than moral disapproval in support of China. Stimson had finally resorted to the device of non-recognition, informing both China and Japan on January 7, 1932, that the United States could not recognize as legal any infringement of American commercial rights in China or the violation of the administrative and territorial integrity of China. The League of Nations eventually supported this non-recognition policy, but Japan ignored it, establishing the puppet state of Manchukuo in the spring of 1932 and finally withdrawing from the League of Nations. Although Stimson's moral sanctions had little effect, he was successful in persuading President-elect Roosevelt to continue the policy of non-recognition of Japanese aggression. Many isolationists feared that Roosevelt would embark on a new crusade against the Japanese, but with the United States preoccupied with the depression and Japan intent on consolidating her gains in Manchuria, the Far Eastern situation eased. Yet, significantly, Roosevelt and Hull were committed to oppose further Japanese aggression in Asia.

The problems of Europe in 1933 were at once less critical and more complex than those of the Far East. The Versailles settlement had left England and France in uneasy control of the European balance of power. Germany had been disarmed by the treaty, and during the early 1920s she had been crippled by inflation. The problem of Germany was one of political stability and economic vitality—potentially the wealthiest and most powerful nation on the continent, her difficulties troubled the victors in the First World War. In the early twenties Germany had turned to the Soviet Union, ignored and rejected by England and France, and the two had agreed at Rapallo on a cautious alignment. The alarmed Western powers had responded by efforts to strengthen the League, and when these failed, they tried traditional diplomacy. At Locarno in 1925, Britain and Italy guaranteed an agreement between Germany, France, and Belgium to respect their common frontiers in the West. In 1926 Germany was admitted to the League of Nations. Although the issue of reparations continued, the major German grievance was disarmament. Under the terms of the Treaty of Versailles, Germany was stripped of her navy and compelled to limit her army to 100,000 men. The victorious powers had pledged themselves to secure general arms limitation in accordance with Wilson's fourth point, but had never done so. When Germany insistently raised the cry of equality in armaments, Britain and France took the preliminary steps toward convening an international disarmament conference at Geneva. After repeated delays the conference opened on February 2, 1932, with an American delegation in attendance.

The disarmament conference moved slowly toward ultimate collapse. Germany demanded equality in arms; France insisted that she could not agree to disarmament without political guarantees for her security. The Soviets called for general and unlimited disarmament, while Britain and the United States advocated limiting "offensive" weapons. When Roosevelt became President, he appointed Norman Davis to head the American delegation. In March 1933 Roosevelt, Hull, and Davis held a series of conferences before Davis left for Geneva. French fear of a rearmed Germany was the great obstacle to agreement, and Davis searched for a way to give France some guarantee of assistance in case of attack by Germany which would be acceptable to Congress. In April Davis cabled home that the United States offer to surrender its traditional neutral rights and agree not to trade with an aggressor in a European conflict. The State Department quickly concurred, and in late April President Roosevelt gave his consent. The State Department was already sponsoring a resolution in Congress, which had originated under Stimson in the Hoover administration, that would permit the President to embargo the export of arms to any country he designated. The House passed this resolution in mid-April, and the administration pressed for Senate approval in order to implement the policy Davis had suggested.

Davis offered the new American proposal to the disarmament conference on May 22, 1933. He told the delegates that if a successful disarmament agreement were achieved, the United States would pledge to meet with other nations when there was a threat to world peace, and if it agreed that one nation was guilty of aggression, "we will refrain from any action tending to defeat such collective effort which these states may thus make to restore peace."[3] Under Davis'

[3]Department of State, *Peace and War: United States Foreign Policy 1931–1941* (Washington, 1943), pp. 188–189.

pledge, though the United States would not join in economic sanctions against an aggressor, it would adjust its policy to avoid defeating measures of collective security adopted by other nations. This was the most advanced position that any official American spokesman had taken on a major issue of world politics since 1919.

Two days later, on May 24, the Senate Foreign Relations Committee met to consider the House resolution which would make the Davis pledge effective. The chairman, Senator Key Pittman of Nevada, best noted for his fondness for silver, liquor, and profanity, cared little for the new departure of the administration, and his committee was dominated by two staunch isolationists, William E. Borah of Idaho and Hiram Johnson of California. Both were Republicans and leaders of the irreconcilables of 1919. Johnson was highly suspicious of the arms embargo resolution, and he insisted that it be amended to apply impartially to all belligerents in any war. Johnson's amendment was designed to change a collective security proposal into an isolationist one, for instead of denying arms to the aggressor, by its terms the President would be compelled to play a weak role, banning arms to the innocent as well as the guilty. Nonetheless, when Pittman confronted Roosevelt with this situation on May 25, the President agreed to accept the Johnson amendment, thereby destroying the policy Davis had announced at Geneva only three days before. An outraged Cordell Hull finally prevailed upon Roosevelt to kill the entire arms embargo resolution in Congress, but the damage had been done. Roosevelt had given way on a major effort to reorient American foreign policy at the first sign of isolationist opposition. There was gloom in the State Department, but among the isolationists on Capital Hill, there was only eagerness to move on from this first victory. As Roosevelt, caught in the midst of domestic crisis, defaulted in his role of leader in foreign policy, Congressional isolationists moved to take his place.

II

The fate of the arms embargo resolution in the Senate revealed the strength of the isolationist leaders in Congress. Johnson and Borah dominated the Foreign Relations Committee. Both were western Progressives who shared the intense nationalism of Teddy Roosevelt without possessing the Republican Roosevelt's broader understanding of world affairs. Although Borah had supported the Kellogg-Briand Pact, his record in foreign affairs was negative; he found a flaw in nearly every proposal and treaty, and his few constructive services came in opposing State Department policies on foreign loans and non-recognition of the Soviet Union. Johnson was even more negative and narrowly vindictive in his view of the world. His single legislative contribution to American foreign policy in more than two decades was the Johnson Act, forbidding private loans to foreign governments in default on their war debt. Johnson and Borah were bitterly suspicious of the British, and they insisted that the United States go its own way in the world, aligning itself with no other nation and defending its own interests, by war if necessary, entirely on its own.

In contrast, many of the other Congressional isolationists abhorred the use of force and favored isolationist policies to avoid involvement in foreign wars. Many who shared the Progressive tradition, notably Senators Robert La Follette, Jr., George Norris, and Gerald P. Nye, reacted against the nationalism of Borah and Johnson; they saw economic forces and special interests as the instigators of war. Norris and La Follette's father had voted against war in 1917, charging that selfish economic interests were behind the conflict, and Nye, although he favored war in 1917, came to share this viewpoint by the 1930s. All three men represented the Middle West, with its ethnic ties to Germany, its interior geographic location, and its agrarian economy—factors which historians have identified with isolationism. Above all, these men viewed the depression as a long-range result of the First World War, and they attributed the causes of that war to greedy manufacturers and bankers who had sought to profit from the wartime trade with the Allies. They were determined to do all they could to prevent future wars and the economic breakdowns that followed.

Outside Congress there was a strong pacifist movement which had gained strength all through the 1920s. Many of the older, conservative peace societies, such as the American Peace Society, the World Peace Foundation, and the Carnegie Endowment for International Peace, continued their educational work, supporting the League of Nations as the best hope for mankind. A large number of more radical pacifist societies had sprung up during and after the First World War. Uncompromising in their aims, they condemned the League because it relied ultimately on force through economic and military sanctions to preserve world peace. Demanding total disarmament as the only way to abolish war, such groups as the National Society for the Prevention of War and the Women's International League for Peace and Freedom sent observers to disarmament conferences, hired lobbyists to appear before Congressional committees, and organized American women and the churches in their cause.

In the early 1930s the failure of the disarmament conferences led the pacifist leaders to search for villains. They found them among the industrialists and financiers who controlled the munitions industry. A series of books and magazine articles appeared in 1933 and 1934 dealing with the "blood brotherhood," the international ring of arms makers who were accused of fomenting wars, sabotaging disarmament, and inciting arms races. With the spotlight focused on the munitions makers, Miss Dorothy Detzer, the skillful and persuasive lobbyist for the Women's International League, believed it was time to press for a Congressional investigation of the arms trade, which she hoped would lead to the nationalization of the munitions industry. She approached Senator George Norris, who strongly approved her idea, and together they went down the roster of the Senate to select the man to conduct the probe. Ruling out senator after senator, they finally had one name left—Gerald P. Nye of North Dakota. With Norris' help,

Miss Detzer succeeded in persuading Nye to introduce a resolution calling for a Senate investigation of the arms trade. As a result of some shrewd parliamentary maneuvering, Nye won approval for his committee, and when Vice-President Garner allowed the committee to name its own chairman, the group surprised the administration by selecting the Republican Nye.

The Nye committee began its public hearings in September, 1934. All summer long a group of investigators had poured through the records of such firms as the Du Pont Company, Remington Arms, and Bethlehem Steel, and had subpoenaed thousands of letters, confidential agreements, and legal memorandums. When the executives of these corporations testified before the committee, they were asked to explain the conduct of their firms. But the committee was interested in exposure, not explanation. The testimony and the official exhibits, which covered the years 1914 to 1934, revealed many unsavory details of the arms trade—the huge profits of munitions makers in the war, the close connections of the arms makers with the War and Navy Departments, the unscrupulous sales techniques used to export arms to Latin America and China. Outside the hearing room Nye made speeches suggesting that American entry into the war was based solely on economic factors. The records of the committee hearings did not substantiate this indictment, but the bold headlines and the dramatic charges that appeared day after day in the daily press brought this message home to the American people.

Walter Millis, a young editorial writer for the New York *Herald Tribune,* reinforced the Nye thesis with his popular historical account, *Road to War: America, 1914-1917.* Although Millis avoided the crude economic charges that Nye made, he showed that American policy from 1914 to 1917 allowed the Allies to develop a huge and increasingly indispensable war trade with the United States that was closed to Germany. Calling the United States "a silent partner of the Entente," Millis levelled his sharpest barbs at Colonel House, who he felt misled Wilson into such an unneutral policy.[4] Millis never reached any specific conclusion, but his book, which became a Book-of-the-Month selection, left the indelible impression that American entry into the World War had been a tragic mistake.

While the isolationists developed their economic theories over American entry into the First World War, they met determined opposition from a small but highly articulate band of internationalists. Although the oratory of Woodrow Wilson had failed to sway the Senate in 1919, this great idealist had won the support of a large number of men for his concept of collective security. In 1922, a group of staunch Wilsonians had gathered together in New York City to found an organization to work for eventual American entry into the League of Nations. Calling itself the League of Nations Non-Partisan Association, this new pressure group was led by John Clarke, who resigned from the Supreme Court to devote himself to the internationalist movement, and George W. Wickersham,

[4]Walter Millis, *Road to War: America, 1914–1917* (Boston, 1935), p. 89.

who had served as Attorney General under Taft. The League of Nations Association centered in the East, and its members lobbied strenuously in 1924 to get the Democratic and Republican parties to support entry into the League of Nations in their party platforms. When this effort failed, the Association changed its goal, and while it affirmed eventual entry into the League, it now focused attention on the drive to gain American membership into the World Court. This judicial body, separate from the League of Nations, was designed to provide an impartial panel of judges to arbitrate international disputes voluntarily submitted to it. Despite endorsement by both Presidents Harding and Coolidge, and by virtually every professional and business group in the nation, the Senate refused to sanction American membership in the Court without adding a reservation which proved unacceptable to the other members.

While the League of Nations Association spent its energy on lost causes in the 1920s, other groups formed with the broader goal of educating the American people on world affairs without advocating any one approach. During the Paris Peace Conference in 1919, members of the American delegation, led by General Tasker H. Bliss, began meeting with members of the British delegation, and laid plans to found an institute for international affairs with branches in England and America. In 1921, the American group, composed of experts on diplomacy from government service and universities, merged with a group of New York businessmen to found the Council on Foreign Relations. The original directors included Norman H. Davis and George Wickersham, and though the organization refused to champion specific policies, it became the headquarters for the internationalist viewpoint in foreign policy, publishing the distinguished periodical *Foreign Affairs,* and bringing together regularly leaders of business and finance with academic and government specialists.

The Foreign Policy Association was also born at the close of the World War. A liberal group led by Charles A. Beard and Herbert Croly met in New York City in the spring of 1918 to back Wilson's fourteen points. They formed a group known as the League of Free Nations Association, changing into the Foreign Policy Association after the defeat of the Treaty and the League in the Senate. Unlike the Council on Foreign Relations, which concentrated only on the elite, the Foreign Policy Association set out to reach the entire American public. It established a research department in 1925, and sent out a weekly bulletin to newspaper editors to insure the dissemination of accurate reports on world affairs. By the 1930s the Foreign Policy Association had developed a wide range of publications designed to make the American people internationally conscious and aware of their responsibility for peace.

In the 1930s the internationalists, despite repeated setbacks and frustrations, appeared to grow in strength as world events bore out their prophecies. In the previous decade their warnings of eventual war unless all nations united in collective security seemed unreal. With the Manchurian crisis and the advent of Hitler, internationalists spoke with new vigor, confident that they had the only sane solution to world problems. They renewed their pleas for American membership on the World Court, and finally in January 1935 the Senate again debated this question. To the dismay of the internationalists, an avalanche of last-minute letters and telegrams stirred up by Father Coughlin and the Hearst press resulted in the defeat of the World Court protocol by seven votes in the Senate. Internationalism was still a minority view.

III

Most Americans in the 1930s were neither isolationists nor internationalists. Rather than adhering to any dogmatic views of foreign policy, they simply ignored the world. They no longer had any specific goals in their foreign policy beyond the naive desire to live and let live. The sense of mission which had powered America's rise to world power had burnt itself out in Wilson's great crusade, and most Americans were content to drift. This indifference meant that American foreign policy would be framed not in Washington but in foreign capitals—in London and Paris, in Moscow and Rome, and mainly in Berlin and Tokyo. With the President deeply involved in overcoming the depression, Congress dominated by isolationists, and the people apathetic toward international affairs, the United States played the role of innocent bystander as the world edged slowly toward war.

15. Death March

Donald Knox

The battle for the Philippines produced one of the most ghastly episodes of World War II when thousands of sick, hungry, exhausted American and Filipino troops surrendered to the Japanese 14th Army on Bataan and were hastily evacuated from the area in a forced march up the peninsula. By the Japanese military code, a soldier who surrendered was a traitor, worthy of the utmost contempt; the prisoners were treated accordingly. In the book Death March: The Survivors of Bataan *Donald Knox interviewed eighty of the survivors and set down the devastating experience they lived through entirely in their own words. The following excerpt begins with the surrender on April 9, 1942.*

Chicago *Herald American*, April 10: Announcement of the fall of Bataan was made in a brief communiqué . . . followed later by a statement from Secretary of War Stimson that the fate of the encircled defenders is not known, although they apparently face death or surrender.

Captain Mark Wohlfeld: We dropped all our guns and stuff on the ground. No fear. Relief. Standing in a file. There was a heavy concentration of Jap planes hitting the Filipinos off to the West. Here's the damned cease-fire and they're still plastering the poor Filipinos on the other side of the ridge. . . . We were lined up on a dirt road. The day was beginning like all the others—hot!

Soon we heard a lot of hubbub at the forward end of the line, way ahead of us around the bend in the road, and we saw our first Japanese. The first ones were artillerymen carrying a mountain howitzer. They were cheerful-looking little fellows and they smiled as they walked by. They were all covered in sweat, and we were amazed at the weight they carried. One carried a wheel, another the tube, another the trail, another the packs of the fellows carrying the piece. They all had flies around their heads. Having been in the jungle for a while, they were filthy.

After them came the infantry and they were a lot more vicious. They started to go through our pockets. Some knew a little English and hollered, "Go you to hell! Go you to hell!" One of the Japs went over to Colonel Sewell and showed that he wanted the colonel to take off his wedding ring. Sewell kept refusing. About then a Jap came up to me and cleaned me out. Then he reached in my back pocket. Suddenly he jumped back and the bayonet came up real fast between my eyes. I reached into my pocket and found a rifle clip I'd forgotten about. Quickly I dropped it on the ground. The Jap took his rifle and cracked me across the head. I fell. My head was covered in blood. When I looked up I saw Sewell couldn't get his wedding ring off, and the Jap was about to take his bayonet and cut it off along with the finger. Sewell saw me and he reached over to get some of my blood which he used to wiggle the ring off. Then he was slapped and kicked.

Captain Loyd Mills: After relieving me of my weapons and taking my wristwatch and rings, this big Jap lieutenant asked, "Do you like Roosevelt?" And I thought, "Oh, Christ, what am I going to say now?" If I say the wrong thing I've had it. I told him that Roosevelt was my commander and that I did what he told me to do. He slapped me on the back. "You O.K.," he said. "You army, me army, too. Are you hungry?" We stayed with them all that day and night. They were front-line troops, so we got better treatment from them than we did from the service troops later who were our guards. . . .

Private First Class John Falconer: When the order to surrender came, it was a great relief to me. I should have been very wary, very fearful, but I wasn't. I thought it was a beautiful day. We found some abandoned trucks and some food. I had, right then, one of the best meals I've ever eaten in my life. I had creamed peas on toast. While we waited for the Japanese we sang songs.

The first Japs we saw were bone tired. They marched right past us. One Jap infantry private was so exhausted that he stumbled and fell in front of us Americans. A Jap officer gave some command, two riflemen came up, picked up the fallen soldier, took him off the road where we couldn't see him. Then we heard a shot and the two Japs returned alone.

Sergeant Ralph Levenberg: I had a pair of especially made tinted rimless glasses. I got pulled out of the line by this Jap guard who wanted my glasses. When he pulled them off I tried to motion to him that he wouldn't be able to see out of them, but he kept grunting and making it very clear that he was bound and determined to have a pair of American sunglasses. About then came along the tallest Jap I'd ever seen in my life. A lieutenant. He yelled, and this little guard froze at attention. The lieutenant came over and returned the glasses to me and indicated I should put them away. Then he turned on this private who was still at complete attention. The officer removed a small sword sheath from his belt and began beating this guard in the face with it, murmuring Japanese comments to him the whole time. That guard never wavered until he dropped completely unconscious. His face was just absolutely like he'd been run over with a tractor. I got back in line and kept my glasses in my pocket.

Captain Loyd Mills: At one stop a Japanese sergeant, who spoke beautiful Oxford-type English, came up to me. He wasn't one of our guards but happened to be around. He said something to me that I've always remembered: "You are going to find a lot of bad Japanese and you are going to find a lot of good ones. Please don't think that all the Japanese are alike as far as the treatment you are going to receive." Then he opened up a can of sardines, and with some rice, gave them to me and the men around me. It was the first real food I'd had in days.

With the surrender of Bataan, General Homma [the Japanese commanding officer] still faced the problem of subduing the American garrison on Corregidor, a short two miles away in Manila Bay. Only when Corregidor surrendered could Japan claim her most valuable prize—the Philippines. For the Japanese 14th Army the campaign was not yet over. Before this decisive battle could begin, however, it was necessary for the Japanese to remove the enormous number of prisoners which Major General Edward P. King had just surrendered. . . . Anticipating this problem in late March, an evacuation plan was developed by Homma's staff. The plan was simple; the captives would walk out of Bataan as far as San Fernando. There, they would be shipped by rail to a prison camp [Camp O'Donnell] in central Luzon. From Mariveles on Bataan's southern tip to San Fernando is almost sixty miles. Plans to feed and care for the prisoners along the road were proposed and agreed upon. Unfortunately for the men of the Luzon Force, the Japanese plan for their evacuation was based on three assumptions, all of which proved false. The first miscalculation assumed the surrendered force to be in good physical condition. The second error was in not allowing enough time to work out all the details of a proper evacuation. Lastly, the Japanese made a faulty estimate in the number of troops they would have to move. They assumed the figure would be between forty and fifty thousand men.

Because of the chaos that followed the disintegration of the Luzon Force, it is impossible even today to give a precise number to the men who took part in the march out of Bataan. . . . An educated guess, however, puts sixty two thousand Filipinos and ten thousand Americans on the march.

Sergeant Ralph Levenberg: Mariveles. Now that was confusion! It reminded me of what it might have been like when the Jews exited Egypt into the desert—no one knowing where they were going or what they should take or how long it would take to get where they were going. Mariveles—tanks, trucks, cars, horses, artillery—like a Philippines Times Square. . . . And everything buried in dust, horrendous amounts of dust being churned up by the tanks and trucks. You realized that Homma's shock troops were coming down Bataan on their way to taking Corregidor. The Japanese were just in a rush to get us out of their way. Our officers were milling around, trying to find out what was going on. The Japanese officers also seemed confused as to what they were supposed to do with this pack of hungry, sick, bedraggled men they had captured.

Private First Class Blair Robinett: My group came up the road from Mariveles another half mile or so when a Jap soldier stepped out, came across, and took my canteen out of its cover. He took a drink, filled his canteen out of mine, poured the rest of my water on the ground, and dropped the canteen at my feet.

I thought he was going to walk back to the line of Jap troops standing across the road, so I bent over to pick up my canteen. But he turned around and hit me on the head with his rifle butt. Put a crease in the top of my head that I still have. I fell face down on the cobblestones. I crawled back up to my knees, debating whether to pick up the canteen again. I figured the best course of action was to stand up and leave the canteen alone. Soon as the Jap troops moved off, I squatted down and picked it up. .. .

We moved down the ridge a ways when we saw this GI. He was sick, I figured he had come out of the hospital that was in tents out under the trees. He was wobbling along, uneasy on his feet. There were Japanese infantry and tanks coming down the road alongside us. One of these Jap soldiers, I don't know whether he was on our side or if he deliberately came across the road, but he grabbed this sick guy by the arm and guided him to the middle of the road. Then he just flipped him out across the road. The guy hit the cobblestone about five feet in front of a tank and the tank pulled on across him. Well, it killed him quick. There must have been ten tanks in that column, and every one of them came up there right across the body. When the last tank left there was no way you could tell there'd ever been a man there. But his uniform was embedded in the cobblestones. The man disappeared, but his uniform had been pressed until it had become part of the ground.

Now we knew, if there had been any doubts before, we were in for a bad time.

Sergeant Ralph Levenberg: One of the tricks that the Japs used to play on us—thought it was funny, too—was when they would be riding on the back of a truck, they would have these long black snake whips, and they'd whip that thing out and get some poor bastard by the neck or torso and drag him behind their truck. 'Course if one of our guys was quick enough he didn't get dragged too far. But, if the Japs got a sick guy. . . .

The thing that burned itself into my mind for days and days was the imprint of a body in the road that had been run over, I don't know how many times. It was paper thin, but the shape was very clear. It was as if the guy was still pleading for somebody to reach down and pick him up.

Sergeant Charles Cook: By the second day I'd thrown my tent half away, my pistol belt away, and everything else extra. I had cut a piece out of my mosquito netting, just enough to cover my face and hands when I laid down. These little squares and my canteen are the only things I carried. Everything else weighed a ton. All I was interested in after a while was trying to take one step at a time. . . .

I know one time I broke ranks to fill my canteen with water, I heard this Jap holler. He was running up to me. So I ran through the back of the barrio, jumping fences and scattering chickens. I came back to the column and just mixed in with the men. The guard never found me. I don't know which day this was, it was just on the walk.

Captain Loyd Mills: The nights were the worst times for me. We walked all day, from early morning until dusk. Then we were put into barbed-wire enclosures in which the conditions were nearly indescribable. Filth and defecation all over the place. The smell was terrible. These same enclosures had been used every night, and when my group got to them, they were covered by the filth of five or six nights.

I had dysentery pretty bad, but I didn't worry about it because there wasn't anything you could do about it. You didn't stop on the March because you were dead if you did. They didn't mess around with you. You didn't have time to pull out and go over and squat. You would just release wherever you were. Generally right on yourself, or somebody else if they happened to be in your way. There was nothing else to do. Without food it was water more than anything. . . .

Private Leon Beck: They'd halt us at these big artesian wells. There'd be a four-inch pipe coming up out of the ground which was connected to a well, and the water would be flowing full force out of it. There were hundreds of these wells all over Bataan. They'd halt us intentionally in front of these wells so we could see the water and they wouldn't let us have any. Anyone who would make a break for the water would be shot or bayoneted. Then they were left there. Finally it got so bad further along the road that you never got away from the stench of death. There were bodies laying all along the road in various degrees of decomposition—swollen, burst open, maggots crawling by the thousands—black, featureless corpses. And they stank!

Sometimes they'd make us stand at attention two or three hours. They'd just stop us and make us stand still. If you got caught sloughing off, shifting your weight from one foot to another, you'd get beaten. I remember very distinctly being beaten once. They hit me with a stalk of sugar cane, which is a pretty heavy instrument. Sugar cane grows anywhere from a half inch to three inches in diameter and has a very hard skin on it. It doesn't wear out very easy. And they beat me all about the head and shoulders. I can only remember being fed three times, and that consisted of walking past a gasoline drum that they were boiling rice in. You'd hold your hands out and a Filipino or a Japanese, depending on who was serving, would throw a spoonful of rice in your hands, and the next one would throw some salt on it, and you kept right on walking while eating out of your hands. . . . And the weather was hot, hot, hot. The sun comes up hot, and it goes down hot, and it stays hot at night. It was just plain hell hot. . . .

Sergeant Forrest Knox: We were waiting in the sun. In an open rice paddy. We stayed there without water till a half dozen men had passed out from the heat. Then we were ripe. The guards put us on the road and double-timed us. Every kilometer they changed the guards because they could not stand to double-time in the sun either. After a couple of miles you could hear the shooting start at the tail of the column as the clean-up squad went to work. The old Indian gauntlet with an Oriental twist. . . .

Private Leon Beck: When it came daylight the Japanese would wake you up, make you form columns of four and stand at attention. Maybe once or twice they would allow an individual to collect a bunch of canteens so that he could go and get water. Then again maybe they wouldn't. It depended on the individual guards you were with.

First thing we would try to do is get all the men who were in the worst shape up to the front of the columns. That way as they got tired, and the men who were helping them wore out, we could pass them slowly back through the column taking turns holding them or helping them. We knew if a man reached a point where he couldn't walk any more, he was going to be killed. So we tried to take turns helping the sick and injured. Sometimes we would prevail upon the guards to let us regroup and we'd be able to put the sick back up front. Sometimes we couldn't.

Staff Sergeant Harold Feiner: I don't know if the guards were Korean or Taiwanese. I was so miserable on that Death March that I couldn't tell you what they were. I know one thing about them, though—they were mean, sadistic, brutal. And yet, on the March I was befriended.

I had been hit at Cabcaben and had a piece of Corregidor shrapnel in my leg. It was the size of a piece of pencil lead and was laying along my shin bone. I had wrapped an old white towel around it and had managed to walk about fifteen miles, but I was getting weaker and more feverish the further I went. I was in bad shape. Guys had to help me. They would kind of hold onto me. If you fell, you were dead. They bayoneted you right away. . . . If you fell, bingo, you were dead.

We finally stopped for the night near a small stream and I laid down. About an hour later this guy comes crawling along. He looked like an Italian, swarthy, kind of muscular. "Hey, fellows, any of you guys need any help?" he was whispering. "I'm a doctor." Didn't give us his name. When he got to me, he stopped and I told him about my leg. Just then a young guard saw us and came over. The first thing they did was hit you with their rifle butts. He spoke atrocious English and he yelled for us to separate. The doctor kept talking, and asked him would it be all right if he took the shrapnel out of my leg. "Wait, wait, wait," and he ran out into the road to see if anyone was coming. Then he came back and said, "Hurry, hurry. "I remember the doctor saying, "Soldier, this is going to hurt. If you can take it, I'll get it out." He never had to worry about me hurting. As soon as he touched it, barn, I passed out. He took it out and wrapped a hand towel around my shin. When he left he said, "Yeah, well, I hope to God you make it. God bless you." He disappeared and I never got to know his name.

The Jap guard came up to me during the night and gave me a cup of sweetened chocolate, tasted like milk. I hadn't had any food and no water for days. I didn't speak one single word of Japanese then, but he could speak a little English, but with a really horrible accent. "Someday me go Hollywood, me going to be movie star." That's the way he talked. He made me laugh. All through the night he gave me something, because he knew I needed strength. In the morning he was gone. His squad had been replaced by another. The orders were given, "Everybody up, up, up." We got in line and I found I couldn't walk. My leg hurt so much. Some guys held me up and I was carried about a hundred feet to the road. There we were told to stop and sit down. Then we were told to get up. We waited about a half an hour before we were permitted to sit down again. Then we were turned around and marched back to where we started. Wait . . . rest . . . wait . . . turn around . . . go back. We did this the whole day. I never had to walk, and by the time we started out the next day I had enough strength to limp along on my own. I'm not a religious man, but God said keep those men there, we want to save that man. I don't know what it was. I know I wouldn't have made it, if I had to march that day.

Maybe a day or so later we came to a river. I was still in fairly bad shape. There were a lot of little rivers, and because it was the dry season, they were shallow. The bridge had been knocked out and the Japanese had reconstructed an engineering bridge. Since their troops were crossing it when we arrived, we were made to march down the bank, cross the river, and march up the other side. Sounds simple. We were told not to touch the water. Some of the guys managed to drag their towels in the water and got some water that way. One man, however, reached over and tried to cup his hands and drink some. He was twelve feet from me. They shot him. Some guards on the bridge just popped him off Going up the other side was hard for me with my leg. I kept sliding on the slimy clay. Finally some guys helped me up.

When we got to the top of the bank, there was a little bend in the road before it crossed the bridge. At that point some Jap sentries were stationed and they were laughing at our struggles. When I got to the top—mind you, I was still crippled—for some reason, maybe because I needed help, one of the sentries took his rifle by the barrel and swung it at me and broke the ribs on my right side. Then I walked with broken ribs and a wounded leg. But I got to San Fernando. Had lots of help. But, hell, guys got there with less than me.

Private First Class Blair Robinett: There was something I couldn't figure out. Looking down, I saw one footprint in the dust. It was dark and it was a perfect footprint shape. Only one, though. Now, I couldn't imagine how a one-legged man could be walking. Finally, I saw a man in front of me limping badly and his leg had blood running down it. Then I figured out how I could see one print. It was being left by the blood. A mile or so later his limp was so bad that he dropped out of the line.

Corporal Robert Wolfersberger: I could see some artillery pieces by the side of the road and some Japs taking a break in the shade. Some of them had tied a big pole onto a tree so that it could swing back and forth. With this they were taking turns raking it through the column of men. It was a big game to them, seeing how many of us they could knock down with one swoosh of this pile driver across the road. Some guys would duck or fall down, and the guy behind would stumble. It created a lot of confusion.

Of course we had a grapevine that worked like a telephone. Word traveled pretty fast. If there was trouble up ahead the word would come back down the column, and those who could, would walk more lightly. When we saw the trucks carrying infantry, we learned to get as far off the road as we could. The Jap troops would carry bamboo sticks—rifle butts were heavy—and they'd lean out and swat you as they went by. If they didn't have sticks, they had stones or knotted ropes. They'd just swing whatever they had and see if they could hit you.

Second Lieutenant Kermit Lay: There was a big tin warehouse or granary somewhere along the March that they packed us into one night. You could sit or lay down but there was no water and it was very hot. And it stank! The next morning across the road the Japs had dug a hole and had some Filipino soldiers burying some dead men, except not everyone was dead. One poor soul kept trying to claw his way out of the hole. The Jap guards really started giving these Filipinos a hard time, trying to get them to cover this man up faster. Finally a Jap came over, took a shovel and beat him on the head with it. Then he had the Filipinos cover him up.

Private First Class Blair Robinett: One morning they moved us out into what I imagine was a *camote,* or sweet potato field. We were crowded up against one another, column after column moved in. Side by side we sat with our arms folded, heads bowed with the sun beating down on the back of our necks. I sat there three or four hours. The heat tore into the middle of the field. . . . What I remember next is a guard poking me with his bayonet trying to get me on my feet. I looked up at him and said, "Go ahead, you son of a bitch, do it." An American Air Force sergeant was standing alongside me, I don't know who he was, but he reached down and grabbed me and pulled me to my feet and into the line. He and somebody else held me between them when we began to walk. I couldn't manage to stand up. I told them they should leave me. "Oh, no," he said, "couldn't do that. You need something inside you." He had his blouse tucked into his pants and there was a bulge around his waist. He reached into his shirt and came out with a raw sweet potato. After I'd eaten one or two of them, I was back in business again.

Corporal Hubert Gater: Late in the day my group had been herded into a field surrounded by three strands of barbed-wire. It could have been the town square or close to it. There were a number of Filipino and American soldiers already there. We were so tired, hungry, thirsty, and many so sick or wounded, that we didn't at first notice the condition of those that were there. We would never forget it by the time we left the next day. Fortunately, it was close to dark and we didn't have to sit under the tropical sun. It had been another long, hot day without food and very little water. . . .

Sometime after dark the Japs brought some cans of rice to the enclosure gate. A five-gallon can for each hundred men. These cans were not full. Who cared? Those close to the gate were fed. There was not enough to go around. There was no crowding or pushing. A friend helped a friend. Many didn't care. Besides being tired, many were at the last stage of malaria. Just to be left alone in the grass or dirt to rest, sleep, or die. To have at least one close friend, a buddy to hold you in his arms and comfort you as you died, was enough. The few that still had faith and courage would have lost it if they could have foreseen the future... .

Later I talked to men at Camp O'Donnell who were behind us and arrived at San Fernando a day or two later. The dead had not been buried. The same terrible odor had doubled, and the sick and dying almost filled the area.

Sergeant Charles Cook: The last night outside of San Fernando I walked all night. They changed guards from flatbed trucks. They wouldn't let us stop. All night long. .. . Around dawn I began to feel that my shoes were full of sand. Somewhere we got a short break and I took my shoes off. They weren't full of sand, my feet were just burned up. I had about ten thousand teeny blisters, no bigger than a pin, on the bottom of my feet.

I must have been in one of the first groups that got into the boxcars, because I don't remember hearing a rumor about them. To know that we were there at the railroad station meant riding instead of walking. That was a good feeling, but it turned out worse than the March.

Corporal Hubert Gater: Shortly after noon all that could walk were lined up outside the barbed wire and marched a few blocks to the railroad.

In the months ahead we would realize that each time we left the sick, they would never be seen again.

There was a train and a few boxcars. The Filipino trains are smaller than ours and the boxcars about two-thirds the size we used. Our spirits rose. We were going to ride instead of more marching. In a few minutes we all wished we had continued to march. The box cats had sat in the tropical sun with the doors closed.

The Japs divided us into groups of one hundred men for each car. One Jap guard was assigned to a car. He pulled the door back and motioned inside. The heat from inside hit us in the face. We stalled for time, but the Jap guard with his bayonet motioned us to climb in and he meant business. We all knew by now to openly resist them would be fatal.

We jammed in-standing room only. Into the oven we went and, protest be damned, the doors were closed. The three hours that followed are almost indescribable. Men fainting with no place to fall. Those with dysentery had no control of themselves. As the car swayed, the urine, and the sweat, and the vomit rolled three inches deep back and forth around and in our shoes. Very little complaining.

Private First Class Jack Brady: It seems to me that once in a while our train would stop, and the Jap guards would open the doors so we could get some fresh air. Then is when we'd get the dead ones out. If we could, we'd lift the corpses and pass them over to the door. There was no way we could have passed them through. . . .

Corporal Hubert Gater: We arrived at the small town of Capas. The boxcar doors were opened and we were ordered out. Sit down and be counted. Who could have escaped from that oven? While the Japs were making sure of the count, it gave us the opportunity to take off our shoes and pour the filth on the ground.

After a brief rest, we were told to get up and line up in a column of twos. Then we started marching down a dirt road the last five or six miles to Camp O'Donnell.

Some had marched all the way. A few had come by truck. Those that marched all the way suffered more. . . . It wasn't the miles, it was the continuous delays along the March. The change of Jap command and guards. Standing in place for two or three hours, waiting for the order to start marching again. The lack of food and water, the rundown condition of the men before the start. A combination of all these things would make O'Donnell just one big graveyard.

O'Donnell was only one of the graveyards. Later in the war those still alive were moved to labor camps in Japan where many more starved or were worked to death. Altogether about ten thousand Americans made the Death March: one thousand died. Another five thousand died later while in Japanese hands. Donald Knox, who conducted these interviews, is a television documentary producer based in Minneapolis. He reports that recalling these events—even thirty-five years later—was still so painful for many of the survivors that they would make him stop the tape recorder while they cried.

16. The Biggest Decision: Why We Had to Drop the Atomic Bomb

Robert James Maddox

On August 6, 1945 the world was changed forever with the detonation of an atomic bomb over the Japanese city of Hiroshima, followed three days later with the use of another bomb over Nagasaki. For the next fifty years mankind would live under the threat and fear that these terrible weapons of destruction would be used again. In the age of the Cold War with its reliance on the MAD (mutually assured destruction) policy of the United States and the Soviet Union, it became fashionable among historical revisionists and politically correct pundits to condemn the president who made the decision to use the bombs in 1945. Harry Truman, the plain spoken man from Missouri, never second guessed his decision. For Truman the bombs brought a swift end to the war against Japan and prevented the massive loss of American lives that would have occurred in an invasion of the Japanese islands. Robert James Maddox, author of Weapons of War: Hiroshima Fifty Years Later, *gives an account in this article of the reasons for Truman's decision and the efforts that went into the making of that decision.*

On the morning of August 6, 1945, the American B-29 *Enola Gay* dropped an atomic bomb on the Japanese city of Hiroshima. Three days later another B-29, *Bock's Car,* released one over Nagasaki. Both caused enormous casualties and physical destruction. These two cataclysmic events have preyed upon the American conscience ever since. The furor over the Smithsonian Institution's *Enola Gay* exhibit and over the mushroom-cloud postage stamp last autumn are merely the most obvious examples. Harry S. Truman and other officials claimed that the bombs caused Japan to surrender, thereby avoiding a bloody invasion. Critics have accused them of at best failing to explore alternatives, at worst of using the bombs primarily to make the Soviet Union "more manageable" rather than to defeat a Japan they knew already was on the verge of capitulation.

By any rational calculation Japan was a beaten nation by the summer of 1945. Conventional bombing had reduced many of its cities to rubble, blockade had strangled its importation of vitally needed materials, and its navy had sustained such heavy losses as to be powerless to interfere with the invasion everyone knew was coming. By late June advancing American forces had completed the conquest of Okinawa, which lay only 350 miles from the southernmost Japanese home island of Kyushu. They now stood poised for the final onslaught.

Rational calculations did not determine Japan's position. Although a peace fiction within the government wished to end the war—provided certain conditions were met—militants were prepared to fight on regardless of consequences. They claimed to welcome an invasion of the home islands, promising to inflict such hideous casualties that the United States would retreat from its announced policy of unconditional surrender. The militarists held effective power over the government and were capable of defying the emperor, as they had in the past, on the ground that his civilian advisers were misleading him.

Okinawa provided a preview of what invasion of the home islands would entail. Since April 1 the Japanese had fought with a ferocity that mocked any notion that their will to resist was eroding. They had inflicted nearly 50,000 casualties on the invaders, many resulting from the first large-scale use of kamikazes. They also had dispatched the superbattleship *Yamato* on a suicide mission to Okinawa, where, after attacking American ships offshore, it was to plunge ashore to become a huge, doomed steel fortress. *Yamato* was sunk shortly after leaving port, but its mission symbolized Japan's willingness to sacrifice everything in an apparently hopeless cause.

The Japanese could be expected to defend their sacred homeland with even greater fervor, and kamikazes flying at short range promised to be even more devastating than at Okinawa. The Japanese had more than 2,000,000 troops in the home islands, were training millions of irregulars, and for some time had been conserving aircraft that might have been used to protect Japanese cities against American bombers.

Reports from Tokyo indicated that Japan meant to fight the war to a finish. On June 8 an imperial conference adopted "The Fundamental Policy to Be Followed Henceforth in the Conduct of the War," which pledged to "prosecute the war to the bitter end in order to uphold the national polity, protect the imperial land, and accomplish the objectives for which we went to war." Truman had no reason to believe that the proclamation meant anything other than what it said.

Against this background, while fighting on Okinawa still continued, the President had his naval chief of staff Adm. William D. Leahy, notify the Joint Chiefs of Staff (JCS) and the Secretaries of War and Navy that a meeting would be held at the White House on June 18. The night before the conference Truman wrote in his diary that "I have to decide Japanese strategy—shall we invade Japan proper or shall we bomb and blockade? That is my hardest decision to date. But I'll make it when I have all the facts."

Truman met with the chiefs at three-thirty in the afternoon. Present were Army Chief of Staff Gen. George C. Marshall, Army Air Force's Gen. Ira C. Eaker (sitting in for the Army Air Force's chief of staff, Henry H. Arnold, who was on an inspection tour of installations in the Pacific), Navy Chief of Staff Adm. Ernest J. King, Leahy (also a member of the JCS), Secretary of the Navy James Forrestal, Secretary of War Henry L. Stimson, and Assistant Secretary of War John J. McCloy. Truman opened the meeting, then asked Marshall for his views. Marshall was the dominant figure on the JCS. He was Truman's most trusted military adviser, as he had been President Franklin D. Roosevelt's.

Marshall reported that the chiefs, supported by the Pacific commanders Gen. Douglas MacArthur and Adm. Chester W. Nimitz, agreed that an invasion of Kyushu "appears to be the least costly worthwhile operation following Okinawa." Lodgment in Kyushu, he said, was necessary to make blockade and bombardment more effective and to serve as a staging area for the invasion of Japan's main island of Honshu. The chiefs recommended a target date of November 1 for the first phase, code-named Olympic because delay would give the Japanese more time to prepare and because bad weather might postpone the invasion "and hence the end of the war" for up to six months. Marshall said that in his opinion, Olympic was only course to pursue." The chiefs also proposed that Operation Cornet be launched against Honshu on March 1, 1946.

Leahy's memorandum calling the meeting had asked for casualty projections which that invasion might be expected to produce. Marshall stated that campaigns in the Pacific had been so diverse "it is considered wrong" to make total estimates. All he would say was that casualties during the first thirty days on Kyushu should not exceed those sustained in taking Luzon in the Philippines-3 1,000 men killed, wounded, or missing in action. "It is a grim fact," Marshall said, "that there is not an easy, bloodless way to victory in war." Leahy estimated a higher casualty rate similar to Okinawa, and King guessed somewhere in between.

King and Eaker, speaking for the Navy and the Army Air Forces respectively, endorsed Marshall's proposals. King said that he had become convinced that Kyushu was "the key to the success of any siege operations." He recommended that "we should do Kyushu now" and begin preparations for invading Honshu. Eaker "agreed completely" with Marshall. He said he had just received a message from Arnold also expressing "complete agreement." Air Force plans called for the use of forty groups of heavy bombers, which "could not be deployed without the use of airfields on Kyushu." Stimson and Forrestal concurred.

Truman summed up. He considered "the Kyushu plan all right from the military standpoint" and directed the chiefs to "go ahead with it." He said he "had hoped that there was a possibility of preventing an Okinawa from one end of Japan to the other," but "he was clear on the situation now" and was "quite sure" the chiefs should proceed with the plan. Just before the meeting adjourned, McCloy raised the possibility of avoiding an invasion by warning the Japanese that the United States would employ atomic weapons if there were no surrender. The ensuing discussion was inconclusive because the first test was a month away and no one could be sure the weapons would work.

In his memoirs Truman claimed that using atomic bombs prevented an invasion that would have cost 500,000 American lives. Other officials mentioned the same or even higher figures. Critics have assailed such statements as gross exaggerations designed to forestall scrutiny of Truman's real motives. They have given wide publicity to a report prepared by the Joint War Plans Committee (JWPC) for the chiefs' meeting with Truman. The committee estimated that the invasion of Kyushu, followed by that of Honshu, as the chiefs proposed, would cost approximately 40,000 dead, 150,000 wounded, and 3,500 missing in action for a total of 193,500 casualties.

That those responsible for a decision should exaggerate the consequences of alternatives is commonplace. Some who cite the JWPC report profess to see more sinister motives, insisting that such "low" casualty projections call into question the very idea that atomic bombs were used to avoid heavy losses. By discrediting that justification as a cover-up, they seek to bolster their contention that the bombs really were used to permit the employment of "atomic diplomacy" against the Soviet Union.

The notion that 193,500 anticipated casualties were too insignificant to have caused Truman to resort to atomic bombs might seem bizarre to anyone other than an academic, but let it pass. Those who have cited the JWPC report in countless op-ed pieces in newspapers and in magazine articles have created a myth by omitting key considerations: First, the report itself is studded with qualifications that casualties "are not subject to accurate estimate" and that the projection "is admittedly only an educated guess." Second, the figures never were conveyed to Truman. They were excised at high military echelons, which is why Marshall cited only estimates for the first thirty days on Kyushu. And indeed, subsequent Japanese troop buildups on Kyushu rendered the JWPC estimates totally irrelevant by the time the first atomic bomb was dropped.

Another myth that has attained wide attention is that at least several of Truman's top military advisers later informed him that using atomic bombs against Japan would be militarily unnecessary or immoral, or both. There is no persuasive evidence that any of them did so. None of the Joint Chiefs ever made such a claim, although one inventive author has tried to make it appear that Leahy did by braiding together several unrelated passages from the admiral's memoirs. Actually, two days after Hiroshima, Truman told aides that Leahy had "said up to the last that it wouldn't go off."

Neither MacArthur nor Nimitz ever communicated to Truman any change of mind about the need for invasion or expressed reservations about using the bombs. When first informed about their imminent use only days before Hiroshima, MacArthur responded with a lecture on the future of atomic warfare and even after Hiroshima strongly recommended that the invasion go forward. Nimitz, from whose jurisdiction the atomic strikes would be launched, was notified in early 1945. "This sounds fine," he told the courier, "but this is only February. Can't we get one sooner?" Nimitz later would join Air Force generals Carl D. Spaatz, Nathan Twining, and Curtis LeMay in recommending that a third bomb be dropped on Tokyo.

Only Dwight D. Eisenhower later claimed to have remonstrated against the use of the bomb. In his *Crusade in Europe,* published in 1948, he wrote that when Secretary Stimson informed him during the Potsdam Conference of plans to use the bomb, he replied that he hoped "we would never have to use such a thing against any enemy," because he did not want the United States to be the first to use such a weapon. He added, "My views were merely personal and immediate reactions; they were not based on any analysis of the subject."

Eisenhower's recollections grew more colorful as the years went on. A later account of his meeting with Stimson had it taking place at Ike's headquarters in Frankfurt on the very day news arrived of the successful atomic test in New Mexico. "We'd had a nice evening at headquarters in Germany," he remembered. Then, after dinner, "Stimson got this cable saying that the bomb had been perfected and was ready to be dropped. The cable was in code ... 'the lamb is born' or some damn thing like that." In this version Eisenhower claimed to have protested vehemently that "the Japanese were ready to surrender and it wasn't necessary to hit them with that awful thing." "Well," Eisenhower concluded, "the old gentleman got furious."

The best that can be said about Eisenhower's memory is that it had become flawed by the passage of time. Stimson was in Potsdam and Eisenhower in Frankfurt on July 16, when word came of the successful test. Aside from a brief conversation at a flag-raising ceremony in Berlin on July 20, the only other time they met was at Ike's headquarters on July 27. By then orders already had been sent to the Pacific to use the bombs if Japan had not yet surrendered. Notes made by one of Stimson's aides indicate that there was a discussion of atomic bombs, but there is no mention of any protest on Eisenhower's part. Even if there had been, two factors must be kept in mind. Eisenhower had commanded Allied forces in Europe, and his opinion on how close Japan was to surrender would have carried no special weight. More important, Stimson left for home immediately after the meeting and could not have personally conveyed Ike's sentiments to the President, who did not return to Washington until after Hiroshima.

On July 8 the Combined Intelligence Committee submitted to the American and British Combined Chiefs of Staff a report entitled "Estimate of the Enemy Situation." The committee predicted that as Japan's position continued to deteriorate, it might "make a serious effort to the USSR [then a neutral] as a mediator in ending the war." Tokyo also would put out "intermittent peace feelers" to "weaken the determination of the United Nations to fight to the bitter end, or to create inter-allied dissension." While the Japanese people would be willing to make large concessions to end the war, "For a surrender to be acceptable to the Japanese army, it would be necessary for the military leaders to believe that it would not entail discrediting warrior tradition and that it would permit the ultimate resurgence of a military Japan."

Small wonder that American officials remained unimpressed when Japan proceeded to do exactly what the committee predicted. On July 12 Japanese Foreign Minister Shigenori Togo instructed Ambassador Naotaki Sato in Moscow to inform the Soviets that the emperor wished to send a personal envoy, Prince Fuminaro Konoye, in an attempt to restore peace with all possible speed." Although he realized Konoye could not reach Moscow before the Soviet leader Joseph Stalin and Foreign Minister V. M. Molotov left to attend a Big Three meeting scheduled to begin in Potsdam on the fifteenth, Togo sought to have negotiations begin as soon as they returned.

American officials had long since been able to read Japanese diplomatic traffic through a process known as the magic intercepts. Army intelligence (G-2) prepared for General Marshall its interpretation of Togo's message the next day. The report listed several possible constructions, the most probable being that the Japanese "governing clique" was making a coordinated effort to "stave off defeat" through Soviet intervention and an "appeal to war weariness in the United States." The report added that Undersecretary of State Joseph C. Grew, who had spent ten years in Japan as ambassador, "agrees with these conclusions."

Some have claimed that Togo's overture to the Soviet Union, together with attempts by some minor Japanese officials in Switzerland and other neutral countries to get peace talks started through the Office of Strategic Services (OSS), constituted clear evidence that the Japanese were near surrender. Their sole prerequisite was retention of their sacred emperor, whose unique cultural/religious status within the Japanese polity they would not compromise. If only the United States had extended assurances about the emperor, according to this view, much bloodshed and the atomic bombs would have been unnecessary.

A careful reading of the MAGIC intercepts of subsequent exchanges between Togo and Sato provides no evidence that retention of the emperor was the sole obstacle to peace. What they show instead is that the Japanese Foreign Office was trying to cut a deal through the Soviet Union that would have permitted Japan to retain its political system and its prewar empire intact. Even the most lenient American official could not have countenanced such a settlement.

Togo on July 17 informed Sato that "we are not asking the Russians' mediation in *anything like unconditional surrender* [emphasis added]." During the following weeks Sato pleaded with his superiors to abandon hope of Soviet intercession and to approach the United States directly to find out what peace terms would be offered. "There *is*.. . no alternative but immediate unconditional surrender," he cabled on July 31, and he bluntly informed Togo that "your way of looking at things and the actual situation in the Eastern Area may be seen to be absolutely contradictory." The Foreign Ministry ignored his pleas and continued to seek Soviet help even after Hiroshima.

"Peace feelers" by Japanese officials abroad seemed no more promising from the American point of view. Although several of the consular personnel and military attachés engaged in these activities claimed important connections at home, none produced verification. Had the Japanese government sought only an assurance about the emperor, all it had to do was grant one of these men authority to begin talks through the OSS. Its failure to do so led American officials to assume that those involved were either well-meaning individuals acting alone or that they were being orchestrated by Tokyo. Grew characterized such "peace feelers" as "familiar weapons of psychological warfare" designed to "divide the Allies."

Some American officials, such as Stimson and Grew, nonetheless wanted to signal the Japanese that they might retain the emperorship in the form of a constitutional monarchy. Such an assurance might remove the last stumbling block to surrender, if not when it was issued, then later. Only an imperial rescript would bring about an orderly surrender, they argued, without which Japanese forces would fight to the last man regardless of what the government in Tokyo did. Besides, the emperor could serve as a stabilizing factor during the transition to peacetime.

There were many arguments against an American initiative. Some opposed retaining such an undemocratic institution on principle and because they feared it might later serve as a rallying point for future militarism. Should that happen, as one assistant Secretary of State put it, "those lives already spent will have been sacrificed in vain, and lives will be lost again in the future." Japanese hard-liners were certain to exploit an overture as evidence that losses sustained at Okinawa had weakened American resolve and to argue that continued resistance would bring further concessions. Stalin, who earlier had told an American envoy that he favored abolishing the emperorship because the ineffectual Hirohito might be succeeded by "an energetic and vigorous figure who could cause trouble," was just as certain to interpret it as a treacherous effort to end the war before the Soviets could share in the spoils.

There were domestic considerations as well. Roosevelt had announced the unconditional surrender policy in early 1943, and it since had become a slogan of the war. He also had advocated that peoples everywhere should have the right to choose their own form of government, and Truman had publicly pledged to carry out his predecessor's legacies. For him to have formally *guaranteed* continuance of the emperorship, as opposed to merely accepting it on American terms pending free elections, as he later did, would have constituted a blatant repudiation of his own promises.

Nor was that all. Regardless of the emperor's actual role in Japanese aggression, which is still debated, much wartime propaganda had encouraged Americans to regard Hirohito as no *less* a war criminal than Adolf Hitler or Benito Mussolini. Although Truman said on several occasions that he had no objection to retaining the emperor, he understandably refused to make the first move. The ultimatum he issued from Potsdam on July 26 did not refer specifically to the emperorship. All it said was that occupation forces would be removed after "a peaceful and responsible" government had been established according to the "freely expressed will of the Japanese people." When the Japanese rejected the ultimatum rather than at last inquire whether they might retain the emperor, Truman permitted the plans for using the bombs to go forward.

Reliance on MAGIC intercepts and the "peace feelers" to gauge how near Japan was to surrender is misleading in any case. The army, not the Foreign Office, controlled the situation. Intercepts of Japanese military communications, designated ULTRA, provided no reason to believe the army was even considering surrender. Japanese Imperial Headquarters had correctly guessed that the next operation after Okinawa would be Kyushu and was making every effort to bolster its defenses there.

General Marshall reported on July 24 that there were "approximately 500,000 troops Kyushu" and that more were on the way. ULTRA identified new units arriving almost daily. MacArthur's G-2 reported on July 29 that "this threatening developments if not checked, may grow to a point where we attack on a ratio of one (1) to one (1) which is not the recipe for victory." By the time the first atomic bomb fell, ULTRA indicated that there were 560,000 troops in southern Kyushu (the actual figure was closer to 900,000), and projections for November 1 placed the number at 680,000. A report, for medical purposes, of July 31 estimated that total battle and nonbattle casualties might run as high as 394,859 *for the Kyushu operation alone.* This figure did not include those men expected to be killed outright, for obviously they would require no medical attention. Marshall regarded Japanese defenses as so formidable that even after Hiroshima he asked MacArthur to consider alternate landing sites and began contemplating the use of atomic bombs as tactical weapons to support the invasion.

The thirty-day casualty projection of 31,000 Marshall had given Truman at the June 18 strategy meeting had become meaningless. It had been based on the assumption that the Japanese had about 350,000 defenders in Kyushu and that naval and air interdiction would preclude significant reinforcement. But the Japanese buildup since that time meant that the defenders would have nearly twice the number of troops available by "X-day" than earlier assumed. The assertion that apprehensions about casualties are insufficient to explain Truman's use of the bombs, therefore, cannot be taken seriously. On the contrary, as Winston Churchill wrote after a conversation with him at Potsdam, Truman was tormented by "the terrible responsibilities that rested upon him in regard to the unlimited effusions of American blood."

Some historians have argued that while the first bomb *might* have been required to achieve Japanese surrender, dropping the second constituted a needless barbarism. The record shows otherwise. American officials believed more than one bomb would be necessary because they assumed Japanese hard-liners would minimize the first explosion or attempt to explain it away as some sort of natural catastrophe, precisely what they did. The Japanese minister of war, for instance, at first refused even to admit that the Hiroshima bomb was atomic. A few hours after Nagasaki he told the cabinet that "the Americans appeared to have one hundred atomic bombs ... they could drop three per day. The next target might well be Tokyo."

Even after both bombs bad fallen and Russia entered the war, Japanese militants insisted on such lenient peace terms that moderates knew there was no sense even transmitting them to the United States. Hirohito had to intervene personally on two occasions during the next few days to induce hard-liners to abandon their conditions and to accept the American stipulation that the emperor's authority "shall be subject to the Supreme Commander of the Allied Powers." That the militarists would have accepted such a settlement before the bombs is farfetched, to say the least.

Some writers have argued that the cumulative effects of battlefield defeats, conventional bombing, and naval blockade already had defeated Japan. Even without extending assurances about the emperor, all the United States had to do was wait. The most frequently cited basis for this contention is the *United States Strategic Bombing Survey* published in 1946, which stated that Japan would have surrendered by November 1 "even if the atomic bombs had not been dropped, even if Russia had not entered the war, and even if no invasion had been planned or contemplated." Recent scholarship by the historian Robert P. Newman and others has demonstrated that the survey was "cooked" by those who prepared it to arrive at such a conclusion. No matter. This or any other document based on information available only after the war ended is irrelevant with regard to what Truman could have known at the time.

What often goes unremarked is that when the bombs were dropped, fighting was still going on in the Philippines, China, and elsewhere. Every day that the war continued thousands of prisoners of war had to live and die in abysmal conditions, and there were rumors that the Japanese intended to slaughter them if the homeland was invaded. Truman was Commander in Chief of the American armed forces, and he had a duty to the men under his command not shared by those sitting in moral judgment decades later. Available evidence points to the conclusion that he acted for the reason he said he did: to end a bloody war that would have become even bloodier had invasion proved necessary. One can only imagine what would have happened if tens of thousands of American boys had died or been wounded on Japanese soil and then it had become known that Truman had chosen not to use weapons that might have ended the war months sooner.

IV

The Cold War and Beyond: Civil Rights and the War on Terror 1946 – Present

17. Letter from Birmingham City Jail

Martin Luther King, Jr.

Martin Luther King, Jr., (1929-1968), Baptist minister and civil rights leader, was an advocate of nonviolent political and social change. In 1963, King helped organize a series of demonstrations in Birmingham, Alabama, protesting racial prejudice and segregation. Local authorities arrested King, and while in jail he wrote the inspiring letter below setting forth his ideas on a nonviolent strategy to force Americans to confront the unjustness of discrimination. This letter stirred many Americans, great and small, black and white, to join the civil rights movement.

My dear Fellow Clergymen,

While confined here in the Birmingham city jail, I came across your recent statement calling our present activities "unwise and untimely." Seldom, if ever, do I pause to answer criticism of my work and ideas. If I sought to answer all of the criticisms that cross my desk, my secretaries would be engaged in little else in the course of the day, and I would have no time for constructive work. But since I feel that you are men of genuine good will and your criticisms are sincerely set forth, I would like to answer your statement in what I hope will be patient and reasonable terms.

I think I should give the reason for my being in Birmingham, since you have been influenced by the argument of "outsiders coming in." I have the honor of serving as president of the Southern Christian Leadership Conference, an organization operating in every southern state, with headquarters in Atlanta, Georgia. We have some eighty-five affiliate organizations all across the South—one being the Alabama Christian Movement for Human Rights. Whenever necessary and possible we share staff, educational and financial resources with our affiliates. Several months ago our local affiliate here in Birmingham invited us to be on call to engage in a nonviolent direct-action program if such were deemed necessary. We readily consented and when the hour came we lived up to our promises. So I am here, along with several members of my staff, because we were invited here. I am here because I have basic organizational ties here.

Beyond this, I am in Birmingham because injustice is here. Just as the eighth century prophets left their little villages and carried their "thus saith the Lord" far beyond the boundaries of their hometowns; and just as the Apostle Paul left his little village of Tarsus and carried the gospel of Jesus Christ to practically every hamlet and city of the Graeco-Roman world, I too am compelled to carry the gospel of freedom beyond my particular hometown. Like Paul, I must constantly respond to the Macedonian call for aid.

Moreover, I am cognizant of the interrelatedness of all communities and states. I cannot sit idly by in Atlanta and not be concerned about what happens in

Birmingham. Injustice anywhere is a threat to justice everywhere. We are caught in an inescapable network of mutuality, tied in a single garment of destiny. Whatever affects one directly affects all indirectly. Never again can we afford to live with the narrow, provincial "outside agitator" idea. Anyone who lives in the United States can never be considered an outsider anywhere in this country.

You deplore the demonstrations that are presently taking place in Birmingham. But I am sorry that your statement did not express a similar concern for the conditions that brought the demonstrations into being. I am sure that each of you would want to go beyond the superficial social analyst who looks merely at effects, and does not grapple with underlying causes. I would not hesitate to say that it is unfortunate that so-called demonstrations are taking place in Birmingham at this time, but I would say in more emphatic terms that it is even more unfortunate that the white power structure of this city left the Negro community with no other alternative.

In any nonviolent campaign there are four basic steps: (1) collection of the facts to determine whether injustices are alive, (2) negotiation, (3) self-purification, and (4) direct action. We have gone through all of these steps in Birmingham. There can be no gainsaying of the fact that racial injustice engulfs this community.

Birmingham is probably the most thoroughly segregated city in the United States. Its ugly record of police brutality is known in every section of this country. Its unjust treatment of Negroes in the courts is a notorious reality. There have been more unsolved bombings of Negro homes and churches in Birmingham than any city in this nation. These are the hard, brutal and unbelievable facts. On the basis of these conditions Negro leaders sought to negotiate with the city fathers. But the political leaders consistently refused to engage in good faith negotiation.

Then came the opportunity last September to talk with some of the leaders of the economic community. In these negotiating sessions certain promises were made by the merchants—such as the promise to remove the humiliating racial signs from the stores. On the basis of these promises Rev. Shuttlesworth and the leaders of the Alabama Christian Movement for Human Rights agreed to call a moratorium on any type of demonstrations. As the weeks and months unfolded we realized that we were the victims of a broken promise. The signs remained. Like so many experiences of the past we were confronted with blasted hopes, and the dark shadow of a deep disappointment settled upon us. So we had no alternative except that of preparing for direct action, whereby we would present our very bodies as a means of laying our case before the conscience of the local and national community. We were not unmindful of the difficulties involved. So we decided to go through a process of self-purification. We started having workshops on nonviolence and repeatedly asked ourselves the questions, "Are you able to accept blows without retaliating?" "Are you able to endure the ordeals of jail?" We decided to set our direct-action program around the Easter season, realizing that with the exception of Christmas, this was the largest shopping period of the year. Knowing that a strong economic withdrawal program would be the by-product of direct action, we felt that this was the best time to bring pressure on the merchants for the needed changes. Then it occurred to us that the March election was ahead so we speedily decided to postpone action until after election day. When we discovered Mr. Connor was in the run-off, we decided again to postpone action so that the demonstrations could not be used to cloud the issues. At this time we agreed to begin our nonviolent witness the day after the run-off.

This reveals that we did not move irresponsibly into direct action. We too wanted to see Mr. Connor defeated; so we went through postponement after postponement to aid in this community need. After this we felt that direct action could be delayed no longer.

You may well ask, "Why direct action? Why sit-ins, marches, etc.? Isn't negotiation a better path?" You are exactly right in your call for negotiation. Indeed, this is the purpose of direct action. Nonviolent direct action seeks to create such a crisis and establish such creative tension that a community that has constantly refused to negotiate is forced to confront the issue. It seeks so to dramatize the issue that it can no longer be ignored. I just referred to the creation of tension as a part of the work of the nonviolent resister. This may sound rather shocking. But I must confess that I am not afraid of the word tension. I have earnestly worked and preached against violent tension, but there is a type of constructive nonviolent tension that is necessary for growth. Just as Socrates felt that it was necessary to create a tension in the mind so that individuals could rise from the bondage of myths and half-truths to the unfettered realm of creative analysis and objective appraisal, we must see the need of having nonviolent gadflies to create the kind of tension in society that will help men to rise from the dark depths of prejudice and racism to the majestic heights of understanding and brotherhood. So the purpose of the direct action is to create a situation so crisis-packed that it will inevitably open the door to negotiation. We, therefore, concur with you in your call for negotiation. Too long has our beloved Southland been bogged down in the tragic attempt to live in monologue rather than dialogue.

One of the basic points in your statement is that our acts are untimely. Some have asked, "Why didn't you give the new administration time to act?" The only answer that I can give to this inquiry is that the new administration must be prodded about as much as the outgoing one before it acts. We will be sadly mistaken if we feel that the election of Mr. Boutwell will bring the millennium to Birmingham. While Mr. Boutwell is much more articulate and gentle than Mr. Connor, they are both segregationists, dedicated to the task of maintaining the status quo. The hope I see in Mr. Boutwell is that he will be reasonable enough to see the futility of massive resistance to desegregation. But he will not see this without pressure from the devotees of civil rights. My friends, I must say to you that we have not made a single gain in civil rights without determined legal and nonviolent pressure. History is the long and tragic story of the fact that privileged groups seldom give up their privileges voluntarily. Individuals may see the moral light and voluntarily give up their unjust posture; but as Reinhold Niebuhr has reminded us, groups are more immoral than individuals.

We know through painful experience that freedom is never voluntarily given by the oppressor; it must be demanded by the oppressed. Frankly, I have never yet engaged in a direct action movement that was "well-timed," according to the timetable of those who have not suffered unduly from the disease of segregation. For years now I have heard the words "Wait!" It rings in the ear of every Negro with a piercing familiarity. This "Wait" has almost always meant "Never." It has been a tranquilizing thalidomide, relieving the emotional stress for a moment, only to give birth to an ill-formed infant of frustration. We must come to see with the distinguished jurist of yesterday that "justice too long delayed is justice denied." We have waited for more than 340 years for our constitutional and God-given rights. The nations of Asia and Africa are moving with jetlike speed toward the goal of political independence, and we still creep at horse and buggy pace toward the gaining of a cup of coffee at a lunch counter. I guess it *is* easy for those who have never felt the stinging darts of segregation to say "Wait." But when you have seen vicious mobs lynch your mothers and fathers at will and drown your sisters and brothers at whim; when you have seen hate-filled policemen curse, kick, brutalize and even kill your black brothers and sisters with impunity; when you see the vast majority of your twenty million Negro brothers smothering in an airtight cage of poverty in the midst of an affluent society; when you suddenly find your tongue twisted and your speech stammering as you seek to explain to your six-year-old daughter why she can't go to the public amusement park that has just been advertised on television, and see tears welling up in her little eyes when she is told that Funtown is closed to colored children, and see the depressing clouds of inferiority begin to form in her little mental sky, and see her begin to distort her little personality by unconsciously developing a bitterness toward white people; when you have to concoct an answer for a five-year-old son asking in agonizing pathos: "Daddy, why do white people treat colored people so mean?"; when you take a cross-country drive and find it necessary to sleep night after night in the uncomfortable corners of your automobile because no motel will accept you; when you are humiliated day in and day out by nagging signs reading "white" and "colored"; when your first name becomes "nigger" and your middle name becomes "boy" (however old you are) and your last name becomes "John," and when your wife and mother are never given the respected title "Mrs."; when you are harried by day and haunted by night by the fact that you are a Negro, living constantly at tiptoe stance never quite knowing what to expect next, and plagued with inner fears and outer resentments; when you are forever fighting a degenerating sense of "nobodiness"; then you will understand why we find it difficult to wait. There comes a time when the cup of endurance runs over, and men are no longer willing to be plunged into an abyss of injustice where they experience the blackness of corroding despair. I hope, sirs, you can understand our legitimate and unavoidable impatience.

You express a great deal of anxiety over our willingness to break laws. This is certainly a legitimate concern. Since we so diligently urge people to obey the Supreme Court's decision of 1954 outlawing segregation in the public schools, it is rather strange and paradoxical to find us consciously breaking laws. One may well ask, "How can you advocate breaking some laws and obeying others?" The answer is found in the fact that there are two types of laws: there are just and there are *unjust* laws. I would agree with Saint Augustine that "An unjust law is no law at all."

Now what is the difference between the two? How does one determine when a law is just or unjust? A just law is a man-made code that squares with the moral law or the law of God. An unjust law is a code that is out of harmony with the moral law. To put it in the terms of Saint Thomas Aquinas, an unjust law is a human law that is not rooted in eternal and natural law. Any law that uplifts human personality is just. Any law that degrades human personality is unjust. All segregation statutes are unjust because segregation distorts the soul and damages the personality. It gives the segregator a false sense of superiority and the segregated a false sense of inferiority. To use the words of Martin Buber, the great Jewish philosopher, segregation substitutes an "I-it" relationship for the "I-thou" relationship, and ends up relegating persons to the status of things. So segregation is not only politically, economically and sociologically unsound, but it is morally wrong and sinful. Paul Tillich has said that sin is separation. Isn't segregation an existential expression of man's tragic separation, an expression of his awful estrangement, his terrible sinfulness? So I can urge men to disobey segregation ordinances because they are morally wrong.

Let us turn to a more concrete example of just and unjust laws. An unjust law is a code that a majority inflicts on a minority that is not binding on itself. This is difference made legal. On the other hand a just law is a code that a majority compels a minority to follow that it is willing to follow itself. This is sameness made legal.

Let me give another explanation. An unjust law is a code inflicted upon a minority which that minority had no part in enacting or creating because they did not have the unhampered right to vote. Who can say that the legislature of Alabama which set up the segregation laws was democratically elected? Throughout the state of Alabama all types of conniving methods are used to prevent Negroes from becoming registered voters and there are some counties without a single Negro registered to vote despite the fact that the Negro constitutes a majority of the population. Can any law set up in such a state be considered democratically structured?

These are just a few examples of unjust and just laws. There are some instances when a law is just on its face and unjust in its application. For instance, I was arrested Friday on a charge of parading without a permit. Now there is nothing wrong with an ordinance which requires a permit for a parade, but when the ordinance is used to preserve segregation and to deny citizens the First Amendment privilege of peaceful assembly and peaceful protest, then it becomes unjust.

I hope you can see the distinction I am trying to point out. In no sense do I advocate evading or defying the law as the rabid segregationist would do. This would lead to anarchy. One who breaks an unjust law must do it *openly, lovingly* (not hatefully as the white mothers did in New Orleans when they were seen on television screaming, "nigger, nigger, nigger"), and with a willingness to accept the penalty. I submit that an individual who breaks a law that conscience tells him is unjust, and willingly accepts the penalty by staying in jail to arouse the conscience of the community over its injustice, is in reality expressing the very highest respect for law.

Of course, there is nothing new about this kind of civil disobedience. It was seen sublimely in the refusal of Shadrach, Meshach and Abednego to obey the laws of Nebuchadnezzar because a higher moral law was involved. It was practiced superbly by the early Christians who were willing to face hungry lions and the excruciating pain of chopping blocks, before submitting to certain unjust laws of the Roman Empire. To a degree academic freedom is a reality today because Socrates practiced civil disobedience.

We can never forget that everything Hitler did in Germany was "legal" and everything the Hungarian freedom fighters did in Hungary was "illegal." It was "illegal" to aid and comfort a Jew in Hitler's Germany. But I am sure that if I had lived in Germany during that time I would have aided and comforted my Jewish brothers even though it was illegal. If I lived in a Communist country today where certain principles dear to the Christian faith are suppressed, I believe I would openly advocate disobeying these anti-religious laws. I must make two honest confessions to you, my Christian and Jewish brothers. First, I must confess that over the last few

years I have been gravely disappointed with the white moderate. I have almost reached the regrettable conclusion that the Negro's great stumbling block in the stride toward freedom is not the White Citizen's Councilor or the Ku Klux Klanner, but the white moderate who is more devoted to "order" than to justice; who prefers a negative peace which is the absence of tension to a positive peace which is the presence of justice; who constantly says, "I agree with you in the goal you seek, but I can't agree with your methods of direct action"; who paternalistically feels that he can set the timetable for another man's freedom; who lives by the myth of time and who constantly advised the Negro to wait until a "more convenient season." Shallow understanding from people of good will is more frustrating than absolute misunderstanding from people of ill will. Lukewarm acceptance is much more bewildering than outright rejection.

I had hoped that the white moderate would understand that law and order exist for the purpose of establishing justice, and that when they fail to do this they become dangerously structured dams that block the flow of social progress. I had hoped that the white moderate would understand that the present tension of the South is merely a necessary phase of the transition from an obnoxious negative peace, where the Negro passively accepted his unjust plight, to a substance-filled positive peace, where all men will respect the dignity and worth of human personality. Actually, we who engage in nonviolent direct action are not the creators of tension. We merely bring to the surface the hidden tension that is already alive. We bring it out in the open where it can be seen and dealt with. Like a boil that can never be cured as long as it is covered up but must be opened with all its pus-flowing ugliness to the natural medicines of air and light, injustice must likewise be exposed, with all of the tension its exposing creates, to the light of human conscience and the air of national opinion before it can be cured.

In your statement you asserted that our actions, even though peaceful, must be condemned because they precipitate violence. But can this assertion be logically made? Isn't this like condemning the robbed man because his possession of money precipitated the evil act of robbery? Isn't this like condemning Socrates because his unswerving commitment to truth and his philosophical delvings precipitated the misguided popular mind to make him drink the hemlock? Isn't this like condemning Jesus because His unique God-consciousness and never-ceasing devotion to his will precipitated the evil act of crucifixion? We must come to see, as federal courts have consistently affirmed, that it is immoral to urge an individual to withdraw his efforts to gain his basic constitutional rights because the quest precipitates violence. Society must protect the robbed and punish the robber.

I had also hoped that the white moderate would reject the myth of time. I received a letter this morning from a white brother in Texas which said: "All Christians know that the colored people will receive equal rights eventually, but it is possible that you are in too great of a religious hurry. It has taken Christianity almost two thousand years to accomplish what it has. The teachings of Christ take time to come to earth." All that is said here grows out of a tragic misconception of time. It is the strangely irrational notion that there is something in the very flow of time that will inevitably cure all ills. Actually time is neutral. It can be used either destructively or constructively. I am coming to feel that the people of ill will have used time much more effectively than the people of good will. We will have to repent in this generation not merely for the vitriolic words and actions of the bad people, but for the appalling silence of the good people. We must come to see that human progress never rolls in on wheels of inevitability. It comes through the tireless efforts and persistent work of men willing to be co-workers with God, and without this hard work time itself becomes an ally of the forces of social stagnation. We must use time creatively, and forever realize that the time is always ripe to do right. Now is the time to make real the promise of democracy, and transform our pending national elegy into a creative psalm of brotherhood. Now is the time to lift our national policy from the quicksand of racial injustice to the solid rock of human dignity.

You spoke of our activity in Birmingham as extreme. At first I was rather disappointed that fellow clergymen would see my nonviolent efforts as those of the extremist. I started thinking about the fact that I stand in the middle of two opposing forces in the Negro community. One is a force of complacency made up of Negroes who, as a result of long years of oppression, have been so completely drained of self-respect and a sense of "somebodiness" that they have adjusted to segregation, and, of a few Negroes in the middle class who, because of a degree of academic and economic security, and because at points they profit by segregation, have unconsciously become insensitive to the problems of the masses. The other force is one of bitterness and hatred, and comes perilously close to advocating violence. It is expressed in the various black nationalist groups that are springing up over the nation, the largest and best known being Elijah Muhammad's Muslim movement. This movement is nourished by the contemporary frustration over the continued existence of racial discrimination. It is made up of people who have lost faith in America, who have absolutely repudiated Christianity, and who have concluded that the white man is an incurable "devil." I have tried to stand between these two forces, saying that we need not follow the "do-nothingism" of the complacent or the hatred and despair of the black nationalist. There is the more excellent way of love and nonviolent protest. I'm grateful to God that, through the Negro church, the dimension of nonviolence entered our struggle. If this philosophy had not emerged, I am convinced that by now many streets of the South would be flowing with floods of blood. And I am further convinced that if our white brothers dismiss us as "rabble-rousers" and "outside agitators" those of us who are working through the channels of nonviolent direct action and refuse to support our nonviolent efforts, millions of Negroes, out of frustration and despair, will seek solace and security in black nationalist ideologies, a development that will lead inevitably to a frightening racial nightmare.

Oppressed people cannot remain oppressed forever. The urge for freedom will eventually come. This is what happened to the American Negro. Something within has reminded him of his birthright of freedom; something without has reminded him that he can gain it. Consciously and unconsciously, he has been swept in what the Germans call the *Zeitgeist*, and with his black brothers of Africa, and his brown and yellow brothers of Asia, South America and the Caribbean, he is moving with a sense of cosmic urgency toward the promised land of racial justice. Recognizing this vital urge that has engulfed the Negro community, one should readily understand public demonstrations. The Negro has many pent-up resentments and latent frustrations. He has to get them out. So let him march sometime; let him have his prayer pilgrimages to the city hall; understand why he must have sit-ins and freedom rides. If his repressed emotions do not come out in these nonviolent ways, they will come out in ominous expressions of violence. This *is* not a threat; it is a fact of history. So I have not said to my people "get rid of your discontent." But I have tried to say that this normal and healthy discontent can be channelized through the creative outlet of nonviolent direct action. Now this approach is being dismissed as extremist. I must admit that I was initially disappointed in being so categorized.

But as I continued to think about the matter I gradually gained a bit of satisfaction from being considered an extremist. Was not Jesus an extremist in love—"Love your enemies, bless them that curse you, pray for them that despitefully use you." Was not Amos an extremist for justice—"Let justice roll down like waters and righteousness like a mighty stream." Was not Paul an extremist for the gospel of Jesus Christ—"I bear in my body the marks of the Lord Jesus." *Was* not Martin Luther an extremist—"Here I stand; I can do none other so help me God." Was not John Bunyan an extremist—"I will stay in jail to the end of my days before I make a butchery of my conscience." Was not Abraham Lincoln an extremist—"This nation cannot survive half slave and half free." Was not Thomas Jefferson an extremist—"We hold these truths to be self-evident, that all men are created equal." So the question is not whether we will be extremist but what kind of extremist will we be. Will we be extremists for hate or will we be extremists for love? Will we be extremists for the preservation of injustice—or will we be extremists for the cause of justice? In that dramatic scene on Calvary's hill, three men were crucified. We must not forget that all three were crucified for the same crime—the crime of extremism. Two were extremists for immorality, and thusly fell below their environment. The other, Jesus Christ, was an extremist for love, truth and goodness, and thereby rose above his environment. So, after all, maybe the South, the nation and the world are in dire need of creative extremists.

I had hoped that the white moderate would see this. Maybe I was too optimistic. Maybe I expected too much. I guess I should have realized that few members of a race that has oppressed another race can understand or appreciate the deep groans and passionate yearnings of those that have been oppressed and still fewer have the vision to see that injustice must be rooted out by strong, persistent and determined action. I am thankful, however, that some of our white brothers have grasped the meaning of this social revolution and committed themselves to it. They are still all too small in quantity, but they are big in quality. Some like Ralph McGill, Lillian Smith, Harry Golden and James Dabbs have written about our struggle in eloquent, prophetic and understanding terms. Others have marched with us down nameless streets of the South. They have languished in filthy roach-infested jails, suffering the abuse and brutality of angry policemen who see them as "dirty nigger-lovers." They, unlike so many of their moderate brothers and sisters, have recognized the urgency of the moment and sensed the need for powerful "action" antidotes to combat the disease of segregation.

Let me rush on to mention my other disappointment. I have been so greatly disappointed with the white church and its leadership. Of course, there are some notable exceptions. I am not unmindful of the fact that each of you has taken some significant stands on this issue. I commend you, Rev. Stallings, for your Christian stance on this past Sunday, in welcoming Negroes to your worship service on a non-segregated basis. I commend the Catholic leaders of this state for integrating Springhill College several years ago.

But despite these notable exceptions I must honestly reiterate that I have been disappointed with the church. I do not say that as one of the negative critics who can always find something wrong with the church. I say it as a minister of the gospel, who loves the church; who was nurtured in its bosom; who has been sustained by its spiritual blessings and who will remain true to it as long as the cord of life shall lengthen.

I had the strange feeling when I was suddenly catapulted into the leadership of the bus protest in Montgomery several years ago that we would have the support of the white church. I felt that the white ministers, priests and rabbis of the South would be some of our strongest allies. Instead, some have been outright opponents, refusing to understand the freedom movement and misrepresenting its leaders; all too many others have been more cautious than courageous and have remained silent behind the anesthetizing security of the stained-glass windows.

In spite of my shattered dreams of the past, I came to Birmingham with the hope that the white religious leadership of this community would see the justice of our cause, and with deep moral concern, serve as the channel through which our just grievances would get to the power structure. I had hoped that each of you would understand. But again I have been disappointed. I have heard numerous religious leaders of the South call upon their worshippers to comply with a desegregation decision because it is the law, but I have longed to hear white ministers say, "Follow this decree because integration is morally right and the Negro is your brother." In the midst of blatant injustices inflicted upon the Negro, I have watched white churches stand on the sideline and merely mouth pious irrelevancies and sanctimonious trivialities. In the midst of a mighty struggle to rid our nation of racial and economic injustice, I have heard so many ministers say, "Those are social issues with which the gospel has no real concern," and I have watched so many churches commit themselves to a completely otherworldly religion which made a strange distinction between body and soul, the sacred and the secular.

So here we are moving toward the exit of the twentieth century with a religious community largely adjusted to the status quo, standing as a taillight behind other community agencies rather than a headlight leading men to higher levels of justice.

I have traveled the length and breadth of Alabama, Mississippi and all the other southern states. On sweltering summer days and crisp autumn mornings I have looked at her beautiful churches with their lofty spires pointing heavenward. I have beheld the impressive outlay of her massive religious education buildings. Over and over again I have found myself asking: "What kind of people worship here? Who is their God? Where were their voices when the lips of Governor Barnett dripped with words of interposition and nullification? Where were they when Governor Wallace gave the clarion call for defiance and hatred? Where were their voices of support when tired, bruised and weary Negro men and women decided to rise from the dark dungeons of complacency to the bright hills of creative protest?"

Yes, these questions are still in my mind. In deep disappointment, I have wept over the laxity of the church. But be assured that my tears have been tears of love. There can be no deep disappointment where there is not deep love. Yes, I love the church; I love her sacred walls. How could I do otherwise? I am in the rather unique position of being the son, the grandson and the great-grandson of preachers. Yes, I see the church as the body of Christ. But, oh! How we have blemished and scarred that body through social neglect and fear of being nonconformists.

There was a time when the church was very powerful. It was during that period when the early Christians rejoiced when they were deemed worthy to suffer for what they believed. In those days the church was not merely a thermometer that recorded the ideas and principles of popular opinion; it was a thermostat that transformed the mores of society. Wherever the early Christians entered a town the power structure got disturbed and immediately sought to convict them for being "disturbers of the peace" and "outside agitators." But they went on with the conviction that they were a "colony of heaven," and had to obey God rather than man. They were small in number but big in commitment. They were too God-intoxicated to be "astronomically intimidated." They brought an end to such ancient evils as infanticide and gladiatorial contest.

Things are different now. The contemporary church is often a weak, ineffectual voice with an uncertain sound. It is so often the arch-supporter of the status-quo. Far from being disturbed by the presence of the church, the power structure of the average community is consoled by the church's silent and often vocal sanction of things as they are.

But the judgment of God is upon the church as never before. If the church of today does not recapture the sacrificial spirit of the early church, it will lose its authentic ring, forfeit the loyalty of millions, and be dismissed as an irrelevant social club with no meaning for the twentieth century. I am meeting young people every day whose disappointment with the church has risen to outright disgust.

Maybe again, I have been too optimistic. Is organized religion too inextricably bound to the status quo to save our nation and the world? Maybe I must turn my faith to the inner spiritual church, the church within the church, as the true *ecclesia* and the hope of the world. But again I am thankful to God that some noble souls from the ranks of organized religion have broken loose from the paralyzing chains of conformity and joined us as active partners in the struggle for freedom. They have left their secure congregations and walked the streets of Albany, Georgia, with us. They have gone through the highways of the South on tortuous rides for freedom. Yes, they have gone to jail with us. Some have been kicked out of their churches, and lost support of their bishops and fellow ministers. But they have gone with the faith that right defeated is stronger than evil triumphant. These men have been the leaven in the lump of the race. Their witness has been the spiritual salt that has preserved the true meaning of the gospel in these troubled times. They have carved a tunnel of hope through the dark mountain of disappointment.

I hope the church as a whole will meet the challenge of this decisive hour. But even if the church does not come to the aid of justice, I have no despair about the future. I have no fear about the outcome of our struggle in Birmingham, even if our motives are presently misunderstood. We will reach the goal of freedom in Birmingham and all over the nation, because the goal of America is freedom. Abused and scorned though we may be, our destiny is tied up with the destiny of America. Before the Pilgrims landed at Plymouth we were here. Before the pen of Jefferson etched across the pages of history the majestic words of the Declaration of Independence, we were here. For more than two centuries our foreparents labored in this country without wages; they made cotton king; and they built the homes of their masters in the midst of brutal injustice and shameful humiliation—and yet out of a bottomless vitality they continued to thrive and develop. If the inexpressible cruelties of slavery could not stop us, the opposition we now face will surely fail. We will win our freedom because the sacred heritage of our nation and the eternal will of God are embodied in our echoing demands.

I must close now. But before closing I am impelled to mention one other point in your statement that troubled me profoundly. You warmly commended the Birmingham police force for keeping "order" and "preventing violence." I don't believe you would have so warmly commended the police force if you had seen its angry violent dogs literally biting six unarmed, nonviolent Negroes. I don't believe you would so quickly commend the policemen if you would observe their ugly and inhuman treatment of Negroes here in the city jail; if you would watch them push and curse old Negro women and young Negro girls; if you would see them slap and kick old Negro men and young boys; if you will observe them, as they did on two occasions, refuse to give us food because we wanted to sing our grace together. I'm sorry that I can't join you in your praise for the police department.

It is true that they have been rather disciplined in their public handling of the demonstrators. In this sense they have been rather publicly "nonviolent." But for what purpose? To preserve the evil system of segregation. Over the last few years I have consistently preached that nonviolence demands that the means we use must be as pure as the ends we seek. So I have tried to make it clear that it is wrong to use immoral means to attain moral ends. But now I must affirm that it is just as wrong, or even more so, to use moral means to preserve immoral ends. Maybe Mr. Connor and his policeman have been rather publicly nonviolent, as Chief Pritchett was in Albany, Georgia, but they have used the moral means of nonviolence to maintain the immoral end of flagrant racial injustice. T. S. Eliot has said that there is no greater treason than to do the right deed for the wrong reason.

I wish you had commended the Negro sit-inners and demonstrators of Birmingham for their sublime courage, their willingness to suffer and their amazing discipline in the midst of the most inhuman provocation. One day the South will recognize its real heroes. They will be the James Merediths, courageously and with a majestic sense of purpose facing jeering and hostile mobs and the agonizing loneliness that characterizes the life of the pioneer. They will be old, oppressed, battered Negro women, symbolized in a seventy-two-year-old woman of Montgomery, Alabama, who rose up with a sense of dignity and with her people decided not to ride the segregated buses, and responded to one who inquired about her tiredness with ungrammatical profundity: "My feet is tired, but my soul is rested." They will be the young high school and college students, young ministers of the gospel and a host of their elders courageously and nonviolently sitting-in at lunch counters and willingly going to jail for conscience's sake. One day the South will know that when these disinherited children of God sat down at lunch counters they were in reality standing up for the best in the American dream and the most sacred values in our Judeo-Christian heritage, and thusly, carrying our whole nation back to those great wells of democracy which were dug deep by the Founding Fathers in the formulation of the Constitution and the Declaration of Independence.

Never before have I written a letter this long (or should I say a book?). I'm afraid that it is much too long to take your precious time. I can assure you that it would have been much shorter if I had been writing from a comfortable desk, but what else is there to do when you are alone for days in the dull monotony of a narrow jail cell other than write long letters, think strange thoughts, and pray long prayers?

If I have said anything in this letter that is an overstatement of the truth and is indicative of an unreasonable impatience, I beg you to forgive me. If I have said anything in this letter that is an understatement of the truth and is indicative of my having a patience that makes me patient with anything less than brotherhood, I beg God to forgive me.

I hope this letter finds you strong in the faith. I also hope that circumstances will soon make it possible for me to meet each of you, not as an integrationist or a civil rights leader, but as a fellow clergyman and a Christian brother. Let us all hope that the dark clouds of racial prejudice will soon pass away and the deep fog of misunderstanding will be lifted from our fear-drenched communities and in some not too distant tomorrow the radiant stars of love and brotherhood will shine over our great nation with all of their scintillating beauty.

Yours for the cause of Peace and Brotherhood,
Martin Luther King, Jr.
April 16, 1963

18. Beyond the Feminine Mystique

A Reassessment of Postwar Mass Culture, 1946-1958

Joanne Meyerowitz

In 1963 Betty Friedan published *The Feminine Mystique,* an instant best seller. Friedan argued, often brilliantly, that American women, especially suburban women, suffered from deep discontent. In the postwar era, she wrote, journalists, educators, advertisers, and social scientists had pulled women into the home with an ideological stranglehold, the "feminine mystique." This repressive "image" held that women could "find fulfillment only in sexual passivity, male domination, and nurturing maternal love." It denied "women careers or any commitment outside the home" and "narrowed woman's world down to the home, cut her role back to housewife." In Friedan's formulation, the writers and editors of mass-circulation magazines, especially women's magazines, were the "Frankensteins" who had created this "feminine monster." In her defense of women, Friedan did not choose a typical liberal feminist language of rights, equality, or even justice. Influenced by the new human potential psychology, she argued instead that full-time domesticity stunted women and denied their "basic human need to grow." For Friedan, women and men found personal identity and fulfillment through individual achievement, most notably through careers. Without such growth, she claimed, women would remain unfulfilled and unhappy, and children would suffer at the hands of neurotic mothers.

The Feminine Mystique had an indisputable impact. Hundreds of women have testified that the book changed their lives, and historical accounts often credit it with launching the recent feminist movement. But the book has also had other kinds of historical impact. For a journalistic expose, Friedan's work has had a surprisingly strong influence on historiography. In fact, since Friedan published *The Feminine Mystique,* historians of American women have adopted wholesale her version of the postwar ideology While many historians question Friedan's homogenized account of women's actual experience, virtually all accept her version of the dominant ideology, the conservative promotion of domesticity.

According to this now-standard historical account, postwar authors urged women to return to the home while only a handful of social scientists, trade unionists, and feminists protested. As one recent rendition states: "In the wake of World War II . . . the short-lived affirmation of women's independence gave way to a pervasive endorsement of female subordination and domesticity." Much of this secondary literature relies on a handful of conservative postwar writings, the same writings cited liberally by Friedan. In particular, the work of Dr. Marynia F. Farnham, a viciously antifeminist psychiatrist, and her sidekick, sociologist Ferdinand Lundberg, is invoked repeatedly as typical of the postwar era. In this standard account, the domestic ideology prevailed until such feminists as Friedan triumphed in the 1960s.

When I first began research on the postwar era, I accepted this version of history. But as I investigated the public culture, I encountered what I then considered exceptional evidence—books, articles, and films that contradicted the domestic ideology. I decided to conduct a more systematic investigation. This essay reexamines the middle-class popular discourse on women by surveying mass-circulation monthly magazines of the postwar era (1946-1958). The systematic sample includes nonfiction articles on women in "middlebrow" magazines *(Reader's Digest* and *Coronet),* "highbrow" magazines *(Harper's* and *Atlantic Monthly),* magazines aimed at African Americans *(Ebony* and *Negro Digest),* and those aimed at women *(Ladies' Home Journal* and *Woman's Home Companion).* The sample includes 489 nonfiction articles, ranging from Hollywood gossip to serious considerations of gender. In 1955 these magazines had a combined circulation of over 22 million. Taken together, the magazines reached readers from all classes, races, and genders, but the articles seem to represent the work of middle-class journalists, and articles written by women seem to outnumber ones by men.

My goal in constructing this sample was not to replicate Friedan's magazine research, which focused primarily on short story fiction in four women's magazines. Rather my goal was to test generalizations about postwar mass culture (that is, commodified forms of popular culture) by surveying another side of it. To this end, I chose nonfiction articles in a larger sample of popular magazines. Some of the magazines of smaller circulation, such as *Harper's* and *Negro Digest,* were perhaps outside the "mainstream." But including them in the sample enabled me to incorporate more of the diversity in American society, to investigate the contours of a broader bourgeois culture and some variations within it. Since my conclusions rest on a sample of nonfiction articles in eight popular magazines, they can provide only a tentative portrait of postwar culture. Future studies based on different magazines or on fiction, advertisements, films, television, or radio will no doubt suggest additional layers of complexity in mass culture and different readings of it.

My interpretation of the sample draws in part on recent theories in cultural studies. For Betty Friedan and for some historians, popular magazines represented a repressive force, imposing damaging images on vulnerable American women. Many historians today adopt a different approach in which mass culture is neither monolithic nor unrelentingly repressive. In this view, mass culture is rife with contradictions, ambivalence, and competing voices. We no longer assume that any text has a single, fixed meaning for all readers, and we sometimes find within the mass media subversive, as well as repressive, potential.

With a somewhat different sample and a somewhat different interpretive approach, I come to different conclusions about postwar mass culture than did

Friedan and her followers. Friedan's widely accepted version of the "feminine mystique," I suggest, is only one piece of the postwar cultural puzzle. The popular literature I sampled did not simply glorify domesticity or demand that women return to or stay at home. All of the magazines sampled advocated both the domestic and the nondomestic, sometimes in the same sentence. In this literature, domestic ideals coexisted in ongoing tension with an ethos of individual achievement that celebrated nondomestic activity, individual striving, public service, and public success.

This essay first discusses nonfiction that focused on individual women. Despite frequent references to femininity and domesticity, most of these stories expressed overt admiration for women whose individual striving moved them beyond the home. In contrast to the "happy housewife heroine" whom Friedan found in magazine fiction, these "true stories" presented women as successful public figures. Second, this essay examines nonfiction that directly addressed issues of gender. Such articles often applauded housewives, but they also supported women's wage work and urged greater participation in politics. Further, they often expressed ambivalence about domesticity and presented it as a problem. Here Dr. Farnham and her conservative fellow travelers voiced a distinctive minority position that in no way dominated the mass culture.

The postwar mass culture embraced the same central contradiction—the tension between domestic ideals and individual achievement—that Betty Friedan addressed in *The Feminine Mystique.* In this sense, I argue, Friedan drew on mass culture as much as she countered it. The success of her book stemmed in part from her compelling elaboration of familiar themes.

In popular magazines, the theme of individual achievement rang most clearly in the numerous articles on individual women. These articles appeared with frequency throughout the postwar era: they comprised over 60 percent, or 300, of the 489 nonfiction articles sampled. These articles usually recounted a story of a woman's life or a particularly telling episode in her life. In formulaic accounts, they often constructed what one such article labeled "this Horatio Alger success story—feminine version." Of these articles, 33 percent spotlighted women with unusual talents, jobs, or careers, and another 29 percent focused on prominent entertainers. Typically they related a rise to public success punctuated by a lucky break, a dramatic comeback, a selfless sacrifice, or a persistent struggle to overcome adversity. Such stories appeared in all of the magazines sampled, but they appeared most frequently in the African-American magazines, *Ebony* and *Negro Digest,* and the white "middlebrow" magazines, *Coronet* and *Reader's Digest.* Journalists reworked the formula for different readers: In *Negro Digest,* for example, articles returned repeatedly to black performers who defied racism, in *Reader's Digest* they more often addressed white leaders in community service. In general, though, the articles suggested that the noteworthy woman rose above and beyond ordinary domesticity. Or, as one story stated, "This is the real-life fairy tale of a girl who hurtled from drab obscurity to sudden, startling fame."

At the heart of many such articles lay a bifocal vision of women both as feminine and domestic and as public achievers. In one article, "The Lady Who Licked Crime in Portland," the author, Richard L. Neuberger, juxtaposed domestic stereotypes and newsworthy nondomestic achievement. The woman in question, Dorothy McCullough Lee, was, the article stated, an "ethereally pale housewife" who tipped "the scales at 110 pounds." But more to the point, she was also the mayor of Portland, Oregon, who had defeated, single-handedly it seems, the heavyweights of organized crime. Before winning the mayoral election in 1948, this housewife had opened a law firm and served in the state legislature, both House and Senate, and as Portland's commissioner of public utilities. Despite her "frail, willowy" appearance, the fearless mayor had withstood ridicule, recall petitions, and threatening mail in her "relentless drive" against gambling and prostitution. She was, the article related without further critique, a "violent feminist" who had "intense concern with the status of women." And, according to all, she was "headed for national distinction." The article concluded with an admiring quotation describing Mayor Lee's fancy hats as the plumes of a crusading knight in armor. Here the feminine imagery blended with a metaphor of masculine public service.

The joint endorsement of domestic and nondomestic roles appeared in the numerous stories that offered a postwar version of today's "superwoman," the woman who successfully combines motherhood and career. As Jacqueline Jones has noted, *Ebony* magazine sometimes featured this type of article. One story, for example presented Louise Williams, a mother of two and also the only black mechanic at American Airlines. As *Ebony* reported, "She is a good cook, but an even better mechanic." She was also an inventor and an active member of her union. And, according to *Ebony* she was "never a lazy housewife." Such stories in African-American magazines clearly provided lessons in surmounting racism. In *Ebony's* female version of racial advancement, women often excelled both in the workplace and at home.

Similar articles appeared regularly in magazines geared to white readers. *Coronet* magazine, for example, presented the "amazing" Dorothy Kilgallen, "star reporter," who wrote a syndicated column, ad-libbed a daily radio program, ran forty charity benefits a year, and had "a handsome and successful husband, a beautiful home, [and] two lovely children." The successful combination of home and career made her "Gotham's busiest glamour girl." Articles of this type resolved the tension between domesticity and public achievement superficially by ignoring the difficulties that women usually faced in pursuing both.

While feminine stereotypes sometimes provided convenient foils that enhanced by contrast a women's atypical public accomplishment, they also served as conservative reminders that all women, even publicly successful women, were to maintain traditional gender distinctions. In their opening paragraphs, numerous authors described their successful subjects as pretty, motherly, shapely, happily married, petite, charming, or soft voiced. This emphasis on femininity and domesticity (and the two were often conflated) seems to have cloaked a submerged fear of lesbian, mannish, or man-hating women. This fear surfaced in an unusual article on athlete Babe Didrikson Zaharias. In her early years, the article stated, the Babe's "boyish bob and freakish clothes . . . [her] dislike of femininity" had led observers to dismiss her as an "Amazon." But after her marriage, she "became a woman," a transformation signaled, according to the approving author, by lipstick, polished nails, and "loose, flowing" hair as well as by an interest in the domestic arts of cooking, sewing, and entertaining. In this article, as in others, allusions to femininity and domesticity probably helped legitimate women's public achievements. Authors attempted to reassure readers that conventional gender distinctions and heterosexuality remained intact even as women competed successfully in work, politics, or sports. It is worth noting that in *The Feminine Mystique,* Friedan adopted this very approach. She attempted to legitimate the early feminists by repeated insistence that most of them were feminine, married, and not man-hating. . . .

In the postwar magazines, marriage also presented problems. Although journalists expected most women to marry, they portrayed the search for a husband as a potentially troubling task. An article in *Ebony* stated, "Most women would rather be married than single but there are many who would rather remain single than be tied to the wrong man." The magazines gave readers contrasting advice on how to find a good husband. One article told women, "Don't fear being aggressive!," while another considered "aggressive traits" as "handicaps ... in attracting a husband." Within marriage as well, journalists seemed to anticipate constant problems, including immaturity, incompatibility, and infidelity. They saw divorce as a difficult last resort and often advised both husbands and wives to communicate and adjust.

The issue of "individualism" sometimes arose in the articles on marriage and domesticity. Some authors constructed the housewife problem as a conflict between gender roles and individuality. Often expressed in historical terms, the conflict pitted old-fashioned gender relations in which women were first and foremost doting mothers and submissive wives against modern relations in which women were individual human beings. Postwar authors did not, as Friedan's *Feminine Mystique* would have it, side automatically with "sexual passivity, male domination, and nurturing maternal love." They portrayed the ideal marriage as an equal partnership, with each partner intermingling traditional masculine and feminine roles. One article insisted: "The healthy, emotionally well-balanced male isn't alarmed by the fact that women are human, too, and have an aggressive as well as a passive side. . . . He takes women seriously as individuals." This article and others condemned men who assumed an attitude of superiority. As another article stated, "The dominating husband and submissive wife are things of the past." Yet, to many it seemed that "individualism" could go too far and upset modern marriage. While husbands might do more housework and wives might pursue nondomestic activities, men remained the primary breadwinners and women the keepers of the home. . . .

While all of the magazines endorsed a manicured version of heterosexual appeal, the African-American magazines displayed it most heartily. This may have reflected African-American vernacular traditions, such as the blues, that rejected white middle-class injunctions against public sexual expression. But it also reflected an editorial decision to construct glamour and beauty as political issues in the fight against racism. Articles admired black women's sex appeal in a self-conscious defiance of racist white standards of beauty. In this context what some feminists today might read as sexual "objectification" presented itself as racial advancement, according black womanhood equal treatment with white. Thus, *Ebony*, which in most respects resembled a white family magazine like *Life*, also included some of the mildly risque cheesecake seen in white men's magazines, like *Esquire*. One editorial explained: "Because we live in a society in which standards of physical beauty are most often circumscribed by a static concept of whiteness of skin and blondeness of hair, there is an aching need for someone to shout from the housetops that black women are beautiful."

In a curious bow to individual striving, popular magazines, both black and white, often portrayed beauty and allure as achievements that any woman could attain if she tried hard enough. As the entertainer Dorothy Dandridge explained in *Ebony*, "Every woman can have some sex appeal." While a woman could achieve allure, she should attain it without "vulgarizing" sex or making an "open display" of it. Similarly, in the *Ladies'HomeJournal*, an article proclaimed, "She Turned Herself into a Beauty." This woman's "achievements" included weight loss, better grooming, and medical help for acne, a deformed nose, and a bent back. Another article, in *Coronet*, stated bluntly: "If anything's lacking, she can take immediate steps to remedy it—go to a hairdresser, a psychiatrist, whatever is needed." With a middle-class faith in the individual's ability to rise, articles suggested that individual effort, careful consumerism, and reliance on experts could bring any woman success, even in the realm of beauty and appeal.

Still, despite the magazines' endorsement of feminine beauty and heterosexual allure, Friedan's polemical claim that "American women have been successfully reduced to sex creatures" seems unabashedly hyperbolic. Try as they might, popular magazines could not entirely dictate the responses of readers. In most cases, we have little way of knowing how readers responded to magazine articles, but in the case of sex appeal we have explicit letters of dissent. In the African-American magazines, some readers, women and men both, objected to the photos of semiclad women. One woman complained that the "so-called beauties" were "really a disgrace to all women." And another protested "those girl covers and the . . . so-called realism (just a cover up name for cheapness, coarseness, lewdness, profanity and irreverence)."

In *Ladies' Home Journal*, too, readers responded with rare indignation to one article on sex appeal. In the offending article, "How to Be Loved," movie star Marlene Dietrich lectured housewives on enhancing their allure. Dietrich linked appeal to unadorned self-subordination. "To be completely a woman," she wrote, "you need a master." She advised women to plan their clothes, their conversation, and their meals to please their husbands. After washing their dishes, "like Phoenix out of the ashes," women should emerge "utterly desirable." And they should not grumble. "Some women," Dietrich proclaimed, "could do with a bit of spanking to answer their complaining." The article evoked what the *Journal's* editors called an "intense" response. Sarcastic letter writers objected to Dietrich's call for servile pampering of men and "utterly desirable" behavior. As one writer stated, "How *could you* hand the American woman such an article?" The letter writers portrayed themselves as down-home and unglamorous housewives, "all straight-haired and plain," who could not and would not emulate Dietrich's version of sexual allure. One woman wrote: "I resemble Eleanor Roosevelt more than I do La Dietrich, so that alters the visual effect." Another writer proclaimed: "Pish, tosh and hooey! Could be that Marlene could emerge from a stack of dirty dishes . . . and still be glamorous and desirable, but the housewife and mother I know gets dishpan hands and another twinge in the old back. . . . Marlene should talk about something she understands." For these women, marriage was a working partnership. Their husbands, they claimed, helped with the housework, accepted their scolding, and respected their "whims and fatigue." "Out here where I live," one woman wrote, "reasonably intelligent [married couples) . . . learn to live and work together." These readers used their domestic identities as hardworking housewives, not to berate women of public achievement, but to reject a competing image of women as subservient sexual bait.

A handful of letters, written by only a few readers, scarcely begins to suggest the range of responses that women probably had when reading the magazines. The frequent articles on work, politics, domesticity, and sexuality may have encouraged some women to take pride in, long for, or emulate magazine versions of public participation, home life, or glamour. At the same time, the flood of competing images—of housewives, workers, politicians, and sex bombs—may have inundated women who could not possibly identify with or remake themselves in all of the proffered models.

The response to one article suggests that readers may have chosen among alternative versions of womanhood, appropriating the images that rang true or appealed to them and rejecting the others. In this set of letters, some housewives accepted the "plight of the young mother" as a true description of their experience. They appreciated an article that validated their sense of domestic discontent. For these women, the article was a "morale lifter." "I have no words to tell what it means," one woman wrote, "to have all the facets of housewifery (that seemed to have sprung from my own deficiencies) held up as situations of national import." Other women rejected the article as a "very unfair picture." They resented an article that depicted them as overworked victims who could not cope with their housework. "Oh, for pity's sake," one woman asked, "What old plight am I in that no one has told me about? ... I have four children . . . and I don't put in a forty-hour week. . . . I think it's a great life." In short, both readers and articles were varied enough and ambivalent enough to enable more than one possible reading... .

According to Friedan, the "feminine mystique" emerged full-blown in the mass culture of the late 1940s and 1950s. Friedan compared short story fiction in women's magazines of the late 1930s, late 1940s, and late 1950s, and she also referred to fiction and nonfiction from various magazines of the postwar era. With this evidence, Friedan told a story of declension. In the 1930s, she claimed, women's magazines encouraged women to participate in the wider world outside the home. Short stories featured fictional career women "marching toward some goal or vision of their own." In Friedan's account, this "passionate search for individual identity" ended in the late 1940s. The postwar magazines, she said, narrowed their scope to the housewife in the home and adopted Farnham and Lundberg's antifeminist stance.

My own research suggests a different history. To place my postwar sample in historical context, I supplemented it with comparable samples of nonfiction articles from popular magazines of the Great Depression and World War II. Most striking were the continuities, the themes that recurred throughout the mid-twentieth century. From the 1930s to the 1950s, magazine articles advocated both domestic ideals and nondomestic achievement for women. In the 1930s and 1940s as well as the 1950s, the women's magazines presented housewives with romantic fiction, marriage advice, recipes, fashions, and ads for household products. And in all three decades, popular magazines, including women's magazines, spotlighted women of public achievement, addressed women as workers, and promoted women's participation in community activism and politics. Throughout the mid-twentieth century, conservatives called occasionally for women's subordination and women's rights advocates insisted occasionally on equality. More frequently, though, the magazines asserted both a long-held domestic ideal and a long-held ethos of achievement.

Beyond the common themes though, postwar magazines differed from earlier magazines in emphasis if not in kind. In my samples, the proportion of articles that focused on motherhood, marriage, and housewifery was actually smaller during the 1950s than during either the 1930s or the 1940s. In the earlier decades, the articles on domesticity often expressed the special concerns of the Great Depression or World War II. During the 1930s, numerous articles praised, advised, and encouraged housewives, as families budgeted their money and adult children returned home. A few articles offered reasons why wives or daughters should not pursue jobs or careers, perhaps reflecting a veiled hostility to women in the depression-era workplace. And several articles presented marriage and domesticity as a "great opportunity" or "the best-paying and most soul-satisfying career that any woman can espouse." During World War II, as expected, the magazines promoted women's participation in war industry, the military, and volunteer service. A couple of articles recommended ways of relieving working women's household burdens, and a few lauded women who combined motherhood and career. But the wartime magazines also lavished extensive praise on devoted mothers and loyal wives. Responding to a wartime fear of family breakdown, they stated explicitly that mothers had a primary duty to their children. The author of one such article called on the government to draft women who neglected their children and assign them "to duty in their own homes." Other articles warned women against taking husbands for granted or lowering housekeeping standards. Placed in this context, the postwar promotion of marriage and motherhood seems neither surprising nor anomalous.

The presentation of women's public lives also shifted with the times. In the postwar era, Rosie the Riveter and her challenge to the sexual division of labor vanished from the mass culture. Magazines rarely presented women in heavy industry or in the armed services. In this sense, the postwar mass culture reverted to prewar assumptions about gender roles. But the sample from the 1950s did not represent domestic retreat. In fact, it included more laudatory stories on women who achieved public success than did the samples from either of the earlier decades. The postwar magazines devoted a greater proportion of space to individual women in business, professions, social service, politics, and entertainment. The concept of public service also seems to have changed. *The Ladies' Home Journal* is perhaps emblematic. In the 1930s, the *Journal* launched a campaign, "It's Up to the Women," inviting women to help end the depression. While the campaign acknowledged the work of local women's clubs, its central theme, repeated in several issues, urged housewives to bolster the economy simply by spending more money. In the 1950s, when the *Journal* again asked housewives to join in public service, it invited them to enter mainstream politics as party workers and politicians. Public service had moved beyond the traditionally female sphere.

Why does my version of history differ from Betty Friedan's? The most obvious, and the most gracious, explanation is that we used different, though overlapping, sources. The nonfiction articles I read may well have included more contradictions and more ambivalence than the fiction on which Friedan focused. But there are, I think, additional differences in approach. Friedan did not read the popular magazines incorrectly, but she did, it seems, cite them reductively. For the prewar era, she seems to have chosen the stories that most embraced public achievement; for the postwar era, she seems to have chosen the stories that most embodied domestic ideals. A cursory review of some of Friedan's evidence suggests that her account of change over time may be somewhat skewed. For her prewar study, Friedan omitted the fiction that featured housewives and failed to mention that the "career women" heroines she cited relinquished or planned to relinquish their jobs for marriage and housewifery. In this way, she may have projected an imagined feminist past onto the mass culture of the 1930s. For the postwar era, she cited both fiction and nonfiction stories on domesticity. But she downplayed the articles on domestic problems (belittling one by saying "the bored editors . . . ran a little article"), ignored the articles on individual achievement, and dismissed the articles on political participation with a one-sentence caricature. Her forceful protest against a restrictive domestic ideal neglected the extent to which that ideal was already undermined.

My reassessment of the "feminine mystique" is part of a larger revisionist project. For the past few years, historians have questioned the stereotype of postwar women as quiescent, docile, and domestic. Despite the baby boom and despite discrimination in employment, education, and public office, married women, black and white joined the labor force in increasing numbers, and both married and unmarried women participated actively in politics and reform. Just as women's activities were more varied and more complex than is often acknowledged, so, I argue, was the postwar popular ideology. Postwar magazines, like their prewar and wartime predecessors, rarely presented direct challenges to the conventions of marriage or motherhood, but they only rarely told women to return to or stay at home. They included stories that glorified domesticity, but they also expressed ambivalence about domesticity, endorsed women's nondomestic activity, and celebrated women's public success. They delivered multiple messages, which women could read as sometimes supporting and sometimes subverting the "feminine mystique."

19. Vietnam: A Necessary War

Michael Lind

In the winter of 1950, Moscow was as cold as hell. On the evening of February 14, 1950, in a banquet hall in the Kremlin, three men whose plans would subject Indochina to a half century of warfare, tyranny, and economic stagnation, and inspire political turmoil in the United States and Europe, stood side by side: Joseph Stalin, Mao Zedong, and Ho Chi Minh.

In the 1960s, when the United States committed its own troops to battle in an effort to prevent clients of the Soviet Union and China from conquering Indochina, many opponents of the American intervention claimed that the North Vietnamese leader Ho Chi Minh's communism was superficial, compared to his nationalism. In reality, there was an international communist conspiracy, and Ho Chi Minh was a charter member of it. Beginning in the 1920s, Ho, a founding member of the French Communist party, had been an agent of the Communist International (Comintern), a global network of agents and spies controlled with iron discipline by the Soviet dictatorship. In the 1930s, Ho had lived in the USSR, slavishly approving every twist and turn of Stalin's policy; in the 1940s, he had been a member of the Chinese Communist party, then subordinated to Moscow. Ho Chin Minh owed not merely his prominence but his life to his career in the communist network outside of his homeland. Because he had been out of the country for so many years, he had survived when many other Vietnamese nationalists, noncommunist and communist alike, had been imprisoned or executed by the French or by the Japanese during World War II. . . .

The Cold War was the third world war of the twentieth century. It was a contest for global military and diplomatic primacy between the United States and the Soviet Union, which had emerged as the two strongest military powers after World War II. Because the threat of nuclear escalation prevented all-out conventional war between the two superpowers, the Soviet-American contest was fought in the form of arms races, covert action, ideological campaigns, economic embargoes, and proxy wars in peripheral areas. In three of these—Korea, Indochina, and Afghanistan—one of the two superpowers sent hundreds of thousands of its own troops into battle against clients of the other side.

In the third world war, Indochina was the most fought over territory on earth. The region owed this undesirable honor not to its intrinsic importance but to the fact that in other places where the two superpowers confronted one another they were frozen in a stalemate that could not be broken without the risk of general war. The Soviet Union and the United States fought proxy wars

---

Michael Lind, *Vietnam: The Necessary War* (New York: Free Press, 1999), 1, 4–5, 31–35, 38–41, 52, 54, 60–62, 64–65, 254, 256–257. Reprinted and edited with permission of The Free Press, a Division of Simon & Schuster, Inc.

in Indochina because they dared not engage in major tests of strength in Central Europe or Northeast Asia (after 1953) or even the Middle East. Indochina was strategic because it was peripheral.

Throughout the Cold War, the bloody military struggles in the Indochina theater were shaped indirectly by the tense but bloodless diplomatic struggles in the European theater. By going to war in Korea and simultaneously extending an American military protectorate over Taiwan and French Indochina, the Truman administration signaled its resolve to defend its European allies. American officials swallowed their misgivings about French colonialism and paid for France's effort in its on-going war in Indochina from 1950 until 1954, in the hope of winning French support for the rearmament of Germany. Khrushchev's humiliation of the United States in the Berlin crisis of 1961 persuaded the Kennedy administration that a show of American resolve on the Indochina front was all the more important. In 1968, concern by members of the U.S. foreign policy elite that further escalation in Indochina would endanger America's other commitments, particularly in the European theater, was one of the factors that led the Johnson administration to begin the process of disengagement from the Vietnam War. The Eastern European revolutions of 1989, which led to the collapse of the Soviet Union itself in 1991, deprived communist Vietnam of its superpower protector and ideological model. . . .

The Vietnam War, like the Korean War, the Afghan War, the Greek Civil War, the Taiwan crises, and a number of other conflicts, was at one and the same time a civil war and proxy battle in the Cold War. During the Cold War, Indochina mattered—and it mattered to the Soviet Union and China as well as to the United States.

Examining the Vietnam War in its Cold War context does not necessarily justify it. Indeed, some argue that while it was necessary for the United States to wage the Cold War, success in the Cold War did not require the United States to establish or defend a protectorate over most of Indochina. This is the claim that was made by a number of American "realists" at the time of the Vietnam conflict and in the succeeding decades. Realism, or realpolitik, is the theory of international relations that emphasizes the primacy and legitimacy of power struggles in world politics. Several of the most prominent American realist thinkers—diplomat George Kennan, journalist Walter Lippmann, and scholar Hans Morgenthau, among others—criticized the Vietnam War in particular, and in some cases the Cold War as a whole, as an unnecessary or disproportionate response to the threats posed by Soviet expansionism and communist Chinese revolutionary radicalism. Within the U.S. government in the 1960s, Senator William Fulbright, chairman of the Senate Foreign Relations Committee, and Undersecretary of State George Ball, one of the Democratic party's most influential foreign policy experts, also used the language of realism to criticize what they considered to be an overly ambitious U.S. grand strategy.

The realist critique of the Vietnam War remains very popular today. It permits aging veterans of the sixties left, embarrassed by their former support for Ho Chi Minh's vicious dictatorship and their denunciations of American presidents as war criminals or their avoidance of the draft, to claim that they were right to oppose the war, even if their rationale was mistaken. . . . Finally, the fact that some of the policymakers who played a role in the war, like former Secretary of State Robert McNamara, have claimed that it was a mistake from the beginning has appeared to strengthen the realist critique (even though other policymakers, such as former national security adviser Walt Rostow, continue to argue that the war made sense in terms of U.S. strategy).

In light of all this, it is important to recall that there was, and is, a realist case in favor of the Vietnam War, as well as one against it. If some American realists such as Lippmann, Kennan, and Morgenthau doubted the importance of America's commitment to denying Indochina to the communist bloc, others, such as Walt and Eugene Rostow, Samuel P. Huntington, and John P. Roche, were convinced of the significance of that commitment. The fact that the United States was defeated in Vietnam does not necessarily discredit the strategic logic that inspired the U.S. commitment to South Vietnam, Laos, and Cambodia and their Southeast Asian neighbors. The failure of American policy in Indochina may have resulted from inappropriate military tactics, or the characteristics of the North Vietnamese and South Vietnamese societies and governments, or the support provided Hanoi by the Soviet Union and China, or the peculiarities of American political culture—or some combinations of all of these factors. The case that Indochina was worth a limited American war of some kind, particularly in the circumstances of the Cold War in the 1960s, is compelling in light of what we now know about the pattern and result of the Cold War as a whole.

Contemporary critics of the Johnson administration spoke of its "credibility gap" in connection with the Vietnam War. In addition to having exaggerated the progress of the United States and its South Vietnamese allies in the war, Johnson and his aides were accused of a failure to clearly explain the goal of the war to the American public and the world. Typical of this line of criticism is a comment in 1968 by William R. Corson, a former marine colonel in Vietnam, in his critique of the war, The Betrayal: "The emergence of the credibility gap came from the ill-fated attempts of Secretary [of State Dean] Rusk to justify the war successively as, first, a defense of Vietnamese freedom, then a defense of our national interest, and finally the defense of the world from the yellow peril."

Indeed, Johnson and officials of his administration provided several rationales for the escalation of the U.S. effort in Vietnam. Johnson cited "the deepening shadow of China. The rulers in Hanoi are urged on by Peking." On another occasion he stressed the need to thwart guerrilla warfare as an instrument of communist expansion: "Our strength imposes on us an obligation to assure that this type of aggression does not succeed." Secretary of State Dean Rusk stressed the potential effects of a defeat of U.S. policy in Southeast Asia on America's global alliance system, including "our guarantees to Berlin."

From today's perspective, the Johnson administration does not appear to have been more inconsistent or disingenuous in describing the aims of U.S. foreign policy than other U.S. wartime administrations. During World War II, the Roosevelt administration sometimes justified the U.S. effort in terms of the security of the United States and at other times claimed that the defeat of the Axis powers would help promote a utopian world characterized by the "Four Freedoms." In the run-up to the Gulf War, the Bush administration provided a number of rationales, including the atrocities committed by Saddam Hussein's regime (some of which were exaggerated) and the importance of Middle Eastern oil for American jobs. President Clinton and members of his administration explained the U.S.-led NATO war against Serbia in terms of a number of different rationales: the moral imperative of preventing or reversing the ethnic cleansing of Albanians in Kosovo by the Serbs, the need to demonstrate the military credibility of NATO and the United States, the economic importance of a stable Europe, and the danger that the conflict would expand and draw in Greece and Turkey. Government officials addressing different audiences on different occasions for different purposes may emphasize different goals of foreign policy. The apparent inconsistencies that result are not necessarily evidence of official duplicity or official confusion. Nor does the fact that some official goals were misguided or overemphasized mean that others were not sound.

What is more, the notion of the "credibility gap" ignores the possibility that in escalating the Vietnam War the Johnson administration had several purposes, not just one. By successfully defending South Vietnam against subversion from North Vietnam, a client of the Soviet Union and China, the United States could deter the Soviets, reassure its allies, discourage the adoption of the Chinese and Vietnamese model of revolutionary "people's war" by antiwestern insurgents in developing countries, and encourage the economic development and liberalization of South Vietnam as well as of South Korea and Taiwan, all at the same time.

While the U.S. intervention in Vietnam served a number of complementary purposes, there was a hierarchy among U.S. goals. The administrations of Kennedy, Johnson, and Nixon may not have made the hierarchy as clear as intellectuals would like. Nevertheless, in hindsight it is possible to identify the place assigned to different goals in the hierarchy of purposes by these three presidents and their aides. The chief purpose of the United States in Vietnam was to demonstrate America's credibility as a military power and a reliable ally to its enemies and its allies around the world. The danger was that if the United States were perceived to be lacking in military capacity, political resolve, or both, the Soviet Union and/or China and their proxies would act more aggressively, while U.S. allies, including important industrial democracies such as West Germany and Japan, would be inclined to appease the communist great powers. It was in this global geopolitical context that preventing "falling dominoes"—whether in Southeast Asia proper, or in Third World countries far from Vietnam—was important. Least important of all the U.S. purposes in intervening in Vietnam was promoting liberty, democracy, and prosperity in South Vietnam itself. The defeat of the attempted takeover of South Vietnam by North Vietnam was a necessary, but not sufficient, condition for the evolution of the authoritarian government of South Vietnam toward liberalism and democracy. But America's political goals in South Vietnam were appropriately incidental and subordinate to America's goals in Southeast Asian power politics, which, in turn, were incidental and subordinate to America's global strategy in the third world war. . . .

Credibility, in power politics, is a country's reputation for military capability combined with the political resolve to use it in order to promote its goals. The concern of statesmen with the reputation of their states for military ability and resolve is as old as interstate politics.

The natural concern of U.S. leaders with credibility was heightened into something like an obsession by the peculiar dynamics of the Cold War—a world war fought by means of sieges and duels. Unlike World Wars I and II, the third global conflict of the twentieth century took the form of a half-century siege on the European front and duels or proxy wars in a number of other theaters. The forward deployment of U.S. troops in Central Europe, Japan, and South Korea following the Korean War, together with U.S. efforts to maintain conventional and nuclear superiority, made up the siege aspect of the Cold War. In the long run, the superior military-industrial capability of the United States and its affluent allies was bound to wear down the military-industrial base of the Soviet empire, as long as two conditions were met. The first condition for western success in the Cold War was alliance unity; the alliance of the United States, West Germany, Japan, Britain, France, and the other major democracies could not be split by a Soviet diplomatic strategy of divide-and-rule. Meeting this condition required periodic reaffirmations of alliance unity, like the development of the Euromissiles by NATO in the early 1980s in response to Soviet intimidation. In addition, the American bloc was required to match and surpass the Soviet imperium in the arms race. Because the goal was to spend the Soviet Union into bankruptcy, not merely to defend the western allies against an implausible threat of invasion, the American bloc could not accumulate a sufficiency of nuclear missiles and other weapons and then quit. The arms race was an auction that had to be continued until one side dropped out.

The military-industrial siege of the Soviet empire took far longer than early Cold War leaders such as Truman and Eisenhower and their advisers had expected. In the 1950s, Eisenhower hoped that U.S. troops might be withdrawn from Europe in the next decade. Instead, the siege lasted almost half a century. While manning the siegeworks in Europe and northeast Asia, the United States also had to demonstrate its determination by threatening war, or, if the threat failed, by waging limited war, with the Soviet Union and/or China and their proxies in regions on the periphery of the main theaters of Cold War competition. Sometimes the United States had to fight where it was challenged by its enemies, not where it would have preferred to fight. Because perceived power is power (except in times of war, when actual power is tested), the danger that a strategic retreat will be misinterpreted as evidence of a loss of will or capability is quite real. To refuse to duel is to lose the duel.

Thus defined, credibility became the central strategic concern of the United States in the Cold War. Henry Kissinger described the American interest in Indochina in terms of U.S. credibility in global power politics: "With respect to Indo-China, we are not equating the intrinsic importance of each part of the world, and we are not saying that every part of the world is strategically as important to the United States as any other part of the world.. . . [The question of aid to allies in Indochina] is a fundamental question of how we are viewed by all other people John Foster Dulles made a similar point in calling on the United States to protect the anticommunist remnant of the Chinese Nationalist regime on Taiwan in spring 1950: "If we do not act, it will be everywhere interpreted that we are making another retreat because we dare not risk war."

Who was the intended audience for American displays of credibility? Makers and defenders of U.S. Cold War strategy reasoned that the United States had to deter its enemies and reassure its allies at the same time. In a speech at Johns Hopkins University on April 7, 1965, President Johnson invoked these two reasons for demonstrations of credibility in the context of the war in Indochina. First, he cited the need to reassure America's allies: "Around the globe, from Berlin to Thailand, are people whose well-being rests, in part, on the belief that they can count on us if they are attacked. To leave Vietnam to its fate would shake the confidence of all these people in the value of America's commitment, the value of America's word." Second, President Johnson sought to discourage America's enemies: "The central lesson of our time is that the appetite of aggression is never satisfied. To withdraw from one battlefield means only to prepare for the next. We must say in Southeast Asia, as we did in Europe, in the words of the Bible: 'Hitherto shalt thou come, but no further.'"

Using less orotund language, Johnson adviser John McNaughton, in a memo of March 25, 1965, emphasized American credibility in listing the aims of U.S. policy in Indochina:

> *70%:—To avoid a humiliating defeat (to our reputation* as *a guarantor)*
> *20%:—To keep South Vietnam (and the adjacent territory) from Chinese hands*
> *10%:—To permit the people of South Vietnam to enjoy a better, freer way of life...*

In the mind of the western public, the idea of defeat in the Cold War was associated with nuclear armaggedon. But the defeat of the United States in the global struggle might have resulted from America's backing down in confrontations involving Berlin, or Korea, or Taiwan, or Indochina, or Cuba, or similar contested areas charged with significance by the superpower rivalry. After the first major defeat or retreat, or perhaps the second or third or fourth in a row, confidence in America's military capability, or its determination to use it, would have collapsed. At that point, something akin to a panic in the stock market would have ensued. In a remarkably short period of time—a few years, perhaps even a few months—the worldwide American alliance system would have unraveled, as European, Asian, Middle Eastern, African, and Latin American states hurriedly made deals with Moscow.

Thanks to runaway bandwagoning, the United States would have found itself marginalized in a world now aligned around the Soviet Union (there having been no other military power with global reach and global ambitions at the time). The Soviets might not have had to fire a shot in anger. There need not have been any additional communist revolutions. The same elites might even have remained in power in the same capitals around the world. Indeed, America's alliances such as NATO and the U.S.-Japan alliance might have lasted formally for a few more years, though moribund. But Moscow would have displaced Washington at the apex of the global military hierarchy, and everybody would have known it.

The bandwagon effect is the reason why it was a mistake to argue that the Soviet empire was bound to collapse of overextension. Power in the international arena is relative, not absolute. If the Soviet Union had managed, by means of military intimidation, to divide the alliance of the United States, Western Europe, and Japan, or to frighten the United States into isolationism and appeasement, then it might have achieved and maintained a position as the world's leading military power in relative terms even while it reduced its expenditures on the military. In the same way, the abatement of the Soviet challenge permitted the United States to become relatively more powerful in world politics in the 1990s, even as it slashed its defense spending and overseas troop deployments. . . .

The Cold War, then, was most likely to end with a rapid and more or less bloodless global diplomatic realignment in favor of the superpower that was perceived to be the most militarily powerful and the most politically determined. We know that this is how the Cold War would have ended if the United States had lost, because this is how the Cold War ended when the Soviet Union lost. . . .

It is possible to argue that even if the Soviet Union and China considered the fate of Indochina to be important, the United States could have ceded the region to one or both of the communist great powers with little or no damage to its foreign policy. During the Cold War, minimal realists such as George Ball, George Kennan, and Walter Lippmann advocated a strategy of finite containment limited to the North Atlantic and North Pacific as an alternative to the policy of global containment that the United States actually pursued. Ball wrote that U.S. strategy should focus on "the principal Atlantic nations." The only area of the non-European world of any importance, apart from Japan, was the Middle

East, because of its oil reserves. The Vietnam War (and presumably the Korean War) was based on the mistaken equation of a commitment "in the jungles and rice paddies of a small country on the edge of nowhere with our most important treaty commitments to defend our Western allies in the heart of Europe—the center of world power and hence the center of danger." Like other minimal realists, Ball saw little reason for the United States to oppose Soviet imperial gains anywhere outside of an imaginary border that encircled North America, Western Europe, and the Middle East. Even the nearby nations of the Caribbean and Central America should be "free to create their own versions of chaos." . . .

. . . It might be argued that the "three fronts" of Korea, Taiwan, and Indochina were not as important in Cold War power politics as American presidents from Truman to Nixon believed. The question of whether a given country or region is strategic or not can be approached by means of a simple question: Do the great powers of a given era consider it worth fighting for?

...[B]etween 1946 and 1989, every major military power of the Cold War era—the United States, China, France, the Soviet Union, and the British Commonwealth—sent at least some troops into combat in Indochina or nearby countries in Southeast Asia. If Indochina was a peripheral region of no strategic importance in world politics, it is curious that this fact escaped the attention of policymakers in Washington, Moscow, Beijing, Paris, and London.

If Indochina was a key strategic region during the Cold War for which the two superpowers were willing to fight, directly or indirectly, why was it of strategic importance? The answer has less to do with sea-lanes than with symbolism. The symbolic significance of Indochina in the global rivalry for world primacy between the American bloc and the communist bloc, and in the simultaneous competition within the communist bloc between the Soviet Union and China, arose from the fact that the Cold War was an ideological war as well as a power struggle. . .

Even the relatively moderate Soviet leader Nikita Khrushchev emphasized that Moscow's support for communist revolutionaries in Asia was inspired not by the "national interest" of "Russia" but by the Soviet regime's ideology: "No real Communist would have tried to dissuade Kim Il-Sung from his compelling desire to liberate South Korea from Syngman Rhee and from reactionary American influence. To have done so would have contradicted the Communist view of the world." The Soviet Union was not only a superpower but the headquarters of the global religion of Marxism-Leninism, with zealous adherents in dozens of countries who looked to Moscow not only for military and economic support but for ideological guidance. Mao and his colleagues also viewed support for foreign communists as a test of their commitment to Marxism-Leninism. Zhou Enlai told North Vietnamese leaders in 1971, "Not to support the revolution of the Vietnamese people is like betraying the revolution." This viewpoint can be compared instructively with a recent description of Shiite Iran's foreign policy: "Because Iran sometimes portrays itself as a guardian of Shiites worldwide, experts in the region said today that it may feel under pressure to respond with military force if it can be proven that the Shiites [in Afghanistan] were attacked for reasons of religious faith."

The global alliance that the United States led in the Cold War was far more diverse than the communist bloc; it included liberal democracies, military dictatorships, and Muslim theocracies that shared little more than a common fear of Soviet power and influence. To the disappointment of Americans who wanted the United States to crusade for a "global democratic revolution," U.S. policymakers properly limited the goal of American grand strategy to the negative one of preventing hostile great powers from winning military hegemony over Europe, Asia, or the Eurasian supercontinent as a whole. The democratic wave of the 1990s was a byproduct of America's Cold War victory, not the goal of America's Cold War strategy. U.S. foreign policy had to be narrowly anticommunist because a pro-democratic foreign policy would have prevented the United States from having many allies outside of Western Europe, where most of the world's outnumbered democracies were found during the Cold War. . . .

What conclusions are to be drawn about the morality of the methods used by the United States in the Vietnam War? Johnson administration adviser John McNaughton, in a 1964 memo about U.S. Vietnam policy, stressed how important it was that the United States "emerge from the crisis without unacceptable taint from methods used."

A compelling case can be made that the United States was wrong for moral as well as for practical reasons to rely heavily on a strategy of attrition in South Vietnam between 1965 and 1968, when the war was a mixture of an insurgency and a conventional war. The attrition strategy was more defensible during the predominantly conventional stage of the Vietnam conflict from 1969-75.

The moral alternative to waging the Vietnam War by indiscriminate and disproportionate means, however, was waging it by more discriminate and proportionate means—not abandoning Indochina to Stalinism, to the detriment of both the peoples of Indochina and the U.S.-led alliance system. One can condemn many of the tactics used by the United States in Vietnam without condemning the war as a whole, just as one can condemn the terror bombing of civilians in Germany and Japan during World War II without arguing that the war against the Axis powers was unjust. . . .

Once the Vietnam War is viewed in the context of the Cold War, it looks less like a tragic error than like a battle that could hardly be avoided. The Cold War was fought as a siege in Europe and as a series of duels elsewhere in the world—chiefly, in Korea and Indochina. Both the siege and the duels were necessary. Power in world politics is perceived power, and perceived power is a vector that results from perceived military capability and perceived political will. The U.S. forces stationed in West Germany and Japan demonstrated the capability of the United States to defend its most important allies. U.S. efforts on behalf of minor allies in peripheral regions such as South Korea and South Vietnam and Laos proved that the United States possessed the will to be a reliable ally. Had the United States repeatedly refused to take part in proxy-war duels with the Soviet Union, and with China during its anti-American phase, it seems likely that there would have been a dramatic pro-Soviet realignment in world politics, no matter how many missiles rusted in their silos in the American West and no matter how many U.S. troops remained stationed in West Germany.

Further Reading

Stephen Ambrose, *Nixon* (3 volumes, 1987-1989).

Christian Appy, *Working-Class War: American Combat Soldiers and Vietnam* (1993).

Doris Kearns Goodwin, *Lyndon Johnson and the American Dream* (1977).

George Herring, *America's Longest War* (1986).

Mary Hershberger, *Traveling to Vietnam: American Peace Activists and the War* (1998).

Joan Hoff, *Nixon Reconsidered* (1994).

Frederik Logevall, *Choosing War: The Lost Chance for Peace and the Escalation of War in Vietnam* (1999).

Jonathan Shay, *Achilles in Vietnam: Combat Trauma and the Undoing of Character* (1994).

Marilyn Young, *The Vietnam Wars*, 1945-1990 (1991).

20. Reagan Calls for a Fight Against Sin, Evil, and Communism, 1983

Ronald Reagan

The other day in the East Room of the White House at a meeting there, someone asked me whether I was aware of all the people out there who were praying for the President. And I had to say, "Yes, I am. I've felt it. I believe in intercessionary prayer." But I couldn't help but say to that questioner after he'd asked the question that—or at least say to them that if sometimes when he was praying he got a busy signal, it was just me in there ahead of him. I think I understand how Abraham Lincoln felt when he said, "I have been driven many times to my knees by the overwhelming conviction that I had nowhere else to go." ...

There are a great many God-fearing, dedicated, noble men and women in public life, present company included. And yes, we need your help to keep us ever-mindful of the ideas and the principles that brought us into the public arena in the first place. The basis of those ideals and principles is a commitment to freedom and personal liberty that, itself is grounded in the much deeper realization that freedom prospers only where the blessings of God are avidly sought and humbly accepted....

I think the items that we've discussed here today must be a key part of the nation's political agenda. For the first time the Congress is openly and seriously debating and dealing with the prayer and abortion issues and that's enormous progress right there. I repeat: America is in the midst of a spiritual awakening and a moral renewal. ...

Now, obviously, much of this new political and social consensus I've talked about is based on a positive view of American history, one that takes pride in our country's accomplishments and record. But we must never forget that no government schemes are going to perfect man. We know that living in this world means dealing with what philosophers would call the phenomenology of evil or, as theologians would put it, the doctrine of sin.

There is sin and evil in the world, and we're enjoined by Scripture and the Lord Jesus to oppose it with all our might. Our nation, too, has a legacy of evil with which it must deal. The glory of this land has been its capacity for transcending the moral evils of our past. For example, the long struggle of minority citizens for equal rights, once a source of disunity and civil war is now a point of pride for all Americans. We must never go back. There is no room for racism, anti-Semitism, or other forms of ethnic and racial hatred in this country. . . .

Public Papers of the Presidents of the United States: Ronald Reagan, 1983 (Washington, D.C.: U.S. Government Printing Office, 1984), vol. 1, pp. 359–364.

And this brings me to my final point today. During my first press conference as president, in answer to a direct question, I pointed out that, as good Marxist-Leninists, the Soviet leaders have openly and publicly declared that the only morality they recognize is that which will further their cause, which is world revolution. I think I should point out I was only quoting Lenin, their guiding spirit, who said in 1920 that they repudiate all morality that proceeds from supernatural ideas—that's their name for religion—or ideas that are outside class conceptions. Morality is entirely subordinate to the interests of class war. And everything is moral that is necessary for the annihilation of the old, exploiting social order and for uniting the proletariat. …

Yes, let us pray for the salvation of all of those who live in that totalitarian darkness. Pray they will discover the joy of knowing God. But until they do, let us be aware that while they preach the supremacy of the State, declare its omnipotence over individual man, and predict its eventual domination of all peoples on the earth, they are the focus of evil in the modern world. …

Because [communist leaders] sometimes speak in soothing tones of brotherhood and peace, because, like other dictators before them, they're always making "their final territorial demand," some would have us accept them at their word and accommodate ourselves to their aggressive impulses. But if history teaches anything, it teaches that simpleminded appeasement or wishful thinking about our adversaries is folly. It means the betrayal of our past, the squandering of our freedom.

So, I urge you to speak out against those who would place the United States in a position of military and moral inferiority. …In your discussions of the nuclear freeze proposals, I urge you to beware the temptation of pride—the temptation of blithely declaring yourselves above it all and label both sides equally at fault, to ignore the facts of history and the aggressive impulses of an evil empire, to simply call the arms race a giant misunderstanding and thereby remove yourself from the struggle between right and wrong and good and evil. …

While America's military strength is important, let me add here that I've always maintained that the struggle now going on for the world will never be decided by bombs or rockets, by armies or military might. The real crisis we face today is a spiritual one; at root, it is a test of moral will and faith. …

I believe we shall rise to the challenge. I believe that communism is another sad, bizarre chapter in human history whose last—last pages even now are being written. I believe this because the source of our strength in the quest for human freedom is not material, but spiritual. And because it knows no limitation, it must terrify and ultimately triumph over those who would enslave their fellow man. For in the words of Isaiah: "He giveth power to the faint; and to them that have no might He increased strength. But they that wait upon the Lord shall renew their strength; they shall mount up with wings as eagles; they shall run, and not be weary. …"

Yes, change your world. One of our Founding Fathers, Thomas Paine, said, "We have it within our power to begin the world over again." We can do it, doing together what no one church could do by itself.

God bless you and thank you very much.

21. The Disuniting of America, 1991

Arthur M. Schlesinger, Jr.

Arthur Meier Schlesinger Jr., born Arthur Bancroft Schlesinger (October 15,1917 – February 28,2007), was a Pulitzer Prize recipient and American historian and social critic whose work explored the liberalism of American political leaders including Franklin D. Roosevelt, John F. Kennedy, and Robert F. Kennedy. He published many highly respected books, two of the best known were A Thousand Days: John F. Kennedy in the White House *(1965) and* The Imperial Presidency *(1973) which examined Richard Nixon's presidency.*

In this article, written in 1991, Schlesinger refers to "the end of history" which had been predicted by Francis Fukuyama in an article and later in his book The End of History and the Last Man. *In this book, Fukuyama had predicted that, "What we may be witnessing is not just the end of the Cold War, or the passing of a particular period of post-war history, but the end of history as such: that is, the end point of mankind's ideological evolution and the universalization of Western liberal democracy as the final form of human government."*

The fading away of the cold war has brought an era of ideological conflict to an end. But it has not, as forecast, brought an end to history. One set of hatreds gives way to the next. Lifting the lid of ideological repression in Eastern Europe releases ethnic antagonisms deeply rooted in experience and in memory. The disappearance of ideological competition in the third world removes superpower restraints on national and tribal confrontations. As the era of ideological conflict subsides, humanity enters—or more precisely re-enters—a possibly more dangerous era of ethnic and racial animosity.

The hostility of one tribe for another is among the most instinctive human reactions. Yet, the history of our planet has been in great part the history of the mixing of peoples. Mass migrations have produced mass antagonisms from the beginning of time. Today, as the twentieth century draws to an end, a number of factors—not just the evaporation of the cold war but, more profoundly, the development of swifter modes of communication and transport, the acceleration of population growth, the breakdown of traditional social structures, the flight from tyranny and from want, the dream of a better life somewhere else—converge to drive people as never before across national frontiers and thereby to make the mixing of peoples a major problem for the century that lies darkly ahead.

What happens when people of different ethnic origins, speaking different languages and professing different religions, settle in the same geographical locality and live under the same political sovereignty? Unless a common purpose binds them together, tribal hostilities will drive them apart. Ethnic and racial conflict, it seems evident, will now replace the conflict of ideologies as the explosive issue of our times.

On every side today ethnicity is the cause of the breaking of nations. The Soviet Union, Yugoslavia, India, South Africa are all in crisis. Ethnic tensions disturb and divide Sri Lanka, Burma, Ethiopia, Indonesia, Iraq, Lebanon, Israel, Cyprus, Somalia, Nigeria, Liberia, Angola, Sudan, Zaire, Guyana, Trinidad—you name it. Even nations as stable and civilized as Britain and France, Belgium and Spain and Czechoslovakia, face growing ethnic and racial troubles. "The virus of tribalism," says the *Economist*, ". . risks becoming the AIDS of international politics-lying dormant for years, then flaring up to destroy countries."

Take the case of our neighbor to the north. Canada has long been considered the most sensible and placid of nations. "Rich, peaceful and, by the standards of almost anywhere else, enviably successful," the *Economist* observes: yet today "on the brink of bust-up." Michael Ignatieff (the English-resident son of a Russian-born Canadian diplomat and thus an example of the modern mixing of peoples) writes of Canada, "Here we have one of the five richest nations on earth, a country so uniquely blessed with space and opportunity that the world's poor are beating at the door to get in, and it is tearing itself apart. . . . If one of the top five developed nations on earth can't make a federal, multi-ethnic state work, who else can?"

The answer to that increasingly vital question has been, at least until recently, the United States.

Now how have Americans succeeded in pulling off this almost unprecedented trick? Other countries break up because they fail to give ethnically diverse peoples compelling reasons to see themselves as part of the same nation. The United States has worked, thus far, because it has offered such reasons. What is it then that, in the absence of a common ethnic origin, has held Americans together over two turbulent centuries? For America was a multiethnic country from the start. Hector St. John de Crèvecoeur emigrated from France to the American colonies in 1759, married an American woman, settled on a farm in Orange County, New York, and published his *Letters from an American Farmer* during the American Revolution. This eighteenth-century French American marveled at the astonishing diversity of the other settlers "a mixture of English, Scotch, Irish, French, Dutch, German, and Swedes," a "strange mixture of blood" that you could find in no other country.

He recalled one family whose grandfather was English, whose wife was Dutch, whose son married a French woman, and whose present four sons had married women of different nationalities. "From this promiscuous breed," he wrote, "that race now called Americans have arisen." (The word *race* as used in the eighteenth and nineteenth centuries meant what we mean by nationality today; thus people spoke of "the English race," "the German race," and so on.) What, Crèvecoeur mused, were the characteristics of this suddenly emergent American race? *Letters fiom an American Farmer* propounded a famous question: "What then is the American, this new man?" (Twentieth-century readers must overlook eighteenth-century male obliviousness to the existence of women.)

Crèvecoeur gave his own question its classic answer: "He is an American, who leaving behind him all his ancient prejudices and manners, receives new ones from the new mode of life he has embraced, the new government he obeys, and the new rank he holds. The American is a new man, who acts upon new principles. . . . *Here individuals of all nations are melted into a new race of men.*"

E pluribus unum. The United States had a brilliant solution for the inherent fragility of a multiethnic society: the creation of a brand-new national identity, carried forward by individuals who, in forsaking old loyalties and joining to make new lives, melted away ethnic differences. Those intrepid Europeans who had torn up their roots to brave the wild Atlantic *wanted* to forget a horrid past and to embrace a hopeful future. They *expected* to become Americans. Their goals were escape, deliverance, assimilation. They saw America as *a* transforming nation, banishing dismal memories and developing a unique national character based on common political ideals and shared experiences. The point of America was not to preserve old cultures, but to forge a new *American* culture.

One reason why Canada, despite all its advantages, is so vulnerable to schism is that, as Canadians freely admit, their country lacks such a unique national identity. Attracted variously to Britain, France, and the United States, inclined for generous reasons to a policy of official multiculturalism, Canadians have never developed a strong sense of what it is to be a Canadian. As Sir John Macdonald, their first prime minister, put it, Canada has "too much geography and too little history."

The United States has had plenty of history. From the Revolution on, Americans have had a powerful national creed. The vigorous sense of national identity accounts for our relative success in converting Crevecoeur's "promiscuous breed" into one people and thereby making a multiethnic society work.

This is not to say that the United States has ever fulfilled Crevecoeur's ideal. *New* waves of immigration brought in people who fitted awkwardly into a society that was inescapably English in language, ideals, and institutions. For a long time the Anglo-Americans dominated American culture and politics. The pot did not melt everybody, not even all the white immigrants.

As for the nonwhite peoples—those long in America whom the European newcomers overran and massacred, or those others hauled in against their will from Africa and Asia—deeply bred racism put them all, red Americans, black Americans, yellow Americans, brown Americans, well outside the pale. The curse of racism was the great failure of the American experiment, the glaring contradiction of American ideals and the still crippling disease of American life.

Yet even nonwhite Americans, miserably treated as they were, contributed to the formation of the national identity. They became members, if third-class members, of American society and helped give the common culture new form and flavor. The infusion of non-Anglo stocks and the experience of the New World steadily reconfigured the British legacy and made the United States, as we all know, a very different country today from Britain.

The vision of America as melted into one people prevailed through most of the two centuries of the history of the United States. But the twentieth century has brought forth a new and opposing vision. One world war destroyed the old order of things and launched Woodrow Wilson's doctrine of the self determination of peoples. Twenty years after, a second world war dissolved the western colonial empires and intensified ethnic and racial militancy around the planet. In the United States itself, new laws eased entry for immigrants from South America, Asia, and Africa and altered the composition of the American people.

In a nation marked by an even stranger mixture of blood than Crèvecoeur had known, his celebrated question is asked once more, with a new passion—and a new answer. Today many Americans disavow the historic goal of "a new race of man." The escape from origins yields to the search for roots. The "ancient prejudices and manners" disowned by Crèvecoeur have made a surprising comeback. A cult of ethnicity has arisen both among non-Anglo whites and among nonwhite minorities to denounce the idea of a melting pot, to challenge the concept of "one people," and to protect, promote, and perpetuate separate ethnic and racial communities.

The eruption of ethnicity had many good consequences. The American culture began at last to give shamefully overdue recognition to the achievements of minorities subordinated and spurned during the high noon of Anglo dominance. American education began at last to acknowledge the existence and significance of the great swirling world beyond Europe. All this was to the good. Of course history should be taught from a variety of perspectives. Let our children try to imagine the arrival of Columbus from the viewpoint of those who met him as well as from those who sent him. Living on a shrinking planet, aspiring to global leadership, Americans must learn much more about other races, other cultures, other continents. As they do, they acquire a more complex and invigorating sense of the world—and of themselves.

But, pressed too far, the cult of ethnicity has had bad consequences too. The new ethnic gospel rejects the unifying vision of individuals from all nations melted into a new race. Its underlying philosophy is that America is not a nation of individuals at all but a nation of groups, that ethnicity is the defining experience for most Americans, that ethnic ties are permanent and indelible, and that division into ethnic communities establishes the basic structure of American society and the basic meaning of American history.

Implicit in this philosophy is the classification of all Americans according to ethnic and racial criteria. But while the ethnic interpretation of American history, like the economic interpretation, is valid and illuminating up to a point, it is fatally misleading and wrong when presented as the whole picture. The ethnic interpretation, moreover, reverses the historic theory of America as one people—the theory that has thus far managed to keep American society whole.

Instead of a transformative nation with an identity all its own, America in this new light is seen as preservative of diverse alien identities. Instead of a nation composed of individuals making their own unhampered choices, America increasingly sees itself as composed of groups more or less ineradicable in their ethnic character. The multiethnic dogma abandons historic purposes, replacing assimilation by fragmentation, integration by separatism. It belittles *unum* and glorifies *pluribus*.

The historic idea of a unifying American identity is now in peril in many arenas—in our politics, our voluntary organizations, our churches, our language. And in no arena is the rejection of an overriding national identity more crucial than in our system of education.

The schools and colleges of the republic train the citizens of the future. Our public schools in particular have been the great instrument of assimilation and the great means of forming an American identity. What students are taught in schools affects the way they will thereafter see and treat other Americans, the way they will thereafter conceive the purposes of the republic. The debate about the curriculum is a debate about what it means to be an American.

The militants of ethnicity now contend that a main objective of public education should be the protection, strengthening, celebration, and perpetuation of ethnic origins and identities. Separatism, however, nourishes prejudices, magnifies differences and stirs antagonisms. The consequent increase in ethnic and racial conflict lies behind the hullabaloo over "multiculturalism" and "political correctness," over the iniquities of the "Eurocentric" curriculum, and over the notion that history and literature should be taught not as intellectual disciplines but as therapies whose function is to raise minority self-esteem.

Watching ethnic conflict tear one nation after another apart, one cannot look with complacency at proposals to divide the United States into distinct and immutable ethnic and racial communities, each taught to cherish its own apartness from the rest. One wonders: Will the center hold? or will the melting pot give way to the Tower of Babel?

I don't want to sound apocalyptic about these developments. Education *is* always in ferment, and a good thing too. Schools and colleges have always been battlegrounds for debates over beliefs, philosophies, values. The situation in our universities, I am confident, will soon right itself once the great silent majority of professors cry "enough" and challenge what they know to be voguish nonsense.

The impact of ethnic and racial pressures on our public schools is more troubling. The bonds of national cohesion are sufficiently fragile already. Public education should aim to strengthen those bonds, not to weaken them. If separatist tendencies go on unchecked, the result can only be the fragmentation, resegregation, and tribalization of American life.

I remain optimistic. My impression is that the historic forces driving toward "one people" have not lost their power. For most Americans this is still what the republic is all about. They resist extremes in the argument between "unity first" and "ethnicity first." "Most Americans," Governor Mario Cuomo has well said, can understand both the need to recognize and encourage an enriched diversity as well as the need to ensure that such a broadened multicultural perspective leads to unity and an enriched sense of what being an American is, and not to a destructive factionalism that would tear us apart."

Whatever their self-appointed spokesmen may claim, most American-born members of minority groups, white or nonwhite, while they may cherish particular heritages, still see themselves primarily as Americans and not primarily as Irish or Hungarians or Jews or Africans or Asians. A telling indicator is the rising rate of intermarriage across ethnic, religious, even (increasingly) racial lines. The belief in a unique American identity is far from dead.

But the burden to unify the country does not fall exclusively on the minorities. Assimilation and integration constitute a two-way street. Those who want to join America must be received and welcomed by those who already think they own America. Racism, as I have noted, has been the great national tragedy. In recent times white America has at last begun to confront the racism so deeply and shamefully inbred in our history. But the triumph over racism is incomplete. When old-line Americans, for example, treat people of other nationalities and races as if they were indigestible elements to be shunned and barred, they must not be surprised if minorities gather bitterly unto themselves and damn everybody else. Not only must *they* want assimilation and integration; *we* must want assimilation and integration too. The burden to make this a unified country lies as much with the complacent majority as with the sullen and resentful minorities.

The American population has unquestionably grown more heterogeneous than ever in recent times. But this very heterogeneity makes the quest for unifying ideals and a common culture all the more urgent. And in a world savagely rent by ethnic and racial antagonisms, it is all the more essential that the United States continue as an example of a how a highly differentiated society holds itself together.

Arthur M. Schlesinger, Jr.

22. President Ronald Reagan Sees a Stronger America

2nd Inaugural Address, January, 1985

Ronald Reagan

There are no words adequate to express my thanks for the great honor that you have bestowed on me. I will do my utmost to be deserving of your trust.

This is, as Senator Mathias told us, the 50th time that we the people have celebrated this historic occasion. When the first President—George Washington—placed his hand upon the Bible, he stood less than a single day's journey by horseback from raw, untamed wilderness. There were 4 million Americans in a union of 13 States. Today we are 60 times as many in a union of 50 States. We have lighted the world with our inventions, gone to the aid of mankind wherever in the world there was a cry for help, journeyed to the Moon and safely returned.

So much has changed. And yet we stand together as we did two centuries ago. When I took this oath four years ago, I did so in a time of economic stress. Voices were raised saying we had to look to our past for the greatness and glory. But we, the present-day Americans, are not given to looking backward. In this blessed land, there is always a better tomorrow.

Four years ago, I spoke to you of a new beginning and we have accomplished that. But in another sense, our new beginning is a continuation of that beginning created two centuries ago when, for the first time in history, government, the people said, was not our master, it is our servant; its only power that which we the people allow it to have.

That system has never failed us, but, for a time, we failed the system. We asked things of government that government was not equipped to give. We yielded authority to the National Government that properly belonged to States or to local governments or to the people themselves. We allowed taxes and inflation to rob us of our earnings and savings and watched the great industrial machine that had made us the most productive people on Earth slow down and the number of unemployed increase.

By 1980, we knew it was time to renew our faith, to strive with all our strength toward the ultimate in individual freedom consistent with an orderly society. ...

At the heart of our efforts is one idea vindicated by 25 straight months of economic growth: Freedom and incentives unleash the drive and entrepreneurial genius that are the core of human progress. We have begun to increase the rewards for work, savings, and investment; reduce the increase in the cost and size of government and its interference in people's lives. . . .

Public Papers of the Presidents of the United States: Ronald Reagan, 1985 (Washington, D.C.: U.S. Government Printing Office, 1988), vol. 1, pp. 55–58.

The time has come for a new American emancipation—a great national drive to tear down economic barriers and liberate the spirit of enterprise in the most distressed areas of our country. My friends, together we can do this, and do it we must, so help me God.

From new freedom will spring new opportunities for growth, a more productive, fulfilled and united people, and a stronger America—an America that will lead the technological revolution, and also open its mind and heart and soul to the treasures of literature, music, and poetry, and the values of faith, courage, and love.

A dynamic economy, with more citizens working and paying taxes, will be our strongest tool to bring down budget deficits. But an almost unbroken 50 years of deficit spending has finally brought us to a time of reckoning. …

We must act now to protect future generations from Government's desire to spend its citizens' money and tax them into servitude when the bills come due. Let us make it unconstitutional for the Federal Government to spend more than the Federal Government takes in. ...

History is a ribbon, always unfurling; history is a journey. And as we continue our journey, we think of those who traveled before us. …

A general falls to his knees in the hard snow of Valley Forge; a lonely President paces the darkened halls, and ponders his struggle to preserve the Union; the men of the Alamo call out encouragement to each other; a settler pushes west and sings a song, and the song echoes out forever and fills the unknowing air.

It is the American sound. It is hopeful, big-hearted, idealistic, daring, decent, and fair. That's our heritage; that is our song. We sing it still. For all our problems, our differences, we are together as of old, as we raise our voices to the God who is the Author of this most tender music. And may He continue to hold us close as we fill the world with our sound—sound in unity, affection, and love—one people under God, dedicated to the dream of freedom that He has placed in the human heart, called upon now to pass that dream on to a waiting and hopeful world. God bless you and may God bless America.

23. George Bush's War Message on Iraq March 17, 2003

George W. Bush

After his defeat in the Persian Gulf War in 1991, Sadam Hussein, the President of Iraq, defied the demands of the United Nations to search his country for evidence of "weapons of mass destruction." For years, Sadam stalled for time or refused permission for inspectors to enter his country. Frustrated by this defiance the United States increasingly saw Sadam as a serious threat to stability in the Middle East. Finally, in the spring of 2003, President George W. Bush appeared before Congress and presented his reasons for using military force to remove Sadam from power.

For more than a decade, the United States and other nations have pursued patient and honorable efforts to disarm the Iraqi regime without war.

Peaceful efforts to disarm the Iraqi regime have failed again and again because we arc not dealing with peaceful men. Intelligence gathered by this and other governments leaves no doubt that the Iraq regime continues to possess and conceal some of the most lethal weapons ever devised.

The regime has a history of reckless aggression in the Middle East. It has a deep hatred of America and our friends. And it has aided, trained and harbored terrorists, including operatives of Al Qaeda.

The Untied States and other nations did nothing to deserve or invite this threat, but we will do everything to defeat it. Instead of drifting along toward tragedy, we will set a course toward safety.

America tried to work with the United Nations to address this threat because we wanted to resolve the issue peacefully.

The United Nations Security Council has not lived up to its responsibilities, so we will rise to ours.

Many Iraqis can hear me tonight...And I have a message for them. If we must begin a military campaign, it will be directed against the lawless men who rule your country and not against you...And we will help you to build a new Iraq that is prosperous and free.

It is too late for Saddam Hussein to remain in power. It is not too late for the Iraqi military to act with honor and protect your country by permitting the peaceful entry of coalition forces to eliminate weapons of mass destruction.

I urge every member of the Iraqi military and intelligence services, if war comes, do not fight for a dying regime that is not worth your own life...In any conflict your fate will depend on your actions... War crimes will be prosecuted. War criminals will be punished. And it will be no defense to say I was just following orders.

In recent days American authorities have expelled from the country certain individuals with ties to Iraqi intelligence services. Among other measures I have directed additional security at our airports and increased Coast Guard patrols of major seaports.

We are a peaceful people, yet we're not a fragile people, and we will not be intimidated by thugs and killers. If our enemies dare to strike us, they and all who have aided them will face fearful consequences.

We are now acting because the risks of inaction would be far greater.

The cause of peace requires all free nations to recognize new and undeniable realities. In the 20th century some chose to appease murderous dictators whose threats were allowed to grow into genocide and global war. In this century when evil men plot chemical, biological and nuclear terror, a policy of appeasement could bring destruction of a kind never before seen on this earth. Terrorists and terrorist states do not reveal these threats with fair notice in formal declarations. And responding to such enemies only after they have struck first is not self-defense, it is suicide. The security of the world requires disarming Saddam Hussein now.

...we believe the Iraqi people are deserving and capable of human liberty. And when the dictator has departed, they can set an example to all the Middle East of a vital and peaceful and self-governing nation.

The United States with other countries will work to advance liberty and peace in that region. Our goal will not be achieved overnight. But it can come over time. The power and appeal of human liberty is felt in every life and every land, And the greatest power of freedom is to overcome hatred and violence, and turn the creative gifts of men and women to the pursuits of peace. That is the future we choose. Free nations have a duty to defend our people by uniting against the violent. And tonight, as we have done before, America and our allies accept that responsibility.

May God continue to bless America.

24. President Obama Addresses Muslim World in Cairo - June 4, 2009

Barack Obama

On June 4, 2009, President Barack Obama spoke to the Muslim World at Cairo University. He was attempting to chart a new foreign policy for the United States in its relations with Muslim countries. While recognizing that the tension that existed between the United States and Muslims was "rooted in historical forces that go beyond any current policy debate," he was calling for a new beginning in their relations with each other, "one based upon mutual interests and mutual respect and one that recognized that the United States and Muslim countries share principles of "justice and progress, tolerance, and the dignity of all human beings."

President Obama was trying to reverse the policy that had gone into place after the September 11, 2001, attack on the World Trade Center during the Bush administration. In 2003, as the U.S. prepared to attack Iraq, President Bush stated "We are a peaceful people, yet we're not a fragile people, and we will not be intimidated by thugs and killers. If our enemies dare to strike us, they and all who have aided them will face fearful consequences." Many Americans agreed with the Bush Doctrine of preemptive strikes against potential enemies and promoting democratic regime change and saw Obama as being too apologetic to Muslim countries; others felt that there was a need to improve the image of the United States abroad in the aftermath of retaliation over the attacks on the World Trade Center towers in 2001.

I am honored to be in the timeless city of Cairo, and to be hosted by two remarkable institutions. For over a thousand years, Al-Azhar has stood as a beacon of Islamic learning, and for over a century, Cairo University has been a source of Egypt's advancement. Together, you represent the harmony between tradition and progress. I am grateful for your hospitality, and the hospitality of the people of Egypt. I am also proud to carry with me the goodwill of the American people, and a greeting of peace from Muslim communities in my country: assalaamu alaykum.

We meet at a time of tension between the United States and Muslims around the world - tension rooted in historical forces that go beyond any current policy debate. The relationship between Islam and the West includes centuries of co-existence and cooperation, but also conflict and religious wars. More recently, tension has been fed by colonialism that denied rights and opportunities to many Muslims, and a Cold War in which Muslim-majority countries were too often treated as proxies without regard to their own aspirations. Moreover, the sweeping change brought by modernity and globalization led many Muslims to view the West as hostile to the traditions of Islam.

Violent extremists have exploited these tensions in a small but potent minority of Muslims. The attacks of September 11th, 2001 and the continued efforts of these extremists to engage in violence against civilians has led some in my country to view Islam as inevitably hostile not only to America and Western countries, but also to human rights. This has bred more fear and mistrust.
So long as our relationship is defined by our differences, we will empower those who sow hatred rather than peace, and who promote conflict rather than the cooperation that can help all of our people achieve justice and prosperity. This cycle of suspicion and discord must end.

I have come here to seek a new beginning between the United States and Muslims around the world; one based upon mutual interest and mutual respect; and one based upon the truth that America and Islam are not exclusive, and need not be in competition. Instead, they overlap, and share common principles - principles of justice and progress; tolerance and the dignity of all human beings.

I do so recognizing that change cannot happen overnight. No single speech can eradicate years of mistrust, nor can I answer in the time that I have all the complex questions that brought us to this point. But I am convinced that in order to move forward, we must say openly the things we hold in our hearts, and that too often are said only behind closed doors. There must be a sustained effort to listen to each other; to learn from each other; to respect one another; and to seek common ground. As the Holy Koran tells us, "Be conscious of God and speak always the truth." That is what I will try to do - to speak the truth as best I can, humbled by the task before us, and firm in my belief that the interests we share as human beings are far more powerful than the forces that drive us apart.

Part of this conviction is rooted in my own experience. I am a Christian, but my father came from a Kenyan family that includes generations of Muslims. As a boy, I spent several years in Indonesia and heard the call of the azaan at the break of dawn and the fall of dusk. As a young man, I worked in Chicago communities where many found dignity and peace in their Muslim faith. As a student of history, I also know civilization's debt to Islam. It was Islam - at places like Al-Azhar University - that carried the light of learning through so many centuries, paving the way for Europe's Renaissance and Enlightenment. It was innovation in Muslim communities that developed the order of algebra; our magnetic compass and tools of navigation; our mastery of pens and printing; our understanding of how disease spreads and how it can be healed. Islamic culture has given us majestic arches and soaring spires; timeless poetry and cherished music; elegant calligraphy and places of peaceful contemplation. And throughout history, Islam has demonstrated through words and deeds the possibilities of religious tolerance and racial equality.

I know, too, that Islam has always been a part of America's story. The first nation to recognize my country was Morocco. In signing the Treaty of Tripoli in 1796, our second President John Adams wrote, "The United States has in itself no character of enmity against the laws, religion or tranquility of Muslims." And since our founding, American Muslims have enriched the United States. They have fought in our wars, served in government, stood for civil rights, started businesses, taught at our Universities, excelled in our sports arenas, won Nobel Prizes, built our tallest building, and lit the Olympic Torch. And when the first Muslim-American was recently elected to Congress, he took the oath to defend our Constitution using the same Holy Koran that one of our Founding Fathers - Thomas Jefferson - kept in his personal library.

So I have known Islam on three continents before coming to the region where it was first revealed. That experience guides my conviction that partnership between America and Islam must be based on what Islam is, not what it isn't. And I consider it part of my responsibility as President of the United States to fight against negative stereotypes of Islam wherever they appear.

But that same principle must apply to Muslim perceptions of America. Just as Muslims do not fit a crude stereotype, America is not the crude stereotype of a self-interested empire. The United States has been one of the greatest sources of progress that the world has ever known. We were born out of revolution against an empire. We were founded upon the ideal that all are created equal, and we have shed blood and struggled for centuries to give meaning to those words - within our borders, and around the world. We are shaped by every culture, drawn from every end of the Earth, and dedicated to a simple concept: E pluribus unum: "Out of many, one."

Much has been made of the fact that an African-American with the name Barack Hussein Obama could be elected President. But my personal story is not so unique. The dream of opportunity for all people has not come true for everyone in America, but its promise exists for all who come to our shores - that includes nearly seven million American Muslims in our country today who enjoy incomes and education that are higher than average.

Moreover, freedom in America is indivisible from the freedom to practice one's religion. That is why there is a mosque in every state of our union, and over 1,200 mosques within our borders. That is why the U.S. government has gone to court to protect the right of women and girls to wear the hijab, and to punish those who would deny it.

So let there be no doubt: Islam is a part of America. And I believe that America holds within her the truth that regardless of race, religion, or station in life, all of us share common aspirations - to live in peace and security; to get an education and to work with dignity; to love our families, our communities, and our God. These things we share. This is the hope of all humanity.

Of course, recognizing our common humanity is only the beginning of our task. Words alone cannot meet the needs of our people. These needs will be met only if we act boldly in the years ahead; and if we understand that the challenges we face are shared, and our failure to meet them will hurt us all.

For we have learned from recent experience that when a financial system weakens in one country, prosperity is hurt everywhere. When a new flu infects one human being, all are at risk. When one nation pursues a nuclear weapon, the risk of nuclear attack rises for all nations. When violent extremists operate in one stretch of mountains, people are endangered across an ocean. And when innocents in Bosnia and Darfur are slaughtered, that is a stain on our collective conscience. That is what it means to share this world in the 21st century. That is the responsibility we have to one another as human beings.

This is a difficult responsibility to embrace. For human history has often been a record of nations and tribes subjugating one another to serve their own interests. Yet in this new age, such attitudes are self-defeating. Given our interdependence, any world order that elevates one nation or group of people over another will inevitably fail. So whatever we think of the past, we must not be prisoners of it. Our problems must be dealt with through partnership; progress must be shared.

That does not mean we should ignore sources of tension. Indeed, it suggests the opposite: we must face these tensions squarely. And so in that spirit, let me speak as clearly and plainly as I can about some specific issues that I believe we must finally confront together.

The first issue that we have to confront is violent extremism in all of its forms.

In Ankara, I made clear that America is not - and never will be - at war with Islam. We will, however, relentlessly confront violent extremists who pose a grave threat to our security. Because we reject the same thing that people of all faiths reject: the killing of innocent men, women, and children. And it is my first duty as President to protect the American people.

The situation in Afghanistan demonstrates America's goals, and our need to work together. Over seven years ago, the United States pursued al Qaeda and the Taliban with broad international support. We did not go by choice, we went because of necessity. I am aware that some question or justify the events of 9/11. But let us be clear: al Qaeda killed nearly 3,000 people on that day. The victims were innocent men, women and children from America and many other nations who had done nothing to harm anybody. And yet Al Qaeda chose to ruthlessly murder these people, claimed credit for the attack, and even now states their determination to kill on a massive scale. They have affiliates in many countries and are trying to expand their reach. These are not opinions to be debated; these are facts to be dealt with.

Make no mistake: we do not want to keep our troops in Afghanistan. We seek no military bases there. It is agonizing for America to lose our young men and women. It is costly and politically difficult to continue this conflict. We would gladly bring every single one of our troops home if we could be confident that there were not violent extremists in Afghanistan and Pakistan determined to kill as many Americans as they possibly can. But that is not yet the case.

That's why we're partnering with a coalition of forty-six countries. And despite the costs involved, America's commitment will not weaken. Indeed, none of us should tolerate these extremists. They have killed in many countries. They have killed people of different faiths - more than any other, they have killed Muslims. Their actions are irreconcilable with the rights of human beings, the progress of nations, and with Islam. The Holy Koran teaches that whoever kills an innocent, it is as if he has killed all mankind; and whoever saves a person, it is as if he has saved all mankind. The enduring faith of over a billion people is so much bigger than the narrow hatred of a few. Islam is not part of the problem in combating violent extremism - it is an important part of promoting peace.

We also know that military power alone is not going to solve the problems in Afghanistan and Pakistan. That is why we plan to invest $1.5 billion each year over the next five years to partner with Pakistanis to build schools and hospitals, roads and businesses, and hundreds of millions to help those who have been displaced. And that is why we are providing more than $2.8 billion to help Afghans develop their economy and deliver services that people depend upon.

Let me also address the issue of Iraq. Unlike Afghanistan, Iraq was a war of choice that provoked strong differences in my country and around the world. Although I believe that the Iraqi people are ultimately better off without the tyranny of Saddam Hussein, I also believe that events in Iraq have reminded America of the need to use diplomacy and build international consensus to resolve our problems whenever possible. Indeed, we can recall the words of Thomas Jefferson, who said: "I hope that our wisdom will grow with our power, and teach us that the less we use our power the greater it will be."

Today, America has a dual responsibility: to help Iraq forge a better future - and to leave Iraq to Iraqis. I have made it clear to the Iraqi people that we pursue no bases, and no claim on their territory or resources. Iraq's sovereignty is its own. That is why I ordered the removal of our combat brigades by next August. That is why we will honor our agreement with Iraq's democratically-elected government to remove combat troops from Iraqi cities by July, and to remove all our troops from Iraq by 2012. We will help Iraq train its Security Forces and develop its economy. But we will support a secure and united Iraq as a partner, and never as a patron. And finally, just as America can never tolerate violence by extremists, we must never alter our principles. 9/11 was an enormous trauma to our country. The fear and anger that it provoked was understandable, but in some cases, it led us to act contrary to our ideals. We are taking concrete actions to change course. I have unequivocally prohibited the use of torture by the United States, and I have ordered the prison at Guantanamo Bay closed by early next year.

So America will defend itself respectful of the sovereignty of nations and the rule of law. And we will do so in partnership with Muslim communities which are also threatened. The sooner the extremists are isolated and unwelcome in

Muslim communities, the sooner we will all be safer.

The second major source of tension that we need to discuss is the situation between Israelis, Palestinians and the Arab world.

America's strong bonds with Israel are well known. This bond is unbreakable. It is based upon cultural and historical ties, and the recognition that the aspiration for a Jewish homeland is rooted in a tragic history that cannot be denied.

Around the world, the Jewish people were persecuted for centuries, and anti-Semitism in Europe culminated in an unprecedented Holocaust. Tomorrow, I will visit Buchenwald, which was part of a network of camps where Jews were enslaved, tortured, shot and gassed to death by the Third Reich. Six million Jews were killed - more than the entire Jewish population of Israel today. Denying that fact is baseless, ignorant, and hateful. Threatening Israel with destruction - or repeating vile stereotypes about Jews - is deeply wrong, and only serves to evoke in the minds of Israelis this most painful of memories while preventing the peace that the people of this region deserve.

On the other hand, it is also undeniable that the Palestinian people - Muslims and Christians - have suffered in pursuit of a homeland. For more than sixty years they have endured the pain of dislocation. Many wait in refugee camps in the West Bank, Gaza, and neighboring lands for a life of peace and security that they have never been able to lead. They endure the daily humiliations - large and small - that come with occupation. So let there be no doubt: the situation for the Palestinian people is intolerable. America will not turn our backs on the legitimate Palestinian aspiration for dignity, opportunity, and a state of their own. For decades, there has been a stalemate: two peoples with legitimate aspirations, each with a painful history that makes compromise elusive. It is easy to point fingers - for Palestinians to point to the displacement brought by Israel's founding, and for Israelis to point to the constant hostility and attacks throughout its history from within its borders as well as beyond. But if we see this conflict only from one side or the other, then we will be blind to the truth: the only resolution is for the aspirations of both sides to be met through two states, where Israelis and Palestinians each live in peace and security.

That is in Israel's interest, Palestine's interest, America's interest, and the world's interest. That is why I intend to personally pursue this outcome with all the patience that the task requires. The obligations that the parties have agreed to under the Road Map are clear. For peace to come, it is time for them - and all of us - to live up to our responsibilities.

Palestinians must abandon violence. Resistance through violence and killing is wrong and does not succeed. For centuries, black people in America suffered the lash of the whip as slaves and the humiliation of segregation. But it was not violence that won full and equal rights. It was a peaceful and determined insistence upon the ideals at the center of America's founding. This same story can be told by people from South Africa to South Asia; from Eastern Europe to

Indonesia. It's a story with a simple truth: that violence is a dead end. It is a sign of neither courage nor power to shoot rockets at sleeping children, or to blow up old women on a bus. That is not how moral authority is claimed; that is how it is surrendered.

Now is the time for Palestinians to focus on what they can build. The Palestinian Authority must develop its capacity to govern, with institutions that serve the needs of its people. Hamas does have support among some Palestinians, but they also have responsibilities. To play a role in fulfilling Palestinian aspirations, and to unify the Palestinian people, Hamas must put an end to violence, recognize past agreements, and recognize Israel's right to exist.

At the same time, Israelis must acknowledge that just as Israel's right to exist cannot be denied, neither can Palestine's. The United States does not accept the legitimacy of continued Israeli settlements. This construction violates previous agreements and undermines efforts to achieve peace. It is time for these settlements to stop.

Israel must also live up to its obligations to ensure that Palestinians can live, and work, and develop their society. And just as it devastates Palestinian families, the continuing humanitarian crisis in Gaza does not serve Israel's security; neither does the continuing lack of opportunity in the West Bank. Progress in the daily lives of the Palestinian people must be part of a road to peace, and Israel must take concrete steps to enable such progress.

Finally, the Arab States must recognize that the Arab Peace Initiative was an important beginning, but not the end of their responsibilities. The Arab-Israeli conflict should no longer be used to distract the people of Arab nations from other problems. Instead, it must be a cause for action to help the Palestinian people develop the institutions that will sustain their state; to recognize Israel's legitimacy; and to choose progress over a self-defeating focus on the past.

America will align our policies with those who pursue peace, and say in public what we say in private to Israelis and Palestinians and Arabs. We cannot impose peace. But privately, many Muslims recognize that Israel will not go away. Likewise, many Israelis recognize the need for a Palestinian state. It is time for us to act on what everyone knows to be true. Too many tears have flowed. Too much blood has been shed. All of us have a responsibility to work for the day when the mothers of Israelis and Palestinians can see their children grow up without fear; when the Holy Land of three great faiths is the place of peace that God intended it to be; when Jerusalem is a secure and lasting home for Jews and Christians and Muslims, and a place for all of the children of Abraham to mingle peacefully together as in the story of Isra, when Moses, Jesus, and Mohammed (peace be upon them) joined in prayer.

The third source of tension is our shared interest in the rights and responsibilities of nations on nuclear weapons.

This issue has been a source of tension between the United States and the Islamic Republic of Iran. For many years, Iran has defined itself in part by its opposition to my country, and there is indeed a tumultuous history between us. In the middle of the Cold War, the United States played a role in the overthrow of a democratically- elected Iranian government. Since the Islamic Revolution, Iran has played a role in acts of hostage-taking and violence against U.S. troops and civilians. This history is well known. Rather than remain trapped in the past, I have made it clear to Iran's leaders and people that my country is prepared to move forward. The question, now, is not what Iran is against, but rather what future it wants to build.

It will be hard to overcome decades of mistrust, but we will proceed with courage, rectitude and resolve. There will be many issues to discuss between our two countries, and we are willing to move forward without preconditions on the basis of mutual respect. But it is clear to all concerned that when it comes to nuclear weapons, we have reached a decisive point. This is not simply about America's interests. It is about preventing a nuclear arms race in the Middle East that could lead this region and the world down a hugely dangerous path.

I understand those who protest that some countries have weapons that others do not. No single nation should pick and choose which nations hold nuclear weapons. That is why I strongly reaffirmed America's commitment to seek a world in which no nations hold nuclear weapons. And any nation - including Iran - should have the right to access peaceful nuclear power if it complies with its responsibilities under the nuclear Non-Proliferation Treaty. That commitment is at the core of the Treaty, and it must be kept for all who fully abide by it. And I am hopeful that all countries in the region can share in this goal.

The fourth issue that I will address is democracy.

I know there has been controversy about the promotion of democracy in recent years, and much of this controversy is connected to the war in Iraq. So let me be clear: no system of government can or should be imposed upon one nation by any other.

That does not lessen my commitment, however, to governments that reflect the will of the people. Each nation gives life to this principle in its own way, grounded in the traditions of its own people. America does not presume to know what is best for everyone, just as we would not presume to pick the outcome of a peaceful election. But I do have an unyielding belief that all people yearn for certain things: the ability to speak your mind and have a say in how you are governed; confidence in the rule of law and the equal administration of justice; government that is transparent and doesn't steal from the people; the freedom to live as you choose. Those are not just American ideas, they are human rights, and that is why we will support them everywhere.

There is no straight line to realize this promise. But this much is clear: governments that protect these rights are ultimately more stable, successful and secure. Suppressing ideas never succeeds in making them go away. America respects the right of all peaceful and law-abiding voices to be heard around the world, even if we disagree with them. And we will welcome all elected, peaceful governments - provided they govern with respect for all their people.

This last point is important because there are some who advocate for democracy only when they are out of power; once in power, they are ruthless in suppressing the rights of others. No matter where it takes hold, government of the people and by the people sets a single standard for all who hold power: you must maintain your power through consent, not coercion; you must respect the rights of minorities, and participate with a spirit of tolerance and compromise; you must place the interests of your people and the legitimate workings of the political process above your party. Without these ingredients, elections alone do not make true democracy.

The fifth issue that we must address together is religious freedom.

Islam has a proud tradition of tolerance. We see it in the history of Andalusia and Cordoba during the Inquisition. I saw it firsthand as a child in Indonesia, where devout Christians worshiped freely in an overwhelmingly Muslim country. That is the spirit we need today. People in every country should be free to choose and live their faith based upon the persuasion of the mind, heart, and soul. This tolerance is essential for religion to thrive, but it is being challenged in many different ways.

Among some Muslims, there is a disturbing tendency to measure one's own faith by the rejection of another's. The richness of religious diversity must be upheld - whether it is for Maronites in Lebanon or the Copts in Egypt. And fault lines must be closed among Muslims as well, as the divisions between Sunni and Shia have led to tragic violence, particularly in Iraq.

Freedom of religion is central to the ability of peoples to live together. We must always examine the ways in which we protect it. For instance, in the United States, rules on charitable giving have made it harder for Muslims to fulfill their religious obligation. That is why I am committed to working with American Muslims to ensure that they can fulfill zakat.

Likewise, it is important for Western countries to avoid impeding Muslim citizens from practicing religion as they see fit - for instance, by dictating what clothes a Muslim woman should wear. We cannot disguise hostility towards any religion behind the pretence of liberalism.

Indeed, faith should bring us together. That is why we are forging service projects in America that bring together Christians, Muslims, and Jews. That is why we welcome efforts like Saudi Arabian King Abdullah's Interfaith dialogue and Turkey's leadership in the Alliance of Civilizations. Around the world, we can turn dialogue into Interfaith service, so bridges between peoples lead to action - whether it is combating malaria in Africa, or providing relief after a natural disaster.

The sixth issue that I want to address is women's rights.

I know there is debate about this issue. I reject the view of some in the West that a woman who chooses to cover her hair is somehow less equal, but I do believe that a woman who is denied an education is denied equality. And it is no coincidence that countries where women are well-educated are far more likely to be prosperous.

Now let me be clear: issues of women's equality are by no means simply an issue for Islam. In Turkey, Pakistan, Bangladesh and Indonesia, we have seen Muslim-majority countries elect a woman to lead. Meanwhile, the struggle for women's equality continues in many aspects of American life, and in countries around the world.

Our daughters can contribute just as much to society as our sons, and our common prosperity will be advanced by allowing all humanity - men and women - to reach their full potential. I do not believe that women must make the same choices as men in order to be equal, and I respect those women who choose to live their lives in traditional roles. But it should be their choice. That is why the United States will partner with any Muslim-majority country to support expanded literacy for girls, and to help young women pursue employment through micro-financing that helps people live their dreams.

Finally, I want to discuss economic development and opportunity.

I know that for many, the face of globalization is contradictory. The Internet and television can bring knowledge and information, but also offensive sexuality and mindless violence. Trade can bring new wealth and opportunities, but also huge disruptions and changing communities. In all nations - including my own - this change can bring fear. Fear that because of modernity we will lose of control over our economic choices, our politics, and most importantly our identities - those things we most cherish about our communities, our families, our traditions, and our faith.

But I also know that human progress cannot be denied. There need not be contradiction between development and tradition. Countries like Japan and South Korea grew their economies while maintaining distinct cultures. The same is true for the astonishing progress within Muslim-majority countries from Kuala Lumpur to Dubai. In ancient times and in our times, Muslim communities have been at the forefront of innovation and education.

This is important because no development strategy can be based only upon what comes out of the ground, nor can it be sustained while young people are out of work. Many Gulf States have enjoyed great wealth as a consequence of oil, and some are beginning to focus it on broader development. But all of us must recognize that education and innovation will be the currency of the 21st century, and in too many Muslim communities there remains underinvestment in these areas. I am emphasizing such investments within my country. And while America in the past has focused on oil and gas in this part of the world, we now seek a broader engagement.

On education, we will expand exchange programs, and increase scholarships, like the one that brought my father to America, while encouraging more Americans to study in Muslim communities. And we will match promising Muslim students with internships in America; invest in on-line learning for teachers and children around the world; and create a new online network, so a teenager in Kansas can communicate instantly with a teenager in Cairo.

On economic development, we will create a new corps of business volunteers to partner with counterparts in Muslim-majority countries. And I will host a Summit on Entrepreneurship this year to identify how we can deepen ties between business leaders, foundations and social entrepreneurs in the United States and Muslim communities around the world.

On science and technology, we will launch a new fund to support technological development in Muslim-majority countries, and to help transfer ideas to the marketplace so they can create jobs. We will open centers of scientific excellence in Africa, the Middle East and Southeast Asia, and appoint new Science Envoys to collaborate on programs that develop new sources of energy, create green jobs, digitize records, clean water, and grow new crops. And today I am announcing a new global effort with the Organization of the Islamic Conference to eradicate polio. And we will also expand partnerships with Muslim communities to promote child and maternal health.

All these things must be done in partnership. Americans are ready to join with citizens and governments; community organizations, religious leaders, and businesses in Muslim communities around the world to help our people pursue a better life.

The issues that I have described will not be easy to address. But we have a responsibility to join together on behalf of the world we seek - a world where extremists no longer threaten our people, and American troops have come home; a world where Israelis and Palestinians are each secure in a state of their own, and nuclear energy is used for peaceful purposes; a world where governments serve their citizens, and the rights of all God's children are respected. Those are mutual interests. That is the world we seek. But we can only achieve it together.

I know there are many - Muslim and non-Muslim - who question whether we can forge this new beginning. Some are eager to stoke the flames of division, and to stand in the way of progress. Some suggest that it isn't worth the effort - that we are fated to disagree, and civilizations are doomed to clash. Many more are simply skeptical that real change can occur. There is so much fear, so much mistrust. But if we choose to be bound by the past, we will never move forward. And I want to particularly say this to young people of every faith, in every country - you, more than anyone, have the ability to remake this world.

All of us share this world for but a brief moment in time. The question is whether we spend that time focused on what pushes us apart, or whether we commit ourselves to an effort - a sustained effort - to find common ground, to focus on the future we seek for our children, and to respect the dignity of all human beings.

It is easier to start wars than to end them. It is easier to blame others than to look inward; to see what is different about someone than to find the things we share. But we should choose the right path, not just the easy path. There is also one rule that lies at the heart of every religion - that we do unto others as we would have them do unto us. This truth transcends nations and peoples - a belief that isn't new; that isn't black or white or brown; that isn't Christian, or Muslim or Jew. It's a belief that pulsed in the cradle of civilization, and that still beats in the heart of billions. It's a faith in other people, and it's what brought me here today.

We have the power to make the world we seek, but only if we have the courage to make a new beginning, keeping in mind what has been written.

The Holy Koran tells us, "O mankind! We have created you male and a female; and we have made you into nations and tribes so that you may know one another."

The Talmud tells us: "The whole of the Torah is for the purpose of promoting peace."

The Holy Bible tells us, "Blessed are the peacemakers, for they shall be called sons of God."

The people of the world can live together in peace. We know that is God's vision. Now, that must be our work here on Earth. Thank you. And may God's peace be upon you.

25. History: The Weapon

Arthur M. Schlesinger, Jr.

Writing history is an old and honorable profession with distinctive standards and purposes. The historian's goals are accuracy, analysis, and objectivity in the reconstruction of the past. But history is more than an academic discipline up there in the stratosphere. It also has its own role in the future of nations.

For history is to the nation rather as memory is to the individual. As an individual deprived of memory becomes disoriented and lost, not knowing where he has been or where he is going, so a nation denied a conception of its past will be disabled in dealing with its present and its future. As the means of defining national identity, history becomes a means of shaping history. The writing of history then turns from a meditation into a weapon. "Who controls the past controls the future," runs the Party slogan in George Orwell's 1984; "who controls the present controls the past."

I

Historians do their damnedest to maintain the standards of their trade. Heaven knows how dismally we fall short of our ideals, how sadly our interpretations are dominated and distorted by unconscious preconceptions, how obsessions of race and nation blind us to our own bias. We remain creatures of our times, prisoners of our own experience, swayed hither and yon, like all sinful mortals, by partisanship, prejudice, dogma, by fear and by hope.

The spotlight we flash into the darkness of the past is guided by our own concerns in the present. When new preoccupations arise in our own times and lives, the spotlight shifts, throwing into sharp relief things that were always there but that earlier historians had casually excised from the collective memory. In this sense, the present may be said to re-create the past.

Historians must always strive toward the unattainable ideal of objectivity. But as we respond to contemporary urgencies, we sometimes exploit the past for nonhistorical purposes, taking from the past, or projecting upon it, what suits our own society or ideology. History thus manipulated becomes an instrument less of disinterested intellectual inquiry than of social cohesion and political purpose.

People live by their myths, and some may argue that the facts can be justifiably embroidered if embroiderment serves a higher good, such as the nurture of a nation or the elevation of a race. It may seem more important to maintain a beneficial fiction than to keep history pure—especially when there is no such thing as pure history anyway. This may have been what Plato had in mind when he proposed the idea of the "noble lie" in *The Republic.*

But enthusiasts are all too likely to confuse "noble lies" with reality. The corruption of history by nationalism is instructive. Nationalism remains, after two centuries, the most vital political emotion in the world—far more vital than social ideologies such as communism or fascism or even democracy. But it was not the product of spontaneous generation. "Nationalism is not the awakening of nations to self-consciousness," as Ernest Gellner has said; "it invents nations where they do not exist. . . ." Nationalism was developed by intellectuals in the interest of aspiring elites and thereafter propagated to receptive masses. And it continues to thrive because it taps potent emotions of history and locality to give individual lives meaning in an increasingly baffling universe.

Today the nationalist fever encircles the globe. In the West the contagion convulses Ireland and Israel, divides Belgium, Cyprus, and Canada, arouses Brittany, Corsica, and the Basque country. Nationalism broke up the Soviet Empire and now threatens to break up the Soviet Union itself. In the third world, nationalism, having overthrown Western colonialism, launches a horde of new states, large and micro, often at each other's throats in reenacting ancient quarrels of history.

Within nation-states, nationalism takes the form of ethnicity or tribalism. In country after country across the third world—India, Burma, Sri Lanka, Indonesia, Iraq, Ethiopia, Nigeria, Angola, Trinidad, Guyana—ethnic groups struggle for power and, in desperate cases, for survival. The ethnic upsurge in America, far from being unique, partakes of the global fever.

The invocation of history is indispensable to nations and groups in the process of making themselves. How else can a people establish the legitimacy of its personality, the continuity of its tradition, the correctness of its course?

Often history is invoked to justify the ruling class. "The past," writes the British historian J. H. Plumb, "has always been the handmaid of authority." This is top-dog history, designed to show how noble, virtuous, and inevitable existing power arrangements are. Because it vindicates the status quo and the methods by which power is achieved and maintained, it may be called exculpatory history.

Other times history is invoked to justify the victims of power, to vindicate those who reject the status quo. Isaiah Berlin has described how the "humiliated and defeated Germans" in the early nineteenth century lashed hack against the arrogant French:

> *They discovered in themselves qualities far superior to those of their tormentors. They contrasted their own deep, inner life of the spirit, their own profound humility, their selfless pursuit of true values—simple, noble, sublime—with the rich, worldly, successful, superficial, smooth, heartless, morally empty French. This mood rose to fever pitch during the national resistance to Napoleon, and was indeed the original exemplar of the reaction of many a backward, exploited, or at any rate patronized society, which, resentful of the apparent inferiority*

> *of its status, reacted by turning to real or imaginary triumphs and glories in its past, or enviable attributes of its own national or cultural character. . . . Hence the value of a real or imaginary rich historical past to inferiority-ridden peoples, for it promises, perhaps, an even more glorious future.*

This is underdog history, designed to demonstrate what Bertrand Russell called the "superior virtue of the oppressed" by inventing or exaggerating past glories and purposes. It may be called compensatory history.

Both exculpatory and compensatory history use the past in order to shape the future. For 70 years in the Soviet Union, scholars practiced exculpatory history, sedulously defending every twist of the party line and every whim of the Kremlin dictatorship. Then came Gorbachev; and *glasnost* led in due course to the emancipation of historians.

For the first time ever, Soviet historians became free to write honest history-to describe the purges and the gulags, to demythologize Stalin and even Lenin, to reassess Bukharin and even Trotsky, to condemn the Soviet-Nazi pact of 1939, to pronounce Stalin's U.S.S.R. a totalitarian state, even to doubt the sacred Revolution itself. "A new future requires a new past," said Eric Foner of Columbia after four months as a lecturer at Moscow State University. "To legitimize these far-reaching changes, the press and public officials now paint the history of the Soviet era in the blackest hues." As party-line history was an instrument of dictatorship, honest history is an instrument of democracy.

In Japan the government's dedication to exculpatory history demonstrated persisting unwillingness to accept responsibility for aggressions and atrocities of half a century ago. School textbooks unrepentantly portray the Japanese conquest of Korea and invasion of China in terms so benevolent as to provoke official protests from Seoul and Beijing. Young Japanese are taught to see their country as a victim rather than the cause of the Pacific War.

When the eminent historian Professor Saburo Ienaga tried, as he wrote in the preface to the English edition of his notable book *The Pacific War,* "to show the Japanese people the naked realities," he was subjected to official persecution. Japanese courts upheld the Education Ministry's censorship of Ienaga's factual account of the Japanese "rape of Nanjing" in 1937. As Ienaga observed, the less the young people of Japan are taught the true history of the war, the greater the risk of a "similar danger" in years to come.

By the 1960s German historians had come to accept the crimes of Hitler as a unique German responsibility and to trace Nazism back to nineteenth-century German history and culture. But the revival of German nationalism in the 1980s set off a scholarly campaign to sanitize the national past. The crimes of Hitler, influential historians argued, were not unique, nor were they peculiarly German. All Hitler was doing was imitating genocidal policies invented by Stalin, substituting race for class. Hitler had no doubt done awful things, but other nations had committed comparable atrocities without suffering the same international disfavor. Nazism was deplorable but not fundamental, more a matter of bad luck and aberration.

As Franz Josef Strauss, the conservative leader, said, Germans must not let the vision of their glorious past "be blocked by the sight-screens of those accursed 12 years between 1933 and 1945. German history cannot be presented as an endless chain of mistakes and crimes." Michael Stürmer, a conservative historian, criticizes the German "obsession with their guilt" and calls for a new affirmation of national identity. Sturmer understands the stakes: "Loss of orientation and the search for identity are brothers. . . . Anyone who believes that this has no effect on politics arid the future ignores the fact that in a land without history, lie who fills the memory, defines the concepts, and interprets the past, wins the future."

History is a weapon. Perhaps their own vicissitudes as a nation—from democracy to Nazism to communism back to democracy in half a century—have made Czechs particularly sensitive to the manipulations of history. "The first step in liquidating a people," a historian observes in Milan Kundera's *The Book of Laughter and Forgetting*, "is to erase its memory. Destroy its books, its culture, its history. Then have somebody write new books, manufacture a new culture, invent a new history. Before long the nation will begin to forget what it is and what it was." "The struggle of man against power," says another character, "is the struggle of memory against forgetting."

Vaclav Havel, Czech playwright and president, made a pointed address in the presence of Kurt Waldheim of Austria. "He who fears facing his own past," Havel said, "must necessarily fear what lies before him. . . . Lying can never save us from the lie. Falsifiers of history do not safeguard freedom but imperil it. ... Truth liberates man from fear." Honest history is the weapon of freedom.